*The Magic Mountains*

# The Magic Mountains
*Hill Stations and the British Raj*

DANE KENNEDY

*University of California Press*
BERKELEY    LOS ANGELES    LONDON

University of California Press
Berkeley and Los Angeles, California

University of California Press, Ltd.
London, England

© 1996 by
The Regents of the University of California

Library of Congress Cataloging-in-Publication Data

Kennedy, Dane Keith.
    The magic mountains : hill stations and the British raj / Dane
Kennedy.
        p.   cm.
    Includes bibliographical references and index.
    ISBN 0-520-20188-4. — ISBN 0-520-20189-2 (pbk.)
        1. India—Description and travel.   2. Summer resorts—India.
    3.    India—History—British occupancy, 1765–1947.    I. Title.
DS412.K46   1996
954'.00943—dc20                                                      95–14014
                                                                          CIP

Printed in the United States of America
9  8  7  6  5  4  3  2  1

*For Marty*

# Contents

# Illustrations

# Acknowledgments

This project began with the sort of serendipity that suggested it had promise. On the morning I was to launch my research at the India Office Library, I found myself seated across a hotel breakfast table from a stranger who introduced herself as Anne MacEwen, and as we entered into conversation I learned that she had spent much of her youth in Simla, British India's foremost hill station, where her father was surveyor-general of India. Like many other persons whom happenstance brought my way, Mrs. MacEwen and her mother, Mrs. Sackville Hamilton, graciously shared their memories of life in the hills.

In undertaking this study, I made a professional leap from one continent to another, and this would not have been possible without the generous assistance of a number of institutions and individuals. My initial foray in the London archives was supported by a research award in 1989 from the Social Science Research Council. The Indo-American Fellowship Program financed and facilitated my work in India in 1991. The Davis Humanities Institute at the University of California, Davis, granted me a visiting fellowship in 1989–90: this was an ideal environment in which to formulate general themes and draft early chapters. I am grateful to these institutions for their support. I also appreciate the help I received from the staffs of the India Office Library and Records in London, the Indian National Archives in New Delhi, the Himachal Pradesh State Archives in Shimla, the West Bengal State Archives and the National Library in Calcutta, the Tamil Nadu State Archives in Madras, the Nilgiri Library in Ootacamund, and the interlibrary loan departments of the University of California, Davis, and the University of Nebraska-Lincoln. Lydia Gomes of the Indo-American Fellowship Program smoothed my way to India, while L. S. Suri, Aditi Sen, and other members of the American Institute of Indian Studies eased the bureaucratic and logistical complications that confront a newcomer to that extraordinary country. Joan Curtis and Sandra Pershing provided technical support at the University of Nebraska, as did Judy Lehman, Ann Chamberlain, and Margaret Nelson at the Davis Humanities Institute. Les Howard made the maps with his customary skill.

My intellectual debts are considerable. Tom Metcalf introduced me to the history of colonial India when I was a student at the University of California, Berkeley, and although I wandered rather far afield before being drawn into the study of the raj, Tom has remained a steady source of advice, encouragement, and friendship. So too has Sandy Freitag, a marvel of energy and generosity. Both of them, along with Dipesh Chakrabarty, Bernard Cohn, Frank Conlon, Michael Fisher, David Gilmartin, Eugene Irschick, Barbara Metcalf, and Barbara Ramusack, have made me feel welcome in the community of South Asian scholars. Robert Reed tried to teach me about hill stations in the late 1970s, and I am abashed that the lesson took so long to register. Dan Brower, Kay Flavell, Interpal Grewal, and Norma Landau challenged me to clarify my arguments during my residence at the Davis Humanities Institute. My stay in Shimla was made memorable by conversations with Pamela Kanwar and Professor S. R. Mehrotra. While conducting his own researches, Peter Hoffenberg was kind enough to feed me a number of useful references on hill stations. My friend and colleague Parks Coble read the entire manuscript. At the University of California Press, Lynne Withey expressed an early interest in this project, and she and Barbara Howell shepherded it through the review process with wonderful efficiency, while Erika Büky and Pamela Fischer gave excellent care to the editorial preparation of the manuscript. Finally, this book is dedicated to Marty, who knows why.

# Abbreviations

| | |
|---|---|
| HPSA | Himachal Pradesh State Archives, Shimla |
| ICS | Indian Civil Service |
| INA | Indian National Archives, New Delhi |
| IOL | India Office Library and Records, London |
| PP | Parliamentary Papers |
| TNSA | Tamil Nadu State Archives, Madras |
| WBSA | West Bengal State Archives, Calcutta |

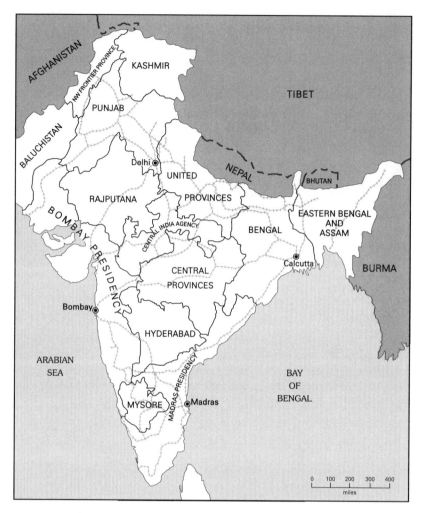

Map 1. British India (c. 1909), with provincial boundaries and major railway routes.

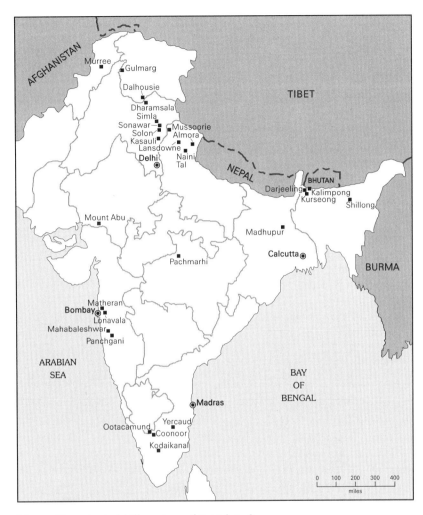

Map 2. The principal hill stations of British India.

# 1    The Hill Stations of British India

Located on peaks that loom like sentinels over heat-shimmering plains, hill stations remain among the most curious monuments to the British colonial presence in India.[1] Their origins can be traced to the effort in the early nineteenth century to establish sanitaria within the subcontinent where European invalids could recover from the heat and disease of the tropics. But hill stations soon assumed an importance that far exceeded their initial therapeutic attraction. To these cloud-enshrouded sanctuaries the British expatriate elite came for seasonal relief not merely from the physical toll of a harsh climate but from the social and psychological toll of an alien culture. Here they established closed communities of their own kind in a setting of their own design. As self-styled guardians of the raj, however, they also sought to supervise their subjects from these commanding heights. Here they established political headquarters and military cantonments, centers of power from whence they issued and executed orders with an Olympian air of omnipotence. Hill stations, in effect, served both as sites of refuge and as sites for surveillance. These were places where the British endeavored at one and the same time to engage with and to disengage from the dominion they ruled. This paradox and its implications for the imperial endeavor give the hill stations their significance.

Hill stations generally have been seen as places where the British went to play. These were the colonial equivalents of Bath or Brighton, cliquish resorts where rakish officers, vampish ladies, ambitious bureaucrats, and bored housewives engaged in endless parties and gossip. Rudyard Kipling did a great deal to engrave this image in the popular mind with his stories about Simla in *Plain Tales from the Hills*. Yet his portrait drew upon perceptions and suspicions that were already widespread among his contemporaries. Despite residents' protestations, the air of scandal settled

---

1. As evidence of the continued popularity of hill stations, see the guidebook by Gillian Wright, *The Hill Stations of India* (Lincolnwood, Ill., 1991).

around Simla soon after its rise to prominence, and it lingers there still.[2] Other hill stations loomed less large in the public eye, but they too established reputations for sportiveness. Here the British appeared to do as they pleased, unrestrained by the demands and debilities that the imperial order inflicted on them in the plains.

For all its hyperbole, this image of the hill station was in certain crucial respects an accurate one. Above all, it conveyed the fact that hill stations sought to isolate their seasonal residents from India's harsher features, to offer them a comforting haven for rest and recreation. This image may explain the general neglect of hill stations by historians: apart from Kiplingesque depictions of Simla and its counterparts in popular narratives of British India, the subject has been all but shrugged aside, dismissed in the historiography of the period as peripheral to the broader issues shaping the colonial experience.[3] One must turn to social scientists, and especially cultural geographers, to find a serious corpus of scholarship on hill stations in India (and other parts of Asia).[4] Their work has tended to stress the

---

2. J. G. Farrell's *The Hill Station* (London, 1987), a historical novel left unfinished by the author's untimely death, paints a portrait of Simla society that Kipling would have found familiar.

3. Most of the historical literature on Indian hill stations has a distinctly nostalgic flavor. See, for instance, Mollie Panter-Downes, *Ooty Preserved: A Victorian Hill Station in India* (New York, 1967); James Lunt, "Simla: The British in India," *History Today* 18, no. 9 (Sept. 1968): 599–605; Michael Edwardes, *Bound to Exile: The Victorians in India* (New York, 1970), chs. 8, 17; Charles Allen, *Plain Tales from the Raj* (London, 1976), ch. 12; Pat Barr and Ray Desmond, *Simla: A Hill Station in British India* (New York, 1978); Jan Morris with Simon Winchester, *Stones of Empire: The Buildings of the Raj* (Oxford, 1983), 198–202; Philip Davies, *Splendours of the Raj: British Architecture in India 1660–1947* (Harmondsworth, 1987), ch. 5; Vipin Pubby, *Simla Then and Now: Summer Capital of the Raj* (New Delhi, 1988); Jahar Sen, *Darjeeling: A Favoured Retreat* (New Delhi, 1989); Raja Bhasin, *Simla: The Summer Capital of British India* (New Delhi, 1992); and Ruskin Bond and Ganesh Saili, *Mussoorie and Landour: Days of Wine and Roses* (New Delhi, 1992). Significantly, none of these titles are the work of academic historians.

4. A seminal introduction to the subject by cultural geographers is J. E. Spencer and W. L. Thomas, "The Hill Stations and Summer Resorts of the Orient," *Geographical Review* 38, no. 4 (Oct. 1948): 637–51. The best more recent works are Monika Bührlein, *Nuwara Eliya: "Hill Station" und Zentraler Ort im Hochland der Insel Ceylon (Sri Lanka)* (Stuttgart, 1991); and Nora Mitchell, "The Indian Hill-Station: Kodaikanal," University of Chicago Department of Geography Research Paper 141, 1972. Other studies include Mary Shaw, "Some South India Hill Stations," *Scottish Geographical Magazine* 59, no. 3 (Jan. 1944): 81–87, and 60, no. 3 (Dec. 1944): 80–85; W. Senftleben, "Some Aspects of the Indian Hill Stations: A Contribution towards a Geography of Tourist Traffic," *Philippine Geographical Journal* 17, no. 1 (Jan.-March 1973): 21–29; Anthony D. King, "Culture, Social Power and Environment: The Hill Station in Colonial Urban Development," *Social*

distinctive form and function of the hill station, a perspective that reaffirms this impression of the stations' exceptionalism. These scholars have shown that the hill station was a variant neither of the traditional Asian city nor of the modern colonial/postcolonial metropolis, both of which thrived by incorporating a combination of commerce, industry, and state institutions. Rather the hill station was a unique urban entity, a seasonal site for the recreational activities of a highly transitory expatriate population, whose memories of a distant homeland it lovingly evoked. Hence, the replication of particular features of the natural and social environment of Britain was central to the hill station's distinctive identity. As one geographer has put it, hill stations "offered isolated, exclusive milieus where sojourners could feel at home."[5]

Both the morphological patterns of the hill stations and the social practices of their British inhabitants furthered this nostalgic intent. In their physical configurations, hill stations had far more affinities with the quaint villages of a romanticized England than with the stark cantonments of a regimented India. Rather than transpose the grid patterns of civil and military stations on the plains to these mountain settings, the British embraced the sinuous contours of the rugged landscape and constructed their cottages along the crests of ridges and around the shores of lakes without apparent premeditation or planning. They hedged the stations' meandering avenues and footpaths with trees and flowers indigenous to their homeland and cultivated English fruit orchards and vegetable gardens in their backyards. Their houses were more often gabled Gothic villas, half-timbered Tudor cottages, gingerbread-ornamented Swiss chalets, and other European architectural imports than the familiar, verandah-enclosed,

---

*Action* 26, no. 3 (July-Sept. 1976): 195–213; Anthony D. King, *Colonial Urban Development: Culture, Social Power and Environment* (London, 1976), ch. 7; Robert R. Reed, "City of Pines: The Origins of Baguio as a Colonial Hill Station and Regional Capital," Center for South and Southeast Asia Studies Research Monograph 13, Berkeley, Calif., 1976; Robert R. Reed, "Remarks on the Colonial Genesis of the Hill Station in Southeast Asia with Particular Reference to the Cities of Buitenzorg (Bogor) and Baguio," *Asian Profile* 4, no. 6 (Dec. 1976): 545–91; Robert R. Reed, "The Colonial Genesis of Hill Stations: The Genting Exception," *Geographical Review* 69, no. 4 (Oct. 1979): 463–68; Jan Pieper, *Die Anglo-Indische Station oder die Kolonialisierung des Götterberges* (Bonn, 1977), 183–95; S. Robert Aiken, "Early Penang Hill Station," *Geographical Review* 77, no. 4 (Oct. 1987): 421–39; and Judith Theresa Kenny, "Constructing an Imperial Hill Station: The Representation of British Authority in Ootacamund" (Ph.D. diss., Syracuse University, 1990); and Nutan Tyagi, *Hill Resorts of U.P. Himalaya: A Geographical Study* (New Delhi, 1991).

5. Aiken, "Early Penang Hill Station," 421.

Public Works bungalows that billeted the British across the rest of the subcontinent. And always at the heart of the stations stood that essential symbol of traditional English values, the Anglican church.

Form followed function: the lives led in the hills replicated the social experiences of the upper middle classes at home. A seemingly endless series of social calls, teas, strolls, picnics, dinners, balls, fetes, races, amateur theatricals, and other festivities dominated the daily routine of residents. While much the same array of social activities occurred wherever the British congregated in India, nowhere else did the pursuit of relaxation and recreation attain such preeminence. The parallels to the spa towns and seaside resorts of England were striking. Visitors came to recuperate from tenacious ills, to relax in a congenial climate, to relish a myriad of leisure activities, and above all to interact with others whose social status and cultural norms mirrored their own. They unpacked and donned their woolens, made their social calls and hosted their "at-homes," exchanged their pleasantries on their promenades along the Mall, and all the while did their best to reinhabit in mind and in manner a world they had left behind.

And yet the fact remains that hill stations were a part of the imperial system—that is, a part of the apparatus that allowed the British to rule India—and a far more integral part than their nostalgic guises suggested. They served as vital centers of political and military power, especially after the 1857 revolt. Pamela Kanwar's study of Simla demonstrates quite clearly that the history of this quintessential hill station was profoundly shaped by its political role as the so-called summer capital of India.[6] While official recognition of its status came in the 1860s, it had already served as the summer residence of governors-general for several decades. By the late nineteenth century, viceroys and their councils were spending at least twice as many months each year in Simla as they were in Calcutta, the historic capital of the raj. This gravitation to the hills occurred at the regional level as well. The governments of Bengal, Bombay, Madras, Assam, United Provinces, and Central Provinces acquired the hill stations of Darjeeling, Mahabaleshwar, Ootacamund, Shillong, Naini Tal, and Pachmarhi as their summer headquarters, and the viceroy shared Simla with the Punjab government. Indeed, nearly every branch of officialdom that had access to a hill station endeavored to spend more of its time and transfer more of its operations there. Military as well as civil authorities established highland

6. Pamela Kanwar, *Imperial Simla* (Delhi, 1990). Similarly, the political significance of Ootacamund is analyzed by Kenny, "Constructing an Imperial Hill Station."

headquarters. Simla became the official residence of the commander-in-chief of the Indian Army. The army's northern command was headquartered in Murree, the Bengal command in Naini Tal, and the southern command in Wellington. Many smaller stations were military cantonments, occupied almost exclusively by troops. Thus, all but a few hill stations in British India had some sort of official imprimatur.

This shift in the bureaucratic axis of the imperial state from the plains to the hills did not go unnoticed by contemporaries. In the late nineteenth century it stirred up a storm of criticism both in India and in England. The commercial and professional elites of Calcutta, Madras, and other Indian metropolises organized rallies and submitted petitions protesting their diminishing access to officialdom in its highland retreats. The secretary of state for India and members of Parliament repeatedly demanded that the central and provincial governments justify the financial and political costs of their annual migrations to the hills. Later, Indian nationalists pointed to the practice as evidence of the aloofness and arrogance of British rule. The viceroy and his officials fought off these attacks with all the skill and tenacity that an entrenched bureaucracy possesses, marshaling a shrewd combination of arguments and inertia to resist any withdrawal from the hill stations. And they had at their backs other critics who urged that all British functions and functionaries relocate to the hills. These individuals envisioned the hill stations as the seedbeds for self-sustaining colonies where civil servants, soldiers, pensioners, and other Europeans could conduct their affairs entirely removed from the plains. All the parties in this debate about hill stations understood that it was a wrangle over access to the state, a struggle for power.

How was it possible for hill stations to serve at once as an integral fixture of British rule in India and as an aloof haven from its entanglements? How could the state and the individual extract such profoundly different uses from the same places? Implicit in these divergent functions lay a dichotomy between the public and the private that coursed through the center of Victorian culture. As social historians have frequently noted, the British at home led bifurcated lives, characterized by the gendered distinction between a male-dominated public sphere of politics and production and a female-dominated private sphere of domesticity and reproduction.[7] Indeed,

---

7. See, for example, Leonore Davidoff and Catherine Hall, *Family Fortunes: Men and Women of the English Middle Class 1780–1850* (London, 1987), esp. 13, 32–33; and Dorothy O. Helly and Susan M. Reverby, eds., *Gendered Domains: Rethinking Public and Private in Women's History* (Ithaca, 1992), Introduction.

it has been suggested by Jürgen Habermas and others that the rise of a public sphere—and, by implication, its private counterpart—was at the core of the development of bourgeois society in eighteenth- and nineteenth-century Europe.[8] In India, where the British suffered heightened concern about the ways that private actions undermined public authority and public power corrupted private judgment, the boundaries between the two spheres were even more sharply drawn. It was considered essential, for instance, that the colonial official assume a public demeanor that disguised the private self. And yet the public and the private did not exist in complete isolation from one another. On the contrary, the two were complementary since each infused the other with meaning.[9] If the Victorians regarded the public and the private as opposing poles of social experience, they nevertheless understood that these polarities stood in dialectical balance. The private and the public, the personal and the political, the individual and the social made up a highly charged grid of currents and countercurrents, and at the points where they intersected community and civic identity were formed. Nowhere within the raj was this intersection of dialectical forces more apparent than in the hill stations.

For the British who lived and worked in India, these highland sites presented a rare opportunity to reproduce the social conditions that gave their homeland its distinctive dynamic. Elsewhere on the subcontinent, the prospects for a bourgeois public sphere as Habermas construes it were limited by the constraints imposed on the British as representatives of the imperial state: these constraints placed them at odds with the civil society that developed among their Indian subjects, whose activities they viewed with suspicion, and it exposed them to those subjects' critical scrutiny, placing their private lives on public display. The authoritarian obligations of power over an alien populace subverted the conditions under which the dialectical interplay between the public and private spheres could take place. Only the hill stations provided a public space where the British could

8. See Jürgen Habermas, *The Structural Transformation of the Public Sphere: An Inquiry into a Category of Bourgeois Society*, trans. Thomas Burger (Cambridge, Mass., 1989); and Craig Calhoun, ed., *Habermas and the Public Sphere* (Cambridge, Mass., 1992). Efforts have been made to apply the Habermasian understanding of the public sphere to the colonial experience, notably in a special issue of *South Asia* 14, no. 1 (1991), edited by Sandria Freitag, and at a conference on "The European Public Sphere and Its Alternatives under Colonialism," held at the University of Chicago in October 1993.

9. Dena Goodman makes this point with regard to European society in "Public Sphere and Private Life: Toward a Synthesis of Current Historiographical Approaches to the Old Regime," *History and Theory* 31, no. 1 (1992): 1–20.

simultaneously pursue their private interests. They provided a public space where the absolutist pretensions of imperial authority could be set aside and the necessity to conform to colonial normative codes could be tempered by the desire to satisfy personal needs. In this public sphere a bourgeois individualist sensibility could be cultivated and the subjective self expressed. Here sociability held sway, debate and gossip flowed freely, and men and women engaged in the personal transactions that became the principal bridge between the separate spheres.

The hill stations' distinctive social function is especially evident when the individuals who pursued private pleasures in these mountain settings are viewed in the aggregate. Whereas the British population of India as a whole consisted overwhelmingly of men, this was not the case in the hill stations (with the exception of the military cantonments). Here the number of women usually equaled and sometimes exceeded the number of men, and children constituted a substantial presence as well. Thus, hill-station communities came closer to the gender and age distributions found in society at home than almost any other clusters of Britons in India. By contrast, the Indian populace of the hill stations lacked the demographic balance it possessed across the rest of the subcontinent. Most of these Indians were adult males who had come in search of work from other areas, where their wives and children and parents remained. In effect, hill stations turned the comparative demographics of colonial India upside down: the Indians were the ones who became fractionated sojourners torn from their social fabric, while the British were the ones who developed relatively stable and sustainable communities. It is no coincidence, therefore, that the main transitions and transactions in the life cycle of the British Indian population frequently took place in the hill stations. These were the preferred places within the subcontinent for women to bear their children, for children to be educated, for young adults to meet and marry, for ambitious officials to make the contacts that furthered their careers, for pensioners to enjoy their retirement, and for invalids to seek their health or meet their death. Taken together, these activities constituted most aspects of the social reproduction of the ruling race.

Thus, what is often seen as the frivolous and fantasylike atmosphere of hill stations was entirely functional to the operation of the raj. With their physical evocation of the tranquil English village and their social replication of respectable English behavior, hill stations helped to imbue their inhabitants with an unmistakable sense of themselves as agents of a superior culture, charged with the responsibility to ensure that the fidelity and determination that had taken them to India did not deteriorate in this physically and morally corrupting land. Those relentless rounds of teas and picnics and dinners served to remind their participants, most of them seasonal refugees from the alien climate and culture of the plains, that they shared a common social identity based on strict standards of conduct and consciousness. As Anthony King has observed, hill stations existed to "maintain the social structure and social behaviour of the British colonial community in India."[10] Private intentions were thereby interwoven with public purposes. Hill stations offered enclaves where the British could restore the physical and psychic energies they needed for their imperial tasks, replicate the social and cultural environments that embodied the values they sought to project, and regulate and reproduce the individual agents who were vital to the continuance of their rule. Paradoxically, then, it was precisely because hill stations were physically removed from the contestation on the Indian plains and were unabashedly imitative of a nostalgically remembered homeland that they played a significant role in the maintenance of the British presence in India. Illusion was essential to their design and operation. Their service to the raj and its rulers ultimately derived from the degree to which they seemed a part of England and apart from India.

The problem with this artifice of isolation and memory is that its defiance of distance could not be sustained. To their dismay, the British watched as the boundaries intended to differentiate the hill stations from the rest of India inexorably eroded under the influx of Indians. They themselves were inadvertently responsible for this outcome since their own presence made these locales accessible from the plains and attractive to its peoples. The British sahibs and memsahibs who made the seasonal pilgrimage to the hills depended on Indian porters, servants, shopkeepers, and others to sustain their comfortable existence: an average of ten or more Indians were employed directly or indirectly in the service of each Briton. Hence, as the hill stations grew more popular as retreats for the British, they also grew more attractive as centers of employment for Indians, most of them migrants from precisely the places that the British were seeking to escape. It must be acknowledged that many Britons were well prepared as a result of the stratifications of class within their home society to ignore the presence of menials, to look past them as if they were invisible, and they used this social skill to sustain an illusion of isolation despite the presence of the domestic servants who inhabited their homes and of the shopkeepers, porters, artisans, and others who occupied the overcrowded station bazaars.

10. King, "Culture, Social Power and Environment," 196.

Yet the sheer scale of the Indian influx eventually forced itself on the consciousness of the British. It manifested itself most often as anxieties about sanitation and disease—a familiar trope for racial fear. As a result, public health measures became common tools for the repair of racial boundaries. Even more subversive to the sanctity of the hill stations were the maharajas, lawyers, merchants, and other upper- and middle-class Indians who began to encroach on these ethnic enclaves in the late nineteenth and early twentieth centuries. Unlike migrant workers, these seeming upstarts possessed the financial resources and cultural standards to demand access to the residential and recreational quarters occupied by the British, to claim the right to participate in the social life of the stations. They intruded into the most intimate and exclusive corners of the space that the British had cleared for their own exclusive use. And yet the responsibility for their appearance on the scene once again lay with the British: if they had not invested so much of their social and political capital in these places, Indians of wealth and influence would not have found them so irresistible. The eventual outcome of these unintended processes was the incorporation of the hill stations within the compass of the Indian realm and their consequent destruction as special spheres of British bourgeois life.

--------

Hill stations sprang up all across British India during the course of the nineteenth century. As one would expect, the largest number arose in the Himalayas, especially in the important area to the west of Nepal, but the British found suitable sites in other parts of the subcontinent as well. The principal requirements for the establishment of a hill station were an elevation high enough to provide respite from the summer heat and a location remote enough to provide isolation from the indigenous multitudes. Matheran, located some fifty miles east of Bombay, may have had the lowest elevation (2,500 feet) of the well-known hill stations, and none of the highland regions in central India provided sites much above 4,000 feet. Wherever possible, however, the British preferred elevations of about 6,000–7,500 feet, which was well above the habitat of malarial mosquitoes. Hill stations ranged across India from Mount Abu in the west to Shillong in the east and from Murree in the north to Kodaikanal in the south.

Exactly how many hill stations were established in British India is difficult to say. Some, such as Cherrapunji in Assam, were essentially stillborn, abandoned in that particular case because the station's annual rainfall exceeded five hundred inches. Others, like Sakesar in Sind, never grew beyond a few bungalows, modest retreats for the few Europeans stationed in the immediate vicinity. An accurate count is made even more difficult because of ambiguities about how a hill station should be defined. Is Alwaye, a hamlet located at an elevation of six hundred feet in the southwestern corner of the subcontinent, a hill station? Nora Mitchell, who has carried out the most detailed geographical study of the subject, thinks so. She identifies close to eighty Indian hill stations that existed during the colonial era.[11] Her list includes not only Alwaye but cities such as Bangalore, Coimbatore, and Poona, which stretch the notion of a hill station beyond what seem to me to be sensible limits. (Her list also excludes the hill stations located in present-day Pakistan, notably Murree.) My own estimate of the number of hill stations in British India is around sixty-five, but sufficient questions can be raised about particular places to make a definitive list all but impossible.

In any case, a precise count of the hill stations is less important than a general appreciation of their distinctive traits. Hill stations were seasonally variable settlements in the cooler elevations of the highlands where the British sought rest and recreation. The sites were in most cases inhabited by relatively few native peoples, though local rajas often held claim to the land. Formal transfer into British hands by treaty or sale or subterfuge was an essential preliminary to the development of hill stations. The only notable exceptions were the Kashmiri stations, which remained under the authority of the maharaja of Kashmir. Perhaps for this reason Gulmarg and its sister stations never became politically important despite the enormous natural appeal of their surroundings. The British had to have full legal rights to the land for them to invest the resources necessary to establish the multitude of social, educational, and political institutions that gave the larger hill stations their importance to the raj.

If all hill stations shared the same basic characteristics, they differed greatly in size, function, and clientele. Mitchell has proposed the following five categories: the official multifunctional hill station, the private multifunctional hill station, the single-purpose hill station, the minor hill station, and the satellite hill station. Among the stations that fall in the first category are Simla, Darjeeling, Naini Tal, and Ootacamund: they were government headquarters as well as social, recreational, and educational centers for the British. Kodaikanal, Matheran, and Mussoorie are examples of stations in the second category: they served much the same array of

---

11. Mitchell, "The Indian Hill-Station," 87. A total of ninety-six hill stations are listed by Mitchell, but perhaps twenty of these (the exact number is difficult to determine from the categories employed in the accompanying map) were founded after independence.

social functions as the first group but did not possess any official purpose. The three remaining categories are a good deal more difficult to distinguish from one another: many stations could be described with equal justice as minor, single-purpose, and satellites of larger stations. Rather than quibble over these somewhat nebulous distinctions, it may be more useful to classify the smaller hill stations by the clientele they accommodated. Most were cantonments for British troops—at least twenty-five stations existed almost exclusively for this purpose. Others held enclaves of missionaries, planters, pensioners, railway workers, and so on. Dharmkot, for instance, was dominated by Presbyterian missionaries, Yercaud by coffee planters, Lonavala by employees of the Bombay railway system, and Madhupur by retired civil servants. The occupational-cum-class attributes of their patrons was the measure most often applied by the British themselves to distinguish one hill station from another.

Small stations sometimes clustered around large official ones, producing a pattern of association that echoed the stratification within the British colonial community at large. Simla had at least six satellite stations in its orbit: Dagshai, Jutogh, and Kasauli were military cantonments, though Kasauli also had a sizable civilian population by the late nineteenth century; Solon was a military convalescent station and site of a large brewery; Sabathu was a military convalescent station and sanitarium for American Presbyterian missionaries; and Sonawar was the home of the Lawrence Military Asylum for the children of British soldiers. Other satellite stations could be found around Dalhousie, Darjeeling, Naini Tal, and Ootacamund. This pattern was most pronounced in the northwest, where strategic interests and other considerations caused the British to maintain a large civil and military presence in highland stations. Elsewhere the clustering of hill stations was less noticeable: official multipurpose stations like Pachmarhi and Shillong stood alone, and Mahabaleshwar had just one neighbor that could be considered a satellite—Panchgani. Although Mitchell organizes all of the Indian hill stations into clusters, most of these groupings are merely geographical, not functional.

A clear chronological pattern can be discerned in the development of hill stations, a pattern shaped by a variable mixture of political, social, military, medical, and technological factors. Monika Bührlein identifies three stages in the evolution of the Ceylonese hill station of Nuwara Eliya—sanitarium to high refuge (1819–72), high refuge to hill station (1872–96), and hill station to town (1892–1948).[12] While the particulars of this periodization

12. Bührlein, *Nuwara Eliya*, passim.

may be distinctive to Nuwara Eliya, a similar sequence of stages applied to the hill stations on the subcontinent. The first settlements appeared in the early 1820s, following the consolidation by the British of those massive territorial gains that came from the regional wars of the late eighteenth and early nineteenth centuries. The defeat of the kingdom of Nepal in 1815 opened the door to the Himalayas, where Simla, Mussoorie, and Almora soon arose in the northwest, followed a decade later by Darjeeling in the northeast. From the start, these highland sites attracted visitors in search of rest and relaxation, but they also served as forward positions in the strategic reconnaissance of neighboring states and as launching pads for commercial probes into central Asia. Mahabaleshwar was founded within a decade of the defeat in 1818 of the Peshwa, which concluded the war against the Marathas. The establishment of Cherrapunji was made possible by the acquisition of Assam in 1824. In the south, the relationship between the conquest of territory and the establishment of sanitaria was less direct. It took nearly thirty years after the defeat of Tipu Sultan in 1792 for the British to explore and settle southern India's highest mountains, the Nilgiris. Once again, however, the crucial decade was the 1820s. This chronological coincidence was partly just that, but one factor that transcended the particularisms of each region was the great cholera pandemic of 1817–21, probably the first of its kind to sweep across the entire subcontinent. Striking at a time when the British were establishing a large and enduring presence in India, this traumatic event accentuated their fear of the tropical environment and their desire for a haven from its scourges.

It was above all as sanitaria, then, that the first hill stations had their origins and acquired their reputations. Most of the residents and visitors in the early years were civil and military officials from neighboring lowlands who sought a general restoration of spirits or recovery from specific infirmities. The founding fathers of highland settlements were invariably British East India Company servants, but they acted as often without as with the encouragement and support of the government. Soon, however, places like Simla, Mahabaleshwar, and Ootacamund received visits from governors and governors-general, and the development of hill stations became a matter of state policy. Roads were cleared by labor corps or convicts, bungalows were built with official monies, convalescent depots were established for invalid troops, and medical data were collected by government physicians. Most civil and military authorities were soon convinced of the therapeutic value of hill stations. Their support provided the sanction around midcentury for a second round of initiatives to locate sites for hill stations. For those stations whose precise date of origin can be determined, nearly twice as many (twenty-three versus twelve) were founded in the 1840s and 1850s as in the 1820s and 1830s. They included multipurpose stations like Mount Abu, Dalhousie, Dharamsala, Kodaikanal, Matheran, Murree, Naini Tal, and Panchgani, and others intended exclusively as garrison or convalescent depots for troops, such as Dagshai, Jalapahar, Jutogh, Kasauli, Sanawar, Senchal, and Wellington. Although the disaster in Afghanistan in 1844 and the victory against the Sikhs in 1849 provided both strategic motives and opportunities for the founding of hill stations near the northwest frontier, elsewhere the main impetus lay in the search for places to rest and recuperate from the arduous life on the plains.

The second half of the nineteenth century was the age of consolidation for hill stations. Far fewer new stations were founded in this period (seven in the 1860s, one in the 1870s, five in the 1880s, and one in the 1890s, according to my incomplete census), but existing stations became larger and more important to the British in India. The railway-construction boom that began in the 1850s and continued through the end of the century made a number of hill stations more accessible to more visitors from more areas than before, thereby strengthening their viability as seasonal resorts. The railway also gave a crucial boost to planters, who began to establish tea, coffee, and cinchona estates on the slopes surrounding many hill stations in the latter half of the century. While subject to the vagaries of the international market, these enterprises provided the hill stations that served as their entrepots with a further impetus for growth.

The social prestige of the hill stations also increased in the latter half of the nineteenth century. During this period, Simla, Darjeeling, Mussoorie, Ootacamund, and other hill stations established themselves as the places where people of influence and ambition congregated. They acquired the reputations for parties and scandals that Kipling memorialized. They attracted growing numbers of British women and children for lengthy stays. And they attained something close to a monopoly over the schooling of European children in India. In short, they took on the principal role in the social reproduction of the British ruling elite. In so doing, they fulfilled the task with which they had been charged—to provide a milieu that mirrored England's in its bourgeois public and private spheres.

It is hardly surprising, therefore, that the hill stations also established themselves as places of political importance in this period. One indicator of their growing prominence was the 1850 statute that permitted hill stations to form municipal governments with the authority to tax and regulate their communities. The great turning point, however, was the 1857 revolt, which deepened British anxieties about their security on the plains and heightened their appreciation of the safety of the hills. As a result, civil and military authorities began to shift their headquarters to hill stations wherever feasible and for however long possible. Simla obtained official recognition as the summer capital of the raj in 1864, when the secretary of state for India allowed the imperial council to accompany the viceroy on his annual migration to the hills. By the early 1870s, most of the provincial governments had obtained sanction to establish seasonal headquarters in hill stations. Moreover, the army moved a significant portion of its command operations and British troops into the fastness of the highlands.

Hill stations reached their zenith in the late nineteenth century. The political importance of the official stations was underscored by the inauguration of large and costly public-building projects. Simla's physical appearance was transformed in the 1880s by the construction of the grandiose Viceregal Lodge and an array of other government buildings. Governors' or lieutenant governors' mansions were established in Darjeeling in 1879, Ootacamund in 1880, Mahabaleshwar in 1886, and Naini Tal in 1896. A profusion of clock towers, bandstands, fountains, and statues evidenced a heightened civic pride and prosperity even among the smaller hill stations. As railways extended feeder lines into remote areas, journeys to the hills became increasingly easy and inexpensive, and narrow-gauge lines were completed to Darjeeling in 1881, Ootacamund in 1902, Simla in 1903, and Matheran in 1907. Most hill stations had attained unprecedented popularity by the turn of the century.

Yet these same developments set in motion the forces that would undermine the bourgeois civic character of the hill stations; these forces intruded into the spaces where the British had hitherto been able to establish an exclusive and unfettered social presence characterized by the free interplay between public and private spheres. By the late nineteenth century the plebeian population of servants, porters, shopkeepers, and others had begun to expand beyond the physical capacities of its confined quarters, and the ensuing overcrowded housing, contaminated water, and other manifestations of degraded living and working conditions soon could no longer be ignored by British residents. Nor could the British ignore the entry of increasing numbers of middle- and upper-class Indians into the hill stations in the late nineteenth and early twentieth centuries. They made their presence felt through the purchase and occupation of property in the European wards of the stations and by the proliferation of hotels, clubs, and other social institutions that catered to their class. The hill stations in the vicinity of Bombay were the first to attract prosperous Indians on a significant scale, but the phenomenon quickly spread across the subcontinent. This influx introduced an entirely new dynamic to the hill stations, exposing British social life to the scrutiny of autonomous outsiders and undermining the unique conditions that sustained the articulation of the bourgeois public and private spheres.

Consequently, as Indians became more visible and influential in the hill stations, the British became less so. The end of World War I was an important turning point. The war had confined an exceptionally large number of Europeans to the hill stations, and with its end many of them took the earliest opportunity to book passages to Britain so that children could be placed in boarding schools and families could be seen for the first time in years. What might have been little more than a temporary setback for the hill stations proved much more far-lasting in the context of contiguous developments. The reduction of shipping fares and the recommendations of the Lee Commission (1925) made it possible for an increasing number of Britons in India to take their holidays in England rather than in the hills. The Indianization of the uncovenanted services made it difficult for hill-station schools to maintain their enrollments since they had built their reputations on preparing the sons of domiciled Europeans for government careers. The protests by nationalists and the postwar construction of the new capital in Delhi undermined Simla's position as the center of power of the British raj, and its diminution implied the same for those other hill stations that acted as summer headquarters for provincial governments. By the 1930s, the imperial and provincial governments had severely reduced or entirely terminated their annual migrations to the hills. As the British found fewer reasons to go to hill stations, property values fell, with only Indians coming forth as buyers. A temporary revival in the hill stations' fortunes occurred when the outbreak of World War II isolated the British in India once again, but they had already ceased to serve as genuine centers of political and social power for the colonial elite. In this respect, they merely mirrored the overall pattern of decline and disengagement that characterized the final decades of the British raj.

It must be reiterated that it was not the hill stations themselves that collapsed but rather the colonial purposes they served. Although the stations suffered through a difficult period of adjustment as British power waned, most of them survived the transition to independence and found renewal as holiday resorts for Indians. Indeed, the genesis of their post-colonial configuration can be clearly detected in the tensions and traumas they experienced in the first half of the twentieth century.

————

This book traces the trajectory of the colonial hill stations' rise and fall against the backdrop of British India. While set within a broadly chronological framework, the study is thematically organized. The early chapters examine the attitudes, assumptions, and intentions that underlay the establishment and development of the hill stations. British responses to and representations of these highland sites took the particular forms they did because of the position the British found themselves in as the expatriate rulers of a strange and perilous land. Chapter Two places the medical rationale for the establishment of the hill stations in the context of the larger colonial discourse about the imperilment of Europeans in the tropical environment. The highland landscape is the subject of Chapter Three, which shows that the British interpreted and altered the environment around them to conform to a picturesque aesthetic that evoked memories of their homeland. Chapter Four traces a similar pattern in the British response to the highlands' native inhabitants, whom the British saw as noble savages set apart by their innocence and simplicity from the peoples of the plains.

The private and the public worlds of the hill stations are the subjects of the middle chapters. Chapter Five suggests that hill stations bore a morphological resemblance to English villages and that their residents conducted themselves in much the same manner as the patrons of English spa towns and seaside resorts: these nostalgic simulacra served to restore a sense of cultural identity and communal purpose to people otherwise immersed in an alien environment. These objectives were reinforced by the remarkably high proportion of British inhabitants who were women and children. Chapter Six argues that their presence helped to establish hill stations as nurseries for the ruling race, special places where the biological and ideological reproduction of the agents of empire could be carried out. The public realm of power is the subject of Chapter Seven. It charts the transfer of political and military authority from the plains to the hills and examines the heated debate this transfer aroused. These developments occurred in the aftermath of the 1857 revolt, and they suggest that British authorities had become convinced that they could rule India best when physically removed from its peoples.

The final chapters explore the forces that undermined the imperial purposes of hill stations. The massive influx of Indian laborers to the hill stations and the problems they posed for the British efforts to maintain their sense of distance from the rest of India are discussed in Chapter Eight. Chapter Nine charts the increasing popularity of hill stations with upper- and middle-class Indians and the contiguous decline in their popularity with the British. If the Indianization of the hill stations is a mark of the dramatic changes in power relations that evidenced imperial decline, it is also an indicator of substantial continuities of purpose between the colonial and postcolonial elites. The Conclusion summarizes the main arguments and draws out their implications for our understanding of the colonial project.

As should be clear by this point, this book is not an exercise in nostalgia for a bygone imperial era.[13] Such sentiments have been plentiful in the popular literature on the raj, and especially on the hill stations.[14] The reason should be obvious: the hill stations seemed so far removed from the harsher realities of colonialism that authors striving to cast the British experience in the most entertaining and evocative light possible have found them attractive settings. I seek to show that this impression of the hill stations is entirely though not unwittingly wrong, that these places were in fact profoundly engaged in the complex and refractory processes of colonialism, but the dialectical terms of their engagement allowed those who enjoyed their pleasures and those who told their tales to see them otherwise. The hill stations offer a unique vantage point from which to view the structure and operation of the raj as it developed over the course of the nineteenth century.

I have evoked Thomas Mann's *The Magic Mountain* in my title, and drawn passages from his book as epigraphs for my chapters, not to dress up this book with cultural pretensions, but to point to pertinent parallels between the Alpine realm imagined by Mann and the Indian realms invented by the British. Like the secluded tuberculosis sanitarium that serves as the unlikely site for the novel's wide-ranging debate about the issues

---

13. For a thoughtful commentary on this subject, see Renato Rosaldo, ''Imperialist Nostalgia,'' *Representations* 26 (spring 1989), 107–22.

14. An example is Graeme D. Westlake, *An Introduction to the Hill Stations of India* (New Delhi, 1993).

confronting European society, the hill stations of India were venues of unexpected importance to the issues confronting colonial society. The distance from the bustling and contentious world of the Indian plains did not divorce the British who frequented the hills from the concerns of the raj, though that was often their desire and their critics' fear. Rather, it presented them with a milieu peculiarly well suited for reexamining, reanimating, and refashioning themselves in their roles as agents of imperial power.

# 2 Climate and the Colonial Condition

All interest in disease and death is only another expression of interest in life.
—Thomas Mann, *The Magic Mountain*

Like meat, we *keep* better here [in the hills].
—Emily Eden, *Up the Country*

The initial reason for seeking sanctuary in the Indian highlands was to escape the heat of the plains. To persons born and bred in the cool maritime climate of the British Isles, heat was not merely a cause of discomfort; it was a trope for all that was alien and hostile about the tropics. British anxieties about hot climates have been traced to their earliest encounters with tropical environments.[1] Although beckoned by the apparent natural abundance of the tropical world, they also were repelled by what their personal experiences persuaded them was a correlation between the heat of the tropics and disease, decay, and death. That British sojourners had ample reason to fear for their lives is borne out by mortality statistics: the cost of entry into these new and rich disease environments was high.[2] Yet Western medicine in the tropics failed to attribute this deadly tariff to microbic agents until the late nineteenth century, clinging instead to a climatic or environmental paradigm that emphasized the action of heat.[3]

1. See Karen Ordahl Kupperman, "Fear of Hot Climates in the Anglo-American Colonial Experience," *William and Mary Quarterly*, 3d ser., 41 (April 1984): 213–40.

2. See David Arnold, *Colonizing the Body: State Medicine and Epidemic Disease in Nineteenth-Century India* (Berkeley, 1993), ch. 2; and Philip D. Curtin, *Death by Migration: Europe's Encounter with the Tropical World in the Nineteenth Century* (Cambridge, 1989).

3. Arnold makes this point in *Colonizing the Body*, 23–34. I have traced these attitudes through the late nineteenth and early twentieth centuries in my essay, "The Perils of the Midday Sun: Climatic Anxieties in the Colonial Tropics," in

As one of the leading textbooks of tropical medicine in the nineteenth century put it, "Heat is in fact the great moving power of all other subordinate sources of disease."[4]

As long as the British in India were restricted to coastal enclaves, the sea supplied the principal means of relief from the oppressive temperatures that were held responsible for so many ailments. Invalids frequently took berths on ships that shuttled along the coast or sailed to Cape Town, Mauritius, and other ports. It was not merely the destination but the voyage itself, with its enforced leisure and exposure to cool ocean breezes, which was thought to offer recuperative benefits.

By the early nineteenth century, however, the British were no longer clinging to the coast; they were ruling the greater part of the subcontinent. Their imperial position drew them in ever-increasing numbers to the interior, where the looming expanses of the Himalayas and the highlands of central and southern India offered enticing alternatives to the sea.[5] Colonial authorities began to probe these newly accessible mountain domains. Although strategic and commercial considerations influenced their efforts, especially in the Himalayas, the principal impetus behind these probes was the desire to find refuge from the heat and disease of the plains. This desire was heightened by the devastating cholera epidemic that swept through India in 1817–21.[6] As a senior member of the Indian Medical Board observed in the early 1820s, "The subject [of highland sanitaria] generally has awakened great anxiety on the part of the Government."[7]

———

The preoccupation with climate and health is evident in the circumstances that led to the founding of some of the leading hill stations in colonial India.

*Imperialism and the Natural World,* ed. John M. MacKenzie (Manchester, 1990), 118–40.

4. Sir James Ranald Martin, *Influence of Tropical Climates in Producing the Acute Endemic Diseases of Europeans,* 2d ed. (London, 1861), 45. The original author of this highly influential book was rather more subtle in assessing the role of heat: "From *heat* spring all those effects which originally *predispose* to the reception or operation of other moribific causes." James Johnson, *The Influence of Tropical Climates on European Constitutions,* 3d ed. (New York, 1826), 389 (emphasis in original).

5. For general discussions of the medical rationale for the establishment of hill stations, see Nora Mitchell, "The Indian Hill-Station: Kodaikanal," University of Chicago Department of Geography Research Paper 141, 1972, ch. 2; and Curtin, *Death by Migration,* 47–50.

6. See Arnold, *Colonizing the Body,* ch. 4; and David Arnold, "Cholera and Colonialism in British India," *Past and Present* 113 (Nov. 1986): 118–51.

7. Dr. Olgilvy, c. 1824, in F/4/898/23460, Board's Collection, IOL.

Southern India's Nilgiri plateau, rising some eight thousand feet above sea level, was penetrated by several parties of British officials in the first two decades of the nineteenth century. After touring the area in 1819, John Sullivan, collector for Coimbatore district, began a personal campaign to persuade the government of Madras that the location's "unusually temperate and healthy" climate made it ideal as a "resort of Invalids." In 1821 the medical board of the presidency ordered three assistant surgeons to investigate these claims. Their reports persuaded the board that "we fully anticipate very great advantages from a resort to these Hills," and it recommended that fifty invalid soldiers be sent there to test the region's salubrity. Independently, Sullivan and other officials from neighboring districts established summer residences at Ootacamund, nestled in the heart of the Nilgiris. This nascent community soon attracted a stream of visitors in search of health and leisure. Among them was Sir Thomas Munro, the governor of Madras, who stayed at Ootacamund in 1826. A year later the station was officially recognized as a sanitarium by Munro's successor, Stephen Lushington, who approved the construction of bungalows and a hospital and the appointment of two medical officers and an apothecary. A third medical officer was sent to Kotagiri, a smaller settlement in the eastern part of the plateau. Even though official support for the medical station at Ootacamund was withdrawn in 1834, the reputation of the Nilgiris as a location for the convalescence of Europeans had already been "completely established," according to J. Annesley of the Madras medical board.[8]

At the same time that John Sullivan was establishing the first European house at Ootacamund, Captain Charles Kennedy, the political agent for the hill states along what was then the northwest frontier of British India, was building a timber dwelling on a magnificently forested ridge known as Simla. His predecessor had discovered the site during a hunting expedition in 1819, and Kennedy decided to make it his permanent residence three

8. The remarks by Sullivan and the medical board may be found in F/4/702/19060 and F/4/771/19407, Board's Collection, IOL. Much of the official correspondence on the establishment of health sanitaria in the Nilgiris is reprinted in Parliamentary Papers (PP), *Papers Relative to the Formation of a Sanitarium on the Neilgherries for European Troops*, Session 729, XLI, 1850, including the comment by Annesley (p. 54). John Sullivan's role in the establishment of Ootacamund is described by Paul Hockings, "John Sullivan of Ootacamund," in *Journal of Indian History Golden Jubilee Volume*, ed. T. K. Ravindran (Trivandrum, 1973), 863–71. Also see Sir Frederick Price, *Ootacamund: A History* (Madras, 1908); and Judith Theresa Kenny, "Constructing an Imperial Hill Station: The Representation of British Authority in Ootacamund" (Ph.D. diss., Syracuse University, 1990).

years later. He explained to his superiors: "the climate is particularly salubrious, and I rejoice to say my health has derived infinite benefit from my residence in it."[9] This retreat quickly became a magnet for invalided officers and other Europeans in upper India seeking rest cures. In 1827 Lord Amherst became the first in a long line of governors-general and viceroys who would make the station their summer home. The government formally acquired Simla in 1830 through an exchange agreement with the maharaja of Patiala and the rana of Keonthal, the joint proprietors of the land. By this date some thirty British houses dotted the ridge, and Simla had acquired a name for itself as "the resort of the rich, the idle, and the invalid."[10]

Darjeeling presented a more complicated history than Simla because of its strategically sensitive location. It came to the attention of the British government when Captain G. S. Lloyd and J. W. Grant, commercial resident at Maldah, visited the area in 1827 and recommended its acquisition as a site for a sanitarium. Lord William Bentinck, then governor-general of India, was favorably disposed to the recommendation, noting in a minute "the great saving of European life and the consequent saving of expense that will accrue both to individuals and to the state." He was restrained, however, by the objections of Charles Metcalfe and other members of the governor-general's council, who feared the response of the Nepalese to this encroachment on their eastern border.[11] Several years later, after enjoying stays at Simla and Mussoorie and failing to establish a satisfactory sanitarium at Cherrapunji in Assam, Bentinck authorized Captain Lloyd to persuade the raja of Sikkim to cede Darjeeling to the British, regardless of "the satisfaction or dissatisfaction of the Nepauli Durbar."[12] The government's letter to the raja sought to assure him that "it is solely on account of the climate that the possession of the place is deemed desirable, [because] the cold . . . is understood . . . as peculiarly beneficial to the European con-

9. Quoted in H. Montgomery Hyde, *Simla and the Simla Hill States under British Protection 1815–1835* (Lahore, 1961), 11.

10. Victor Jacquemont, *Letters from India*, vol. 1 (London, 1834), 226. The origins of Simla have been most recently detailed by Raja Bhasin, *Simla: The Summer Capital of British India* (New Delhi, 1992); Pamela Kanwar, *Imperial Simla* (Delhi, 1990); and Vipin Pubby, *Simla Then and Now: Summer Capital of the Raj* (New Delhi, 1988).

11. See minutes on Darjeeling, 17 June 1830–17 October 1833, nos. 1–6, Foreign Dept. Proceedings, INA. Bentinck's minute is reprinted in C. H. Philips, ed., *The Correspondence of Lord William Cavendish Bentinck*, vol. 1 (Oxford, 1977), 457.

12. Minute by Bentinck, 8? January 1835, no. 1, Foreign Dept. Proceedings, INA.

Figure 1. Eden Sanitarium, Darjeeling. From Darjeeling Himalayan Railway Company, *The Darjeeling Himalayan Railway. Illustrated Guide for Tourists* (London, 1896).

stitution when debilitated by the Heat of the plains."[13] Although it is clear that the British also hoped Darjeeling would provide a bridgehead for trade with Tibet, health considerations predominated. Lord Auckland, who succeeded Bentinck as governor-general, reiterated his predecessor's commitment to Darjeeling, proclaiming that he was "unwilling to abandon an object of so much importance to . . . the European inhabitants of Bengal as that of giving them means of access to a healthy climate within one third of the distance from Calcutta to Simla."[14] The enthusiastic attention the Calcutta press gave to the government's efforts demonstrates that the Europeans in Bengal did indeed support the development of Darjeeling as a health resort. And with the appointment of Dr. Arthur Campbell of the Bengal Medical Service as superintendent of the station in 1839, its transformation into the most popular mountain sanitarium in the eastern Himalayas had begun (Figure 1).[15]

13. Government of India to Raja of Sikkim, 11 February 1835, no. 111, Foreign Dept. Proceedings, INA. Also see the remarks in the ensuing treaty, quoted in *Newman's Guide to Darjeeling and Neighbourhood,* 6th ed. (Calcutta, 1919), 52.

14. Minute by Auckland, 16 April 1836, no. 21, Foreign Dept. Proceedings, INA.

15. Evidence of the public interest in Darjeeling can be found in the newspaper articles reprinted in H. Hosten, "The Centenary of Darjeeling," *Bengal: Past and Present* 39, pt. 2, no. 78 (April-June 1930): 106–23; and Fred Pinn, *The Road to Destiny: Darjeeling Letters 1839* (Calcutta, 1986). For general histories of Darjeeling, see E. C. Dozey, *A Concise History of the Darjeeling District since 1835* (Calcutta, 1922); and Jahar Sen, *Darjeeling: A Favoured Retreat* (New Delhi, 1989).

All three presidencies sought health resorts in the hills, and an element of bureaucratic rivalry suffused their efforts. Bengal, of course, could obtain access to the Himalayas, while Madras claimed jurisdiction over the Nilgiris, but Bombay held no territory of equivalent elevation within its domain. Some of its European community journeyed to the Nilgiris, but the desire to find a more accessible convalescent depot, as well as to be free of obligation to Madras officialdom, prompted an investigation of the Western Ghats south of Bombay city. In 1825 Major John Briggs, the British resident for the princely state of Satara, sent his ailing family to the nearby plateau of Mahabaleshwar (elevation 4,500 feet). His subsequent report to the Bombay medical board on the virtues of the location included the engaging claim that while its lower elevation made it considerably warmer than the Nilgiris, this effect had the advantage of causing less shock to the systems of new arrivals. The governor of Bombay, Sir John Malcolm, visited Mahabalesh-war in 1828, and his enthusiasm for the spot led the government to persuade the raja of Satara to give up the territory in exchange for a village. It soon became the principal hill station for the Bombay presidency.[16]

Less than a decade after the first Englishmen had probed the mountain regions of India, then, several highland sites had gained recognition as salubrious retreats from the oppressive heat of the plains. "It is but of late years that public attention has been awakened to the vast advantages of climate which the elevated tracts of this country represent to its European possessors," declared Mahabaleshwar's medical officer in 1830. He gave thanks for "those resources for the preservation and recovery of health, which nature has thus bountifully placed within our reach."[17] These senti-ments, buoyant with the sense of discovery, were widely shared. Here at last a remedy for the fearful cost of residence in the tropics seemed within reach.

Much of the initial euphoria was created by the testimonials of visitors, who praised the invigorating effects of the highland climate. But anecdotal evidence went only so far: authorities demanded statistical proof of the health benefits of the hills. Bentinck, in an 1833 minute, had argued on the

16. See John Briggs's letter to the Bombay medical board (31 May 1826), reprinted in Perin Bharucha, *Mahabaleswar: The Club 1881–1981* (Bombay, c. 1981), app. B; as well as the report on Mahabaleshwar in F/4/1117/29948, Board's Collection, IOL, and the letter from Malcolm to Bentinck in Philips, *Correspon-dence*, vol. 1, 271.

17. James Murray, *Account of Malcolm Pait, on the Mahableshwur Hills* (Bombay, 1863), 1. Murray was the Bombay medical-service surgeon appointed to the Mahabaleshwar sanitarium. His account was originally written in 1830.

basis of medical records from army cantonments in various parts of Bengal that British soldiers stationed closer to the mountains had lower death rates than their counterparts in the lowlands, suggesting a correlation between elevation and survival.[18] But evidence from the hill stations themselves was still fragmentary. Government surgeons stationed in the hills had just begun accumulating and interpreting morbidity and mortality data about their patients. Intent upon demonstrating the relationship between climate and health, they also began to keep careful records of temperature, rainfall, humidity, wind, barometric pressure, and other measures of climatic conditions. The issue, however, was reducible to a single calculation—the death rate.

The preoccupation with mortality rates had particular relevance for the army, whose European ranks had been repeatedly decimated by disease in the first half of the nineteenth century.[19] Virtually all the statistical data concerning the health benefits of hill stations derived from military inquiries. In 1845, for example, Edward Balfour, a Bengal Army surgeon, compared mortality figures for British troops on the plains and in the Nilgiris. His evidence indicated that the annual death rate for the European forces in the three Indian presidencies averaged between 52 and 63 per 1,000 in the late 1820s (compared to 15.9 per 1,000 in Britain). Yet for army officers invalided to the Nilgiris between 1831 and 1834, the rate stood at 27 per 1,000. Balfour never disaggregated the mortality rate for officers in the plains: if he had done so, the contrast with the Nilgiri rate would have been far less stark. He did acknowledge that the figures for enlisted men at the convalescent station in the Nilgiris remained high but argued with some justification that this result was to be expected from a group that had come to the hills because of illness. Whatever the epidemiological weaknesses of Balfour's study, it made a more substantial case than ever before that the hill stations provided real medical benefits to British troops.[20]

Two years later a special committee appointed by the governor-general reviewed the medical evidence from highland sanitaria. Its conclusion was unequivocal: the death rate for European troops stationed in the hills was *half* that of their counterparts in the plains.[21] By midcentury the medical

18. Philips, *Correspondence*, vol. 2, 1169–71.
19. For mortality rates among British soldiers in India, see Curtin, *Death by Migration*, Table 1.1, passim.
20. Edward Balfour, *Statistical Data for Forming Troops and Maintaining Them in Health in Different Climates and Localities* (London, 1845).
21. I have been unable to obtain this 1847 report. It is referred to by the court of directors in a letter to the governor-general, 30 May 1849, in E/4/800/639–43,

efficacy of convalescence stations in the highlands had been demonstrated to the satisfaction of most military authorities. In 1860 the government of India circulated a letter to regional officials declaring that the establishment of hill sanitaria for European troops was "of so important a nature, that . . . no delay should be allowed to take place in doing all that can be done."[22] In 1863 the Parliamentary commission charged with investigating the health of the army in India was sufficiently impressed with the medical evidence concerning hill stations to recommend that a third of the British forces be stationed there on a rotating basis, and only strategic consider-ations prevented it from proposing an even higher percentage for billeting in the hills.[23] Medical opinion in British India was now all but unanimous in its endorsement of hill stations as sanitaria.

Yet the nature of this endorsement demands close scrutiny. Doctors took great care to distinguish those disorders that seemed to respond to con-valescence in the hills from those that did not. They consistently cautioned against sending to hill sanitaria patients who suffered from heart disease, epilepsy, rheumatism, bronchitis, and syphilis—illnesses that in some cases were aggravated by high altitudes or cool temperatures but above all were not classifiable as afflictions associated with tropical conditions. Although a few hill stations eventually acquired reputations as tuberculosis sanitaria (notably Almora, Kurseong, Hazaribagh, and Panchgani), this disease was rarely mentioned in the medical literature, probably because it was less deadly to the British in India than at home. The greatest menaces for the British in nineteenth-century India were malaria, cholera, typhoid fever, hepatitis, and dysentery. Although all these diseases occurred in Europe, their virulence in India made it possible to regard them as tropical afflictions. As such, they were most often invoked in medical assessments of the hills.

Remote highland retreats certainly offered greater immunity from dan-gerous contagions than the densely populated regions of the subcontinent. The etiology of cholera, typhoid fever, hepatitis, and dysentery was directly

India and Bengal Dispatches, IOL. It also forms the basis for the defense of hill sanitaria by the inspector general of hospitals in Duncan MacPherson, *Reports on Mountain and Marine Sanitaria* (Madras, 1862), 31.

22. F. D. Atkinson, secretary to the government of India, Military Department, in *Selections from the Records of the Government of India (Military Department),* no. l: *Report on the Extent and Nature of the Sanitary Establishments for European Troops in India* (Calcutta, 1862), 138. Some insight into the importance authorities gave to highland sanitaria can be gained from the letters and reports reprinted in this volume and two subsequent ones published in *Selections from the Records.*

23. PP, *Report of the Commissioners Appointed to Inquire into the Sanitary State of the Army in India,* XIX, 1863, esp. 150–53.

traceable to environments degraded by human habitation. Soldiers crammed together in unsanitary barracks naturally faced greater risks than did most Europeans. As the French traveler Victor Jacquemont observed: "Europeans are seldom [cholera's] victims, especially *gentlemen;* but the soldiers of the European corps, all Irish . . . , are swept away by it in great numbers."[24] Prior to the late nineteenth century, doctors may not have fully understood the role that contaminated food and water played in the spread of these diseases, but they did appreciate the fact that the retreat to sparsely populated mountain areas reduced the risk of infection. The early reports on the Nilgiris pointedly noted the absence of cholera, which had only recently assumed fearsome proportions in the subcontinent.[25] And medical officials soon observed that the residents of hill stations were less likely to suffer attacks of malaria than their counterparts on the plains, even though they did not understand until the end of the century that the disease occurred in the habitat of the anopheles mosquito.

Health authorities, however, were not able to proclaim the highlands fully free from the so-called zymotic diseases of the tropics. Some of the hill stations at lower elevations were within the anopheles mosquito zone, and visitors to the others often had to pass through dense belts of forest (known as the *terai* along the base of the Himalayas) where it was possible to contract an especially virulent strain of malaria carried by *Anopheles fluviatilis.*[26] Often, of course, those infected manifested no symptoms until after their arrival in the hills, thereby confounding claims of environmental immunity. In midcentury, the inspector general of hospitals remained unpersuaded that hill stations lay beyond some obscure "fever range."[27]

Cholera took little time to find its way to the hill stations: it arrived with the troops, porters, and other transient parties that came up from the plains. Fanny Parks reported an outbreak of cholera in the Mussoorie-Landour bazaar around 1840 that caused most of the hill bearers to take flight.[28] The reputations of Dharamsala and Murree, two predominantly military hill stations, were badly damaged by a series of cholera epidemics. The disease attacked Simla and its satellite stations in 1857, 1867, 1872, 1875, and on various occasions thereafter. It reached epidemic proportions in Shillong in

---

24. Jacquemont, *Letters,* vol. 1, 207.
25. *Papers Relative to the Formation of a Sanitarium,* 2, 45.
26. Leonard Jan Bruce-Chwatt, *Essential Malariology* (London, 1980), 161–62.
27. MacPherson, *Reports on . . . Sanitaria,* 33.
28. Fanny Parks, *Wanderings of a Pilgrim, in Search of the Picturesque,* vol. 2 (London, 1850), 253.

1879. By the end of the century, it had made an appearance in most hill stations.

As the growing populations of the hill stations began to overwhelm their rudimentary water and sewage systems in the late 1800s, water-borne diseases spread. Typhoid fever became endemic in Ootacamund and its neighbor Coonoor in the late 1860s, and many other hill stations were soon similarly afflicted. Outbreaks of dysentery grew increasingly frequent, and chronic diarrhea was common among the residents of hill stations. Its prevalence persuaded medical authorities that they faced a distinctive ailment, which they termed *diarrhoea alba* and attributed to such unlikely causes as the mica content of the water supply. The condition was known as "hill diarrhea" or "the Simla trots." Thus, as hill stations became more populated, their residents faced an escalating risk of contracting some of the very diseases they had sought to escape.[29]

Moreover, prevention was one thing, and cure quite another. Although some medical authorities initially sought to show that the highland climate could restore the health of those afflicted with tropical maladies, experience taught them to temper such claims. The sallow sufferers of hepatitis gained little benefit from residence in the hills. Cholera attacked its victims so swiftly and aggressively that survival was usually determined in a matter of days, if not hours, which meant that those who sought recovery in a mountain sanitarium had already passed the crisis point. This was often true for dysentery as well. The highlands appeared to offer greater promise to malarial invalids, whose condition was usually less acute, but these patients were never entirely freed from the risk of further bouts of fever. Medical authorities quickly lost their illusions about the curative benefits of hill sanitaria. The medical board of Madras observed that the Nilgiris were "not well adapted for the cure of those chronic diseases attributable to a tropical climate." The author of a memorandum on the health of British

29. For the outbreaks of cholera, see W. J. Moore, *Health Resorts for Tropical Invalids in India, at Home, and Abroad* (London, 1881), 28, 44; *Punjab District Gazetteers, Rawalpindi District, 1907*, vol. 28A (Lahore, 1909), 251; W. Martin Towelle, *Towelle's Hand Book and Guide to Simla* (Simla, 1877), 44; and Kenny, "Constructing an Imperial Hill Station," 174. Concerning contaminated water and the problem of typhoid in major hill stations, see R. S. Ellis, *Report on the Stations of Ootacamund and Coonoor* (Madras, 1865); J. L. Ranking, *Report upon the Sanitary Condition of Ootacamund* (Madras, 1868); C. J. Bamber, *Report on an Outbreak of Enteric Fever in Simla during the Summer of 1904* (Lahore, 1904); and *Report of the Simla Sanitary Investigation Committee* (Simla, 1905). Hill diarrhea is discussed in the standard medical textbook, W. J. Moore, *A Manual of the Diseases of India*, 2d ed. (London, 1886), 167–73.

troops said the same for hill stations as a whole: "the climate of the mountains, invaluable in prevention, will not cure disease." And the Parliamentary commission on the sanitary state of the Indian Army concluded that "hill stations are not curative."[30]

What, then, constituted the medical rationale for the hill sanitaria? As their preventative benefits diminished and their curative benefits proved illusory, health authorities increasingly stressed their value as places for convalescence from the physical enfeeblement that came in some measure from repeated attacks of disease but above all from prolonged exposure to the harsh climate of India. Those who, in the parlance of the period, had been "debilitated" by their long residence in the plains could expect to do best from withdrawal to the highlands. "The invalids who derive most benefit from a change to the Hills," observed the senior medical officer at Ootacamund, "are those who labour under no organic disease, but suffer from general debility, the result of a residence in the low country; these cases rally wonderfully and rapidly." Such was the medical magic of the hill stations. The reports from various mountain sites took on an increasingly common character. For Darjeeling's medical officer, the sanitarium was especially suited for patients suffering from "general debility, whether arising from a long residence in the plains or depending on tardy convalescence from fevers and other acute disease." A surgeon with the sanitary commission of Madras made the same point about Yercaud, a hill station in southern India: "it is not . . . to invalids suffering from organic disease that our mountain climates hold out much ground of hope; but rather to those who are simply exhausted in mind and body from prolonged exposure to a high temperature in the low country, and who need rest from work and a cooler air to breathe." Authors of general assessments of the hill stations, such as Dr. D. H. Cullimore in *The Book of Climates*, concurred: "it is as a restorative to those suffering from overwork, or exhausted by the heat of the plains, that tropical hill-stations are the most advantageous."[31] This reasoning represented a shift in the medical advocacy of hill

30. *Papers Relative to the Formation of a Sanitarium*, 66; memo by Dr. J. P. March in *Selections from the Records of the Government of Bengal*, no. 36, pt. 2: *The Maghassani Hills as a Sanitarium* (Calcutta, 1861), 12; and *Report of the Commissioners Appointed to Inquire into the Sanitary State of the Army in India*, 153.

31. George Makay, *Remarks on the Climate, with Advice to Invalids and Others Visiting the Neilgherry Hills* (Madras, 1870), 27; Dr. H. Chapman in H. V. Bayley, *Dorje-ling* (Calcutta, 1838), 35; W. R. Cornish, "The Shervaroy Hills," in

stations from the problematic grounds posed by a clinical assessment of climate and disease to a more socially resonant understanding of the effects of the tropics on the European.

————————

The alacrity with which the British Indian medical establishment conferred invalid status upon those who complained of "debility," which often seemed to mean little more than a general sense of ennui, illustrates the social purposes that underlay the desire to invest the highlands with therapeutic value. It was not uncommon for European sojourners in the tropics to experience lethargy, irritability, depression, nervousness, insomnia, and various other vague symptoms, which were diagnosed in descriptive terms such as "Punjab head," "Burma head," "tropical fatigue," "tropical inertia," and "tropical amnesia." Nothing in the discourse of the doctors suggests that they regarded these maladies to be any less "real" than those of specific organic origin. Their reluctance to make such a distinction may have been due in part to the practical problems of diagnosis: it was seldom certain whether complaints of "debility" were manifestations of physiological disease or derived from psychological or other causes. Moreover, few physicians before the late nineteenth century would have seen the need to distinguish the psychological from the physiological.[32] They treated both indiscriminately, and the mysteries of tropical maladies obscured the distinctions between the two even further. Whether the benefits of a stay in the hills were measurable in careful tabulations of clinic records or in vague expressions of well-being, medical authorities were equally prepared to appropriate the evidence within their own terms of reference and for their own professional advantage. And, in so doing, they spoke to issues that extended far beyond the conventional confines of their practice.

The most conspicuous reason for granting medical significance to the vague malaise that assailed Europeans in India was the scientific justification this supplied to what might otherwise have been regarded as merely a holiday in the hills. Particularly for members of the official community, the surest way to obtain occasional respite from their official responsibil-

————————

*The Hill Ranges of Southern India,* ed. John Shortt (Madras, 1870–83), 34; D. H. Cullimore, *The Book of Climates,* 2d ed. (London, 1891), 13.

32. See Waltraud Ernst, *Mad Tales from the Raj: The European Insane in British India, 1800–1858* (London, 1991), 98, 142–47.

ities in the plain's oppressive heat was by securing a medical leave.[33] The doctors who obliged them in this gambit were themselves servants of the colonial state, and their own experiences with the Indian climate heightened their understanding of their patients' desires to seek rest and relief in the highlands. One can detect the influence of personal experience in the assertion by W. J. Moore, surgeon general for the government of Bombay, that hill stations "be regarded not only as exciting a sanitary effect on the body, but also on the mind: the freedom from the harass of daily work and the change of scene and society, tending to raise and exhilarate the spirits, depressed by the continued influence of the heated plains."[34]

Precedents for this medicalization of leisure can be found in Britain itself. English physicians in the eighteenth and early nineteenth centuries had given scientific legitimation to the seasonal migrations of the landed elite to spa towns such as Bath and Brighton, where they claimed that the mineral waters and the sea air and water were therapeutic. A similar body of professional advice arose in the nineteenth century in connection with the travels of the newly prosperous bourgeoisie to various Mediterranean locations.[35] Like their counterparts in England, doctors in India provided the British elite who ruled the subcontinent with a medical validation for their social assemblages.

Yet the claims of medicine were more than a simple pretext for the exercise of leisure habits that aped fashions in Britain. As "the master narrative of scientific discourse" for the British in nineteenth-century India,[36] medicine was the principal means by which they sought to understand the physical environment and to assess the risks it posed to their personal *and* communal well-being. What the surgeons and other medical authorities had to say about the therapeutic benefits of the hill stations illuminates the broad contours of concern by the British about their status as overlords in an alien land. When the doctors prescribed a "change of climate" for their debilitated patients, the literal and figurative meanings of this counsel were unalterably bound together. Flight from the climatic

33. See D. G. Crawford, *A History of the Indian Medical Service 1600–1913*, vol. 1 (London, 1914), ch. 19, for information about the requirements and conditions for leaves and furloughs.

34. Moore, *Health Resorts*, 3.

35. See Edmund W. Gilbert, *Brighton: Old Ocean's Bauble* (London, 1954), chs. 4, 5; and John Pemble, *The Mediterranean Passion: Victorians and Edwardians in the South* (Oxford, 1987), pt. 2.

36. The phrase comes from Arnold, *Colonizing the Body*, 21.

perils of lowland India entailed flight from the labyrinth of social and cultural hazards that lurked within the colonial environment.

One route of access to these interwoven issues lies in the preoccupation with the problem of "degeneration." Official opinion in nineteenth-century India held that a European population could not be sustained on a permanent basis in the tropical climate of lowland India: colonists would degenerate and die out by the third generation.[37] The high mortality rate among the British in India until the second half of the century certainly gave credence to this forecast, and because the problem of health seemed so closely connected to the issue of degeneration, members of the medical profession frequently assumed the role of authorities on the matter. James Johnson's *The Influence of Tropical Climates on European Constitutions*, the first important British textbook on tropical medicine published in the nineteenth century, opened with the assertion that Europeans degenerated in the tropical climate, and Sir James Ranald Martin, a highly respected expert on tropical medicine who authored later editions of the same work, stated that "the third generation of unmixed European is nowhere to be found in Bengal," an absence he attributed to "the physical degradation resulting from long residence in a hot and pestilential country." A health manual for British women in India gave its readers the unwelcome news that their children would "show early signs of degeneration of both body and mind." It alleged, "If a British family keeps its blood unalloyed, it dies out in a third generation." "I *have* seen the third generation of Europeans reared in Calcutta," declared Sir Joseph Fayrer, president of the medical board of the India Office, "but such are rare, and though there was no marked physical degeneration, yet there was that which would make one look with great misgiving on the prospects of a race so produced."[38] This

37. This concern is examined in my introduction to Richard F. Burton, *Goa, and the Blue Mountains* (Berkeley, 1991), xi–xii; and in David N. Livingstone, "Human Acclimatization: Perspectives on a Contested Field of Inquiry in Science, Medicine and Geography," *History of Science* 25 (1987): 359–94. For the parallel debate about degeneration in European society, see J. Edward Chamberlin and Sander L. Gilman, eds., *Degeneration: The Dark Side of Progress* (New York, 1985); and Daniel Pick, *Faces of Degeneration: A European Disorder, c. 1848–1918* (Cambridge, 1989).

38. Johnson, *Influence of Tropical Climates*, 10; Martin, *Influence of Tropical Climates*, 137, 97; Edward John Tilt, *Health in India for British Women*, 4th ed. (London, 1875), 108, 3; Sir Joseph Fayrer, *Tropical Dysentery and Chronic Diarrhoea* (London, 1881), 345. An especially full exposition of the theory of European degeneration in India can be found in Sir R. Havelock Charles, "Neurasthenia and Its Bearing on the Decay of Northern Peoples in India," *Transactions of the Society of Tropical Medicine and Hygiene* 7, no. 1 (Nov. 1913): 2–31.

concluding clause, oblique though it may have been, was clear enough in intimating that the chief signs of degeneration were evident in something other than physical decay. Martin's use of the adjective "unmixed" and the health manual's reference to "unalloyed blood" made the point more explicitly. The specter of degeneration lay less in the threat of physical extinction than in the prospect of miscegenation and the loss of racial identity.

The policy implications of the problem of degeneration come through most clearly in the testimony to the select committee appointed by Parliament to consider the prospects for European settlement in India in the aftermath of the 1857 revolt. One of the central questions the committee asked was whether the climate of the Indian plains posed an insuperable barrier to permanent colonization. The medical and government witnesses were all but unanimous that it did. They insisted that the physical frame of the European could not withstand the effects of high temperatures and tropical diseases over the long term, and that because manual labor was virtually impossible, the range of opportunities for colonists would be drastically limited. The incantatory theme of degeneration appeared repeatedly in their testimony. Dr. Robert Baikie, the chief medical officer for the Nilgiris, cited the experience of the Portuguese as proof that a settler population would "die out in the third generation."[39] Since the Portuguese in India certainly had not failed to produce biological heirs, it is quite clear that the phrase "die out" was meant in a metaphorical sense and referred to the devolution of notionally pure Portuguese colonists into the mixed-race Goan community. The fear that India would similarly incorporate the offspring of British colonists—alienating them from their national-cum-racial heritage—is apparent in Captain John Ouchterlony's lament that "even if children were reared to maturity [in India], their constitutions would be enfeebled, and the 'Saxon energy' impaired, and I believe that their progeny resulting from the intermarriages of colonists would be found deteriorated in all English or European attributes."[40] For medical and administrative authorities in India, the risks of tropical degeneration were so fearsome that they precluded the possibility of a European settler population's surviving over several generations *as* Europeans.

39. PP, *First Report from the Select Committee on Colonization and Settlement (India)* (1858), Session 1857–58, VII, pt. 1, 54.

40. PP, *Third Report from the Select Committee* (1858), Session 1857–58, VII, pt. 1, 2.

Other witnesses did not share this gloomy assessment. Almost without exception, they were planters and other nonofficial Europeans who saw themselves as permanent residents of India. In a typical statement, the indigo planter John Saunders declared: "I have been 25 years [in India], and have never been seriously ill; and I have had 12 brothers and cousins residing in the same district, and I do not think that any one of them has ever suffered seriously from the climate."[41] Another planter professed his good health but was less confident of the benefits for future generations: "I believe they deteriorate; the second and third generation would be inferior to the first."[42] To guard against this danger, he sent his children back to Britain for their education, and he claimed that other planters did the same. Most of the nonofficial witnesses, however, insisted that India posed no environmental barrier to colonization. "The Bengal climate is a very fine climate," affirmed William Theobald, an agent for Bengal planters and merchants. "The doctors and some other people would make us afraid of it, . . . but I think we have a very comfortable existence. . . . I regard [the climate] as of no importance at all on the question of colonization and settlement."[43] The disdain that the planters and traders felt for the supposed dangers of the tropical climate was motivated not merely by their personal cognizance of health but also by their communal appreciation of the political and economic advantages they stood to gain from an enlarged settler population. Much of their testimony revolved around the resentments they harbored against the Indian government for its policies regarding land tenure, the legal system, and other areas of conflict. From their perspective, colonization by additional Europeans offered the prospect of overturning those policies.

While the debate about tropical degeneration therefore possessed important political ramifications, these ramifications were inseparable in the minds of the climatic pessimists from the danger of racial decline. Their objections to permanent settlement derived not just from the political challenge that colonists posed but from the social precedent they set. Any significant increase in the colonist population was most likely to occur in

41. PP, *Fourth Report from the Select Committee* (1858), Session 1857–58, VII, pt. 2, 219.

42. Josiah Patrick Wise in PP, *Second Report from the Select Committee* (1858), Session 1857–58, VII, pt. 1, 62. A similar statement is offered by another indigo planter, James Thompson MacKenzie, in *Second Report from the Select Committee* (1858), Session 1857–58, VII, pt. 1, 100, 104.

43. PP, *First Report from the Select Committee* (1858), Session 1857–58, VII, pt. 1, 56, 80.

the agricultural realm, where indigo and tea production offered the most successful examples of European enterprise. Yet the planters who pioneered these industries were notorious for their hard drinking, their rough treatment of workers, their brazen liaisons with Indian mistresses, and their plenteous sirings of mixed-race children.[44] Blind though they might be to their own transgressions, they supplied the proponents of the degeneration theory with a stark example of the dangers posed by extended residence in the tropics. They were not, however, the only exemplars of this menace. By the mid-nineteenth century colonial authorities had become profoundly disturbed by the large number of European soldiers, vagrants, prostitutes, orphans, and others who haunted the periphery of British Indian society, exhibiting what these authorities regarded as the early manifestations of degeneration.[45] Their fate was a salutary reminder that the entire European population stood at varying degrees of risk. Conventional opinion held that all women and children were imperiled by the biological weaknesses of their natures, while men were put at risk by the fortunes of their rank and the cravings of their sex. None could disregard the dangers of the tropics.

Within this context the medical discourse about hill stations had broad social significance. For the advocates of highland sanitaria, these remote retreats offered the only territorial means of escape from the subversive effects of the Indian environment. Time and again, witnesses before the select committee invoked the hills as havens from degeneration, and the committee itself concluded, "Few objects of contemplation can be more interesting [for European colonization] than the formation and progress of these establishments in the hills."[46] British officials in India had come to see the hill stations as the only sites where they could establish a lasting presence without imperiling their physical and moral integrity.

Reinforcing the special appeal of the hill stations was the discomfort these places caused for the Indian servants, porters, and others who came there in search of employment. Especially in the early years, migrant

44. See the scathing denunciation of the planters by G. O. Trevelyan, *The Competition Wallah*, 2d ed. (London, 1866), 262–81.

45. See Kenneth Ballhatchet, *Race, Sex and Class under the Raj: Imperial Attitudes and Policies and Their Critics, 1793–1905* (New York, 1980); David Arnold, "European Orphans and Vagrants in India in the Nineteenth Century," *Journal of Imperial and Commonwealth History* 7, no. 2 (Jan. 1979): 104–27; David Arnold, "White Colonization and Labour in Nineteenth-Century India," *Journal of Imperial and Commonwealth History* 9, no. 2 (Jan. 1983): 133–58; and Ernst, *Mad Tales from the Raj.*

46. PP, *Report from the Select Committee* (1859), Session 2, V, iv.

laborers from the plains were poorly prepared for the climatic and institutional conditions in the hills, and they suffered from inadequate clothing
and shelter. An early visitor to the Nilgiris observed, "When [servants']
pores and half-clothed bodies are exposed to the cold after the sun is down,
they always become discontented and often very sick." Thomas Macaulay,
who spent the season in Ootacamund a few years later, noted that his
servants "are coughing and shivering all round me." The Bengali servants
at Mussoorie were "very miserable," according to Emily Eden, sister of the
governor-general Lord Auckland. "They had slept in the open air and were
starved with the cold, and were so afraid of the precipices that they could
not even go to the bazaar to buy food." Later, when Eden's Bengali maid
began to cough and spit blood during a long stay in Simla, she commented,
"I suppose this is a very bad Siberia to them."[47] Siberia indeed. Whatever
concern some Europeans may have felt for the sufferings of the Indian
employees they took with them to the hill stations (and a great many felt
none), the fact that these shivering servants did not do well in the highland
climate served simply to reinforce the notion that this was a realm uniquely
suited to the racial requirements of the British.

Invariably, then, the commentary on hill stations conflated medical and
moral issues, imbuing the stations with the ability to restore not merely
the physical health of Europeans but their social and ethical character as
well. This view was especially evident in remarks about the British soldier,
whose life on the plains was seen as so degraded that it threatened to
undermine the entire European endeavor in India. Dr. William Curran, an
Indian Army surgeon, argued that by stationing soldiers in the hills,
authorities would "hear less of crime, and see scarcely anything of that
intemperance, and of its possible consequence, insanity, which are now so
comparatively common in our army in India." Similarly, an early enthu-
siast for the creation of a convalescent cantonment in the Nilgiris argued
that "the climate would invite [soldiers] to manly sports, and to athletic
exercises," rather than encouraging the alcoholic and sexual excesses that
characterized their leisure time on the plains. The Nilgiris were thought
by the Madras medical board to exert "a favorable moral influence. . . . [on] the European soldier, who is usually less under the influ-

47. Lt. H. Jervis, *Narrative of a Journey to the Falls of the Cavery with an Historical and Descriptive Account of the Neilgherry Hills* (London, 1834), 47; Thomas Babington Macaulay, *Letters,* ed. Thomas Pinney, vol. 3 (Cambridge, 1976), 68; Emily Eden, *Up the Country: Letters from India* (1930; reprint London, 1984), 115, 173.

ence of moral impressions." Another expert explained that "the constant out-of-doors employment and recreation which [soldiers] would be enabled . . . to find and enjoy, would remove them from the influence of that most demoralizing of all agencies, the dull, monotonous irksomeness of the almost constant confinement to barracks, and of the life of utter idleness which they are compelled to in the plains."[48] From this literature arose a quaint but revealing vision of the redemption of the British "Tommy" in a highland Arcadia, where he might eat fresh vegetables grown in his own garden, drink nutritious ale brewed from mountain spring water, and amuse himself in such innocent outdoor activities as collecting butterflies.[49]

---

Roy Macleod has observed that "scientific knowledge, as applied through medicine, is not merely factual knowledge; it also comprises a set of social messages wrapped up in technical language."[50] As is evident from the preceding analysis, the medical interest in hill stations harbored a special set of social messages. The discourse of the doctors may have been couched in the clinical vocabulary and derived from the empirical methods of an emerging scientific discipline, but it addressed a highly charged body of concerns about the precariousness of the European presence in colonial India. The climatic preoccupations of the medical fraternity were a kind of shorthand, comprehensible to all Europeans, for identifying these concerns and suggesting measures for their relief. For this reason the medical rationale for seeking health in the hill stations persisted long after the emergence of cholera, typhoid, and other epidemic diseases had shattered the illusion that the highland sanitaria were inviolable to the microbic perils

48. William Curran, "Further Evidence in Favour of a Hill Residence for European Soldiers in India," *Irish Journal of Medical Science* 52, no. 104 (1871): 415; Major William Murray, *An Account of the Neilgherries, or, Blue Mountains of Coimbatore, in Southern India* (London, 1834), 27; Medical Board Office, Madras Presidency, *Report on the Medical Topography and Statistics of Neilgherry Hills* (Madras, 1844), 32; Capt. J. Ouchterlony, *Geographical and Statistical Memoir of a Survey of the Neilgherry Mountains* (Madras, 1868), 66.

49. This vision was not as far-fetched as it may seem. Visitors both to Darjeeling and to the Nilgiris tell of British soldiers who hunted butterflies to sell to tourists. See L. A. Waddell, *Among the Himalayas* (1899; reprint, Delhi, 1979), 40; and E. F. Burton, *An Indian Olio* (London, 1888), 128.

50. Roy Macleod, "Introduction," in *Disease, Medicine, and Empire: Perspectives on Western Medicine and the Experience of European Expansion,* ed. Roy Macleod and Milton Lewis (London and New York, 1988), 1. Arnold makes much the same point throughout *Colonizing the Body.*

of India.[51] The recommendation that the British withdraw from the heat of the plains and establish seasonal domicile in the distant hills had something more than a strictly somatic intent; it served the symbolic purpose of inscribing the social distance between the British and their Indian subjects on the landscape itself.

51. See, for example, Sir Joseph Fayrer, "The Hill Stations of India as Health Resorts," *British Medical Journal* 1 (June 9, 1900): 1393–97; and F. M. Sandwith, "Hill Stations and Other Health Resorts in the British Tropics," *Journal of Tropical Medicine and Hygiene* 10, no. 22 (Nov. 15, 1907): 361–70.

# 3   Landscapes of Memory

Sing the praises of the atmosphere, so thin and light, well-nigh as
rare as the empty universal ether, free of earthly admixture whether
good or bad, and even without actual sunshine to be preferred to the
rank vapours of the plain.
                              —Thomas Mann, *The Magic Mountain*

Nothing soothes me so much as being alone among
mountain-scenery;—it is like resting in another world.
                              —Sir Thomas Munro writing to his wife
                    from Ootacamund in 1826, quoted in G. R. Gleig,
                    *The Life of Major-General Sir Thomas Munro, Bart.*

When the British first directed their gaze toward the mountainous regions of India in the early nineteenth century, what they saw was mediated by what their heritage had taught them to see. However commonplace the notion that our culture shapes our perceptions of the external
world, it takes on new meaning when the object being perceived is as alien
as India was to the British. The sensory impact of India would have been
difficult if not impossible to process without a shared aesthetic standard
against which these unfamiliar landscapes could be measured and through
which they could be given meaning. As a historian of British tourism
observed: "Travel . . . forces us to measure the unfamiliar by reference to
the familiar: to define the experience of being abroad, we need a concept
of 'home.'"[1] For the imperial sons and daughters of late Georgian and
early Victorian Britain, that concept of home as a physical environment
was embodied in the general notion of the picturesque.

The picturesque arose in the eighteenth century as a signifier of those
scenes of nature that fulfilled certain prescriptions of beauty; these notions
were derived from such varied sources as the Roman pastoral tradition, the
landscapes of Claude Lorrain, and the antiquarian enthusiasm for architectural relics of the past. They became a pliant and pervasive part of the
British aesthetic repertoire, especially for the growing number of persons
who sought edification and pleasure in travel. Whether their journeys took

1. Ian Ousby, *The Englishman's England: Taste, Travel and the Rise of Tourism*
(Cambridge, 1990), 2.

them to popular sites in the British Isles or to more distant destinations, these travelers communicated much of what they saw in the language of the picturesque. Such was the case for the British who ventured into the newly accessible hinterlands of Calcutta, Madras, and other coastal enclaves in the late eighteenth and early nineteenth centuries. Their diaries and sketchbooks invariably employed the descriptive conventions of the picturesque. William Hodges, Thomas and William Daniell, and Henry Salt were particularly effective in making use of these motifs in their lithographs and paintings of India: they concentrated their gaze on scenic vistas, turbulent waterfalls and gentle rivers, dramatic rock formations, curious natural phenomena such as the banyan tree, and grand architectural monuments and ruins, all of which were meant to encourage a contemplative frame of mind.[2]

Especially noteworthy was the selectivity of this vision. The marshy deltas and densely wooded hills and semiarid plains that made up much of India rarely received aesthetic note. The scenes privileged by British pictorial and literary representation were those that conformed most closely to the conventions of the picturesque. The viewer, then, was not merely a passive receptor of natural stimuli but an active agent who channeled and processed messages in a highly selective manner. An observation by Malcolm Andrews in his study of tourism and the picturesque landscape in late-eighteenth-century Britain holds equally for the contemporaneous experience in India: the traveler was "engaged in an experiment in controlled aesthetic response to a range of new and often intimidating visual experiences."[3] The picturesque was an interpretive mechanism that allowed the British to infuse an unfamiliar geography with meaning.

———

Mountains held a special place within the aesthetics of the picturesque.[4] Tours through upland Wales, the Lake and Peak districts, the Scottish

2. See Pratapaditya Pal and Vidya Dehejia, From Merchants to Emperors: British Artists and India 1757–1930 (Ithaca and London, 1986), ch. 3; Mildred Archer and Ronald Lightbown, India Observed: India as Viewed by British Artists 1760–1860 (London, 1982); Mildred Archer, Early Views of India: The Picturesque Journeys of Thomas and William Daniell 1782–1794 (London, 1980); and Jagmohan Mahajan, Picturesque India: Sketches and Travels of Thomas and William Daniell (New Delhi, 1983).

3. Malcolm Andrews, The Search for the Picturesque: Landscape Aesthetics and Tourism in Britain, 1760–1800 (Stanford, 1989), 67.

4. See Marjorie Hope Nicolson, Mountain Gloom and Mountain Glory: The Development of an Aesthetics of the Infinite (Ithaca, 1959).

highlands, and, further afield, the Pyrenees, Tuscany, and the Alps had nourished an appreciation for highland views among the British. There is a dramatic difference, however, between the gentle green hills of Wales and the sheer rock massif of the Alps, a difference not merely of scale but of signification. Among the archetypal images of the picturesque is the pastoral one of verdant rolling hills with cottages nestled in the vales and sheep grazing on the slopes under the drowsy care of shepherds. The representational expectations of visitors to Wales and other highland parts of Britain were suitably served by this bucolic imagery, but it proved entirely inadequate for the encounter with environments as severe and imposing as the Alps. These places demanded a different aesthetic response. Hence the evocation of the sublime, a term that referred to the intense and ambivalent emotions that arose when one confronted nature at its most untamed. Because of their overwhelming immensity, great mountain ranges like the Alps aroused awe and fear in the observer. Such feelings alarmed most Georgian travelers, who preferred to pass through the Alps as quickly as possible, but the Romantic sensibility of the late eighteenth and early nineteenth century led many to embrace the sublime, to seek out bleak environs and savor the intense emotions they inspired. The British carried this aesthetic stance abroad. As a result, those who visited the mountain regions of India were equipped to respond in two distinct registers. The picturesque could be called upon when the surroundings resembled the gentle pastoral highlands of Britain, while the sublime existed to express the conflicting feelings of fear and rapture that arose from the sight of such imposing and unfamiliar terrain as the Alps.

The topography of the Nilgiris and other highland regions of central and southern India consisted for the most part of gently rolling, sparsely wooded plateaus bounded by steep escarpments, a tractable terrain that fitted easily within the pastoral conventions of the picturesque. One of the first accounts of the area around Ootacamund proclaimed it to be "the most picturesque spot," explaining that "the hills throughout the interior present a softened outline and a rounded form, a succession of gentle swells and easy eminences. . . . A thousand streams of crystal clearness . . . preserve the perennial freshness of the wooded vales." Another early visitor to the region evoked the poetry of William Wordsworth and the paintings of Claude Lorrain and Nicholas Poussin in his descriptions. The landscape, he thought, "looked as if it had once been liquid and in the midst of some mighty storm, its waves had been solidified, and all its gulfs and surges perpetuated in the billowy agitation." Romantic rhetoric even infiltrated the supposedly dispassionate reports of medical authorities. "It is difficult

to find appropriate terms to convey an accurate description of these singularly smooth, rounded and undulating hills," gushed the Madras medical
board in its report on the Nilgiris. "They present truly a 'surging scene'
to use an expression of Coleridge, resemble the billows of the sea suddenly
stilled, solidified and fixed, while in their full career of heaving commo-
tion." As this recurrent use of sea imagery suggests, water in motion was
an evocative symbol of the natural world to British sensibilities, and few
scenes were more privileged by the picturesque than waterfalls. The Nilgiris proffered the popular Kalhatti falls and several other cascades for the
British to admire. "A cataract rolling down in the centre of the chasm
completes the grandeur of the scene," pronounced one visitor, "conveying
that unfailing delight which the fall of rushing water affords in every part
of the world." (The iconoclastic Richard Burton, who ridiculed the rhetoric
of the picturesque, was less impressed, remarking dryly that the waterfalls of the Nilgiris "only want water.")[5]

The language used to describe highland territory elsewhere in the
peninsular and central portions of the subcontinent was similarly imbued
with the motifs of the picturesque. An officer sent to explore the Annamullay mountains south of the Nilgiris wrote about "undulating grassy
hills, wooded vallies [sic], rocky crags, overhanging precipices, [and] . . .
green fields." The first Englishman to visit the plateau in the Central
Provinces where the hill station of Pachmarhi would arise wrote with
feeling about its cool climate and striking vistas, and the authors of the
district gazetteer described the scenery as "a maze of gorges and ravines,
sometimes picturesque, and sometimes of great grandeur." Even the relatively unimposing highland terrain in the vicinity of Bombay inspired
visitors to flights of lyricism. One of the earliest officials to view Mahabaleshwar asserted that the "scenery from many positions is both grand
and romantic, reminding one of old England." Another spoke somewhat

5. Major William Murray, *An Account of the Neilgherries, or, Blue Mountains of Coimbatore, in Southern India* (London, 1834), 52; Capt. Robert Mignan, *Notes Extracted from a Private Journal, Written during a Tour through a Part of Malabar, and among the Neilgherries* (Bombay, 1834), 63; Medical Board Office, Madras Presidency, *Report on the Medical Topography and Statistics of Neilgherry Hills* (Madras, 1844), 2–3; Lt. H. Jervis, *Narrative of a Journey to the Falls of the Cavery with an Historical and Descriptive Account of the Neilgherry Hills* (London, 1834), 36–37; Richard F. Burton, *Goa, and the Blue Mountains* (1851; reprint, Berkeley, 1991), 270. The journal of the medical officer who in 1824 investigated the Nilgiri and Shevaroy ranges as locations for sanitaria was, not surprisingly, "thickly sprinkled with quotations from English poets and Virgil," according to Sir Frederick Price, *Ootacamund: A History* (Madras, 1908), 26.

Figure 2. Representing the hill station as a site of the picturesque: an early view of Simla from W. L. L. Scott's *Views in the Himalayas.* Courtesy of the British Library, Oriental and India Office Collections.

hopefully of the location's "Alpine grandeur," then modified the analogy with a description of the "waving hills with the mellow tints of autumn under an Italian sky."[6]

Pictorial representations of these mountain sites communicated similar sentiments (Figure 2). A dozen or more volumes of engravings and lithographs portraying various parts of the Indian highlands were published in the early to middle part of the nineteenth century. Nearly all were the work of British East India Company officers, who were often skilled draftsmen.

6. Lt.-Col. Douglas Hamilton, *Report on the High Ranges of the Annamullay Mountains* (Madras, 1866), 7; Capt. J. Forsyth, *The Highlands of Central India* (London, 1871), 85; G. L. Corbett and R. V. Russell, *Central Provinces District Gazetteers: Hoshangabad District,* vol. A (Calcutta, 1908), 333; Peter Lodwick to the *Bombay Courier,* 1 May 1824, in Perin Bharucha, *Mahabaleswar: The Club 1881–1981* (Bombay, c. 1981), app. A; James Murray, *Account of Malcom Pait, on the Mahableshwur Hills* (Bombay, 1863), 22, 25.

Training in topographical and architectural drawing was standard at the company's military cadet schools, and Haileybury, the training college for company civil servants, employed professional artists to teach its students drawing and watercolor painting.[7] The artistic maxims absorbed in these institutions came into play when officials began to portray the highland landscapes that had come within their domain. Their efforts invariably followed the compositional conventions of European topographical drawing and landscape painting (although the professional artists who turned the sketches into engravings and lithographs certainly played some role in accentuating these picturesque qualities).[8] Most of the images were panoramic views, frequently framed by trees or other devices in the foreground that accentuated the scope and grandeur of the scene. Among the favorite subjects were lakes and wooded valleys nestled among the hills, with ranges of peaks or the hot plains receding in the distance. A stag, an Indian herdsman, or a British couple admiring the view often added pastoral flavor to the scene. Interspersed among these panoramas were more intimate tableaux of striking rock formations, waterfalls, and other motifs of the picturesque.[9] Mildred Archer, the leading authority on British Indian art, believes that Captain Richard Barron's drawings of the Nilgiri hills evoke "a peaceful charm reminiscent of Samuel Palmer's views of Shoreham Valley in Kent," and she observes that the mountains appeared "as a Garden of Eden" in much of this work.[10]

7. Archer and Lightbown, *India Observed*, 12; Pal and Dehejia, *From Merchants to Emperors*, 14.

8. Richard Burton, for one, was suspicious of the interventions of professionals: "I have been able . . . to illustrate my own books. It is only in this way that a correct idea of unfamiliar scenes can be given. Travellers who bring home a few scrawls and put them in the hands of a professional illustrator, have the pleasure of seeing the illustrated paper style applied to the scenery. . . . Even when the drawings are carefully done by the traveller-artist, it is hard to persuade the professional to preserve their peculiarities." Isabel Burton, *The Life of Captain Sir Richard F. Burton*, vol. 1 (London, 1893), 61.

9. See Capt. Richard Barron, *Views in India, Chiefly among the Neelgherry Hills* (London, 1837); H. L. Frazer, *Views of the Neilgherries* (Calcutta, 1856–57); Lt.-Col. James Fullerton, *Views in the Himalaya and Neilgherry Hills* (London, c. 1848); Lt.-Col. Douglas Hamilton, *Sketches of the Shevaroy Hills* (London, 1865); Major E. A. McCurdy, *Three Panoramic Views of Ootacamund* (London, c. 1830); Capt. E. A. McCurdy, *Views of the Neilgherries, or Blue Mountains of Coimbetoor* (London, c. 1830); Alicia Eliza Scott, *Simla Scenes Drawn from Nature* (London, c. 1846); W.L.L. Scott, *Views in the Himalayas* (London, 1852); and Capt. George Powell Thomas, *Views of Simla* (London, c. 1846).

10. Archer and Lightbown, *India Observed*, 108.

The sublime rather than the pastoral, however, was the ambiance that early British travelers usually associated with the Himalayas. The sheer size of these mountains set them apart from the ranges to the south: by the early nineteenth century, the British knew that the highest peaks in the world could be found here, although their full measure remained underestimated. George Francis White's *Views of India, Chiefly among the Himalaya Mountains* (c. 1838) is in many ways characteristic of the initial British response to this soaring scenery. The book is an account of his journey with several friends through the western Himalayas, and it includes a number of handsome lithographs made from his drawings. White's self-proclaimed "ardour in pursuit of the picturesque" pervades the text. From a distance, "the mountain ranges have all the indistinctness which belongs to the land of the faerie, and which, leaving the imagination to luxuriate in its most fanciful creations, lends enchantment to the scene." But on closer inspection "the mind is almost overpowered with astonishment, which, as we survey the gigantic wonders of the scene, is not wholly unmixed with a sensation allied to fear." Indeed, fear is an appropriate response to "a land whose savage aspect was seldom redeemed by scenes of gentle beauty."[11] To tour this unwelcoming land, to experience this fear, was to be presented with a salutary reminder of how puny human beings were when measured against the raw forces of nature.

Herein lay the essence of the sublime, and it pervaded the rhetoric of early British travelers to the Himalayas. Bishop Heber, who visited the Kumaun area in 1824, wrote in his journal that "everything around was so wild and magnificent that man appeared as nothing, and I felt myself as if climbing the steps of the altar of God's great temple."[12] The pseudonymous "Pilgrim" (P. Barron), who wandered through the same area in the early 1840s, was equally affected by his surroundings:

> On [the Himalayas] the eye never wearies to dwell—it affords a kind of enjoyment which springing from the purest of all sources, the fountain head of nature, has a tendency to elevate the feelings of the mind, and to exclude from it the workings of all ungenerous and turbulent passions. . . . [A] feeling from time to time creeps over you, of shrinking from your own insignificance, in the presence of such examples of the stupendous might and power of the great architect of the universe. What an atom in its system a human being appears; and how humiliated you feel, at having ever

11. Lt. George Francis White, *Views in India, Chiefly among the Himalaya Mountains*, ed. Emma Roberts (London and Paris, c. 1838), 38, 19, 32, 40.

12. Bishop Heber, *Bishop Heber in Northern India: Selections from Heber's Journal*, ed. M. A. Laird (Cambridge, 1971), 216.

expected that the gratification of your insignificant desires and wishes could have been anything else but dust in the Balance, to the Creator of works like these.[13]

The British, not unlike the Indians they ruled, felt themselves closer to the gods in these mountains and humbled by the proximity. Given, however, the purposes that these high places were increasingly intended to serve—that is, as sites for sanitaria—there was something problematic about the aesthetics of the sublime. To feel dwarfed and overawed by the untamed forces of nature may have been emotionally edifying for the passing traveler, but it was intensely disturbing to the invalid or other sojourner trying to find sanctuary from the plains. Such respite necessitated a landscape that had been tamed of its danger and reduced to human proportions, which is to say a landscape that had been made picturesque. The war correspondent of the London *Times*, William Howard Russell, made this point during a convalescent stay in Simla: "The landscape suffers from . . . the magnitude of the scale in which it is cast, and it is only by minute and accurate analysis that one comprehends its vastness."[14] The sublime was simply not suited to the purposes of residence. The mountain landscape, or more precisely those of its selected pockets within which hill stations were established, had to be brought within bounds, subdued and domesticated, if it were to serve those who sought physical or psychic relief from the pressures of the colonial tropics.[15]

Partly for this reason, perhaps, the sanitaria established in the Indian highlands became known as "hill stations." To use the word *hill* to refer to stations balanced precariously on the edges of ridges some six to eight thousand feet in elevation seems, on the face of it, a rather odd choice of terminology. It has been argued that the Himalayan stations seemed as though they were situated on little more than hills because they were set against the backdrop of the high country.[16] But the universal adoption of the term *hill station* for highland sanitaria also suggests an etymological effort to minimize the disturbing implications of the sublime. It should be

13. "Pilgrim" [P. Barron], *Notes of Wanderings in the Himmala* (Agra, 1844), 47.

14. William Howard Russell, *My Diary in India*, vol. 2 (London, 1860), 105.

15. Although the context is quite different, the threat of the sublime became a preoccupation for William Wordsworth, who attempted in his later years to develop an aesthetic for its "containment," according to Theresa M. Kelley, *Wordsworth's Revisionary Aesthetics* (Cambridge, 1988), ch. 6.

16. See Fanny Parks, *Wanderings of a Pilgrim, in Search of the Picturesque*, vol. 2 (London, 1850), 228.

noted, for instance, that the Nilgiris were initially described as "mountains" in official reports, but once John Sullivan and others had established permanent residence there, they quickly became "hills." To speak of hill stations rather than mountain stations rhetorically scaled back the overwhelming force of the landscape.

Domesticating the environs of hill stations required not merely a change in terminology but an intervention in the physical world itself. It began, appropriately enough, with the garden, that ancient symbol of peace and refuge where people sought harmony with nature. From the start, hill stations were centers of horticultural experimentation and emendation. The British were delighted to discover that many of the flowers, fruits, and vegetables popular in Britain flourished in the cool mountain climate. Roses, geraniums, fuchsias, lilies, dahlias, heliotropes, buttercups, sweet peas, bluebonnets, and other popular flowers soon graced the grounds of highland cottages and spread through the surrounding countryside. Experimental fruit orchards and vegetable gardens brought forth a cornucopia of cabbages, cauliflowers, lettuce, turnips, parsley, strawberries, apples, pears, plums, and other familiar produce. It has been claimed that the first English apple tree to be transplanted into Indian soil was nurtured in Mussoorie. "Violets, buttercups, wild strawberries and raspberries, and many other old friends abound," wrote Lady Lawrence to her husband from Simla in 1839. "Every house has its garden," a visitor to the Nilgiris effused, "and the verandahs are bowery with trailers, and creepers. . . . Fruit trees also abound, especially the peach, and we have plenty of strawberries, and also home vegetables." More pointedly, a midcentury guide to Darjeeling stated: "Many common English wild flowers bring back to memory the hills and dales and shady nooks and lanes of the fatherland." Memories of England, of course, were central to these horticultural activities.[17]

The casual efforts of individuals to transform the flora of the hill stations were reinforced by the concerted actions of the state. Government nurseries and botanical gardens were established in a number of hill stations to test potential cash crops and to provide local residents with seeds and plants. The venerable Calcutta Botanic Garden, founded in 1786–87, was emulated

17. Lady Lawrence quoted in Sir Herbert Benjamin Edwardes and Herman Merivale, *Life of Sir Henry Lawrence*, 2d ed., vol. 1 (London, 1872), 210; Mrs. Murray Mitchell, *In Southern India* (London, 1885), 351, 354; *Darjeeling*, pamphlet reprinted from *Calcutta Review*, no. 55 (1857): 14.

with particular success in Darjeeling and Ootacamund.[18] The Lloyd Botanical Garden, named after its founder, the official who had negotiated the deed that ceded Darjeeling to the British, covered fourteen acres just below the central portion of the station. The fifty-four-acre Government Botanical Garden at Ootacamund was established in 1848 along the slopes of Dodabetta peak, the highest location in the area. The two gardens played important roles in the development of tea, coffee, cinchona, and other commercial crops, but they also served as pleasure parks for station residents and supplied them with flower and vegetable seeds, cuttings from ornamental shrubs, and shade and fruit trees. Only a few years after its founding, the government garden at Ootacamund was offering for sale fifty-three varieties of apple trees.[19] (Darjeeling was less kind to apple trees and the like: the garden's director concluded in 1886 that the place was "pretty nearly hopeless as a home for any European fruit, except the strawberry."[20]) One of the central aims of the botanical gardens was to make the landscape less alien, to give it a more recognizable and pleasing appearance to those for whom it became a sanctuary.

These gardens held a deeper meaning for the British *mentalité*. European botanical gardens originated in the sixteenth and seventeenth centuries as a result of the discovery of the New World and its flora; they attempted to draw together representative samples of the entire plant kingdom in a new Garden of Eden.[21] While any serious hopes of achieving such a comprehensive collection had been abandoned by the nineteenth century, botanical gardens retained symbolic associations with Eden. Those who strolled along the secluded paths in the Darjeeling and Ootacamund gardens sought the sense of peace and purity that the Christian faith identified with the original home of Adam and Eve.

While the botanical gardens at Ootacamund and Darjeeling were exceptionally large and important, a number of other hill stations had public gardens and nurseries that served local needs. There was one in Mussoorie

18. See Edward W. Ellsworth, *Science and Social Science Research in British India, 1780–1880* (New York, 1991), ch. 6; and Daniel R. Headrick, *The Tentacles of Imperialism: Technology Transfer in the Age of Imperialism, 1850–1940* (New York, 1988), ch. 7.

19. *Report on the Government Botanical and Horticultural Gardens, Ootacamund, for the Year 1854–55* (Madras, 1856), Appendix.

20. "Annual Report of Royal Botanic Gardens for Year 1885–86," July 1886, Medical Branch, Municipal, Proceedings of the Lieutenant Governor of Bengal, WBSA.

21. See John Prest, *The Garden of Eden: The Botanic Garden and the Recreation of Paradise* (New Haven, 1981).

as early as 1827, and by the latter part of the century the station had two botanical gardens. Simla's municipal government established a nursery at Annandale, a large, level glade directly below the main ridge of the station, where plants, flowers, and fruit trees were sold to the public in the late nineteenth and early twentieth centuries. Coonoor had the much admired Sim's Park, a thirty-acre public garden founded in 1874. Panchgani was the site of a government nursery, and the visitor Margaret Denning claimed that it sent "every day a basket of fresh fruit and vegetables . . . to every house." The Chaubattia fruit garden near Ranikhet grew apples, pears, peaches, apricots, plums, cherries, sweet chestnuts, quince, currants, gooseberries, figs, mulberries, strawberries, and blackberries on its fifty acres, and it offered seedlings and grafts for sale. Several experimental fruit orchards were scattered across the Nilgiris. Each of these gardens dispersed European plants to local residents, helping to transform the local environments in such a way that they became like home for the British.[22]

In the Himalayan stations, efforts to transform the landscape seldom went beyond these horticultural interventions; the rugged ridges prevented much more. For instance, even though the British regarded lakes as an important feature of the picturesque landscape, and even though, as was demonstrated on English country estates, they were willing to dig artificial lakes where natural ones did not exist, none of the Himalayan resorts possessed the topography suitable for such a project. (Naini Tal had the rare distinction of a natural lake.) "Everybody who has visited the hills," noted George White, "regrets the absence of those large bodies of water which alone are wanting to fill up the coup-d'oeil."[23]

In the less perpendicular terrain of India's central and southern highlands, however, hydraulic engineering of this sort was undertaken with great gusto. At Ootacamund, Sullivan dammed a stream running through the valley in 1823, thereby creating the lake that became the station's most celebrated feature. "This beautiful piece of water," wrote one enraptured visitor, "winds in a serpentine course among the hills, gently rising from its bands, and clothed with the softest verdure, . . . affording one of the

22. Edwin T. Atkinson, *The Himalayan Gazetteer*, vol. 3, pt. 1 (1882; reprint, Delhi, 1973), 601; Annual Report of the Simla Municipality, 1887–88, HPSA; W. Francis, *The Nilgiris* (Madras, 1908), 206; *Gazetteer of the Bombay Presidency*, vol. 19: *Satara* (Bombay, 1885), 534; Margaret B. Denning, *Mosaics from India* (Chicago, 1902), 199; H. G. Walton, *Almora: A Gazetteer*, vol. 35 (Allahabad, 1911), 25; *Madras District Gazetteers, Statistical Appendix for the Nilgiri District* (Madras, 1928), 45–47.
23. White, *Views in India*, 40.

Figure 3.   The artificial lake at Shillong. From Eastern Bengal State Railway, *From the Hooghly to the Himalayas* (Bombay, 1913).

most scenic, healthful, and agreeable drives of which India, or perhaps any part of the world, can boast."[24] Artificial lakes were created with similar intent at the hill stations of Kodaikanal, Mahabaleshwar, Matheran, Panchgani, Shillong (Figure 3), Wellington, and Yercaud.

So popular were lakes as an aesthetic improvement to the hill station's landscape that at least one intrepid investigator made the mirage of a lake the central feature of his geographical report. When Lieutenant-Colonel (later General) Douglas Hamilton informed the Madras government of his search for a convalescent site in the Palni mountains of southern India, he described the place he considered best suited for such a station as being located near a lake. As the report progressed, however, it became clear that what Hamilton initially had termed a lake was no such thing: it was a valley where he thought he detected evidence of an ancient lake bed. The distinction seemed scarcely worthy of note to Hamilton, so persuaded was he that this location offered the most picturesque environment for a settlement. "Let but the lake be reconstructed and a road made to it, and this

24. Capt. Henry Harkness, *A Description of a Singular Aboriginal Race Inhabiting the Summit of the Neilgherry Hills* (London, 1832), 5.

magnificent sheet of water . . . will of itself attract residents to its vicinity."[25] Paul Carter has observed with reference to colonial Australia that British explorers sometimes described features of the landscape as rivers or mountains when these terms were inappropriate. He finds in this practice an effort "to differentiate the landscape," and the effect was less to describe places than to invent them. "Geographical class names . . . rendered the world visible, bringing it within the horizon of discourse."[26] Hamilton's imaginary lake represents an invention of just this sort. It distinguished a particular place within the Palni hills, rendering it visible as a site for a convalescent station. This incident in linguistic invention, in turn, helps us to understand that the lakes which appeared at Ootacamund and elsewhere were inventions as well, introduced by the British as part of their effort to reshape the landscape so that it would conform to their cultural expectations.

The result was to domesticate the disorderly, to familiarize the unfamiliar, to model these highland spaces in the likeness of favored landscapes at home. The climate and flora of Darjeeling "recalled that of England" for Joseph Hooker, while Ootacamund made the same impression on Macaulay. Captain George Thomas compared the summer months in Simla to an "English spring . . . [with a] thousand *English* blossoms." The environs of Naini Tal were described as "the Westmoreland of Kumaun." An Eastern Bengal State Railway brochure suggested that Shillong was like "parts of Hampshire and Surrey"; an agent for tea planters compared it to "Surrey or Cotswold Hills." Pachmarhi was said to resemble "a fine English park." Ootacamund seemed like "Malvern at the fairest season" to the Bishop of Calcutta, "some sweet spot in the Scottish Highlands" to the missionary John W. Dulles, and "the mountains and hills of Cumberland and Westmorland" to the sportswoman Isabel Savory. For Lord Lytton, viceroy of India, it was "a paradise. . . . The afternoon was rainy and the road muddy, but such beautiful *English* rain, such delicious *English* mud. Imagine Hertfordshire lands, Devonshire downs, Westmoreland lakes, Scotch troutstreams, and Lusitanian views!" Similarly, Mussoorie reminded Fanny Parks of the Isle of Wight and caused her to exclaim: "How delicious is this coldness in the Hills!—it is just as wet, windy, and wretched as in England." A paternalistic army surgeon who advocated the billeting of British troops in hill stations believed that the Himalayas in general would stir memories of home for the army's Celtic ranks: "those Scotch and Irish soldiers who

25. Lt.-Col. Douglas Hamilton, *Report on the Pulni Mountains* (Madras, 1864), 4.

26. Paul Carter, *The Road to Botany Bay: An Essay in Spatial History* (London, 1987), 50, 51.

constitute so large a portion of the British army would find in the Himalayas a soil and sky not much different from their own, they would here feed upon food and vegetables like those they were accustomed to at home, and be brought into daily contact with a simple race . . . who delight in the sound of a pipe which closely resembles the wild minstrelsy of their own native glens."[27]

Over time, hill stations were drawn so tightly within the aesthetic confines of British landscape traditions that they became divorced from the surrounding environment, particularly when that environment was as intimidating as the Himalayas. Within the stations the natural world had been cut to human scale, so that luxuriant gardens and quaint cottages, thick stands of trees and wide pedestrian malls, meandering lanes and shimmering lakes all existed in harmonious juxtaposition. Beyond the stations loomed nature in the raw, an elemental force, its scale and strength dwarfing humankind. Increasingly, those who wished to savor the thrill of the sublime had to do so outside the confines of the hill station. Guidebooks directed visitors to distant sites where they could gaze upon snow-capped peaks, torrent-worn gorges, and other natural wonders. Even though breathtaking vistas were available from the centers of many hill stations, the British inhabitants privileged sights that stood beyond municipal boundaries, designated places that received evocative names and attracted organized parties. Within the stations' confines, inhabitants' vision tended to narrow, focusing on flower-bedecked homes comfortably nestled along hillsides or upon the shores of artificial lakes.

---

By their very nature, representations give an oblique reading of the objects they represent, a frame of reference that furthers the ends of those who set its parameters and that imposes their intentions on the image. The

27. Joseph Dalton Hooker, *Himalayan Journals,* vol. 1 (London, 1854), 109; Thomas Babington Macaulay, *Letters,* vol. 3 (Cambridge, 1976), 58, 59; Thomas, *Views of Simla,* 5 (emphasis in original); H. R. Neville, *Naini Tal: A Gazetteer, Being Volume XXXIV of the District Gazetteers of the United Provinces of Agra and Oudh* (Allahabad, 1904), 12; Eastern Bengal State Railway, *From the Hooghly to the Himalayas* (Bombay, 1913), 47; Hyde Clarke, "The English Stations in the Hill Regions of India," *Journal of the Statistical Society* 44 (Sept. 1881): 532; Forsyth, *Highlands of Central India,* 85; Bishop of Calcutta quoted in Jervis, *Narrative of a Journey,* 20; Rev. John W. Dulles, *Life in India; or Madras, the Neilgherries, and Calcutta* (Philadelphia, 1855), 441; Isabel Savory, *A Sportswoman in India* (London, 1900), 330; Lord Lytton quoted in Lady Betty Balfour, *The History of Lord Lytton's Indian Administration, 1876 to 1880* (London, 1899), 220 (emphasis in original); Parks, *Wanderings of a Pilgrim,* vol. 2, 229, 239; William Curran, "The Himalayas as a Health Resort," *Practitioner* (Jan. 1871): 42.

pleasant picture that the British painted of hill-station landscapes and the collateral program they undertook to make the environment even more picturesque disguised a complicated and troubling reality. Although the British did indeed transform the environs of hill stations, this transformation did not accord entirely with their ideals. One of the foremost environmental repercussions of their entry into the highlands was deforestation.

The assault on the forests began in the early nineteenth century with the growth of a commercial market for timber.[28] The Kumaun/Garhwal region was one of the earliest centers for the cutting of timber for export to the plains: from the 1820s onward visitors to Mussoorie, Almora, and surrounding areas remarked upon the denuded hillsides.[29] After midcentury the railroad-construction boom produced an enormous demand for wood for use as railway ties. Entire forests of sal and other trees disappeared from the Himalayan foothills. The contemporaneous introduction of tea and other plantation crops to Darjeeling, Assam, and the Nilgiris led to the massive clearing of wooded tracts in these regions. The Darjeeling district gazetteer stated in 1876 that "the forest has almost entirely disappeared in many parts, owing to the spread of cultivation."[30] The demand for fuel and building material by the growing populations of the hill stations also contributed to the problem. Local stands of trees quickly fell to the axes of the founding residents, and encroachments on surrounding timber areas intensified as the stations expanded. Simla consumed some 85,000 cubic feet of timber per year toward the end of the nineteenth century. During the station's great public-construction boom of the 1880s the figure reached 250,000 cubic feet per year.[31]

---

28. The leading authority on this topic is Richard P. Tucker, whose work includes "The British Colonial System and the Forests of the Western Himalayas, 1815–1914," in *Global Deforestation and the Nineteenth-Century World Economy*, ed. Richard P. Tucker and J. F. Richards (Durham, 1983), 146–66; and "The Depletion of India's Forests under British Imperialism: Planters, Foresters, and Peasants in Assam and Kerala," in *The Ends of the Earth: Perspectives on Modern Environmental History*, ed. Donald Worster (Cambridge, 1988), 118–40. For a useful overview of the British impact on colonial forest lands, see Richard H. Grove, "Colonial Conservation, Ecological Hegemony and Popular Resistance: Towards a Global Synthesis," in *Imperialism and the Natural World*, ed. John M. MacKenzie (Manchester, 1990), 15–50.

29. Heber, *Bishop Heber*, 221; "Pilgrim," *Notes of Wanderings*, 128, 165; and "Mountaineer," *A Summer Ramble in the Himalayas* (London, 1860), 4–5, 13.

30. W. W. Hunter, *A Statistical Account of Bengal*, vol. 10: *Districts of Darjiling and Jalpaiguri, and State of Kuch Behar* (London, 1876), 19.

31. Report by Lalla Chajju Ram, municipal forest ranger, to Simla Municipality, 5 Sept. 1894, Simla Municipal Proceedings, vol. 6, 1893–94, HPSA.

Adding to the commercial or developmental pressures on the forests was the conviction—widely held by the British in the first half of the nineteenth century—that illness lurked in thick stands of indigenous growth. Even though most hill stations were believed to be above the so-called fever zone, many authorities insisted on a prophylactic policy of clearing out brush, trees, and other "vegetative matter" that might harbor disease. In Darjeeling, for example, the presence of a small fly with an irritating bite caused officials in the late 1830s to recommend that most of the trees within the station be cut down.[32] A medical officer who arrived shortly thereafter found that the summit had indeed been cleared. In his opinion, this improved the view, but he felt that still more vegetation needed to be removed.[33] In Mussoorie, where commercial demand had wiped out the forests, Thornton's *Gazetteer* concluded that "the injurious effect to the scenery has been more than compensated by increased salubrity."[34]

Others, however, lamented the disappearance of the forests, and their influence grew as the depredations increased. One reason they objected was aesthetic: chopping down all the trees around a hill station made it difficult to sustain the illusion that residents were nestled in the picturesque bosom of nature. Another reason was pragmatic: the destruction of forest cover caused erosion and landslides. They were also increasingly convinced that deforestation caused a rise in temperatures and a decline in rainfall.[35] A visitor to the Nilgiris expressed this concern about the climatic effects of deforestation as early as 1834. It gradually gained currency and by the latter part of the century was offered to explain such phenomena as the apparent increase in summer temperatures in Mahabaleshwar and Mussoorie and the diminution in winter snowfall at Darjeeling.[36] Lastly, the medical

32. Letters and a memorandum by Capt. G. A. Lloyd and Surgeon Henry Chapman, 19 June 1837, no. 39, Foreign Dept. Proceedings, INA.

33. J. T. Pearson, "A Note on Darjeeling," 1839, reprinted in Fred Pinn, *The Road to Destiny: Darjeeling Letters 1839* (Calcutta, 1986), 101.

34. Quoted in Hyde Clarke, *Colonization, Defence and Railways in Our Indian Empire* (London, 1857), 101.

35. The origins and spread of this "dessication" theory are traced by Richard Grove, "Conserving Eden: The (European) East India Companies and Their Environmental Policies on St. Helena, Mauritius, and in Western India, 1660 to 1854," *Comparative Studies in Society and History* 35, no. 2 (April 1993): 318–51.

36. Mignan, *Notes Extracted from a Private Journal*, 137; J. C. Lisboa, "Short Notes on the Present Altered Climate of Mahableshwar and Its Causes," in Roa Bahadur D. B. Parasnis, *Mahabaleshwar* (Bombay, 1916), app. 2; N. M. Dastur, *Pocket Book of Mahabaleshwar and Panchgani* (Poona, 1944), 47–48; H. G. Walton, *Dehra Dun: A Gazetteer, District Gazetteers of the United Provinces of Agra*

rationale for removing trees from stations began to weaken around mid-century. John Strachey, writing in 1861, deplored the "mischief" that had been caused in both the hills and the plains by "the ignorant notion which is so commonly prevalent that trees are prejudicial to health."[37] Quite the reverse came to be viewed as true. "Careful protection of existing trees," insisted the Simla Municipality, "and planting in vacant spaces are considered very necessary to maintain and improve the beauty and salubrity of the station."[38] By the second half of the nineteenth century, it was the absence rather than the presence of trees that aroused anxiety.

As the adverse effects of deforestation became increasingly apparent, a conservationist impulse took shape that would profoundly affect the physical appearance of hill stations.[39] Even in the early years some efforts had been made to conserve woodland: both Simla and Ootacamund had regulations in the 1830s requiring residents to obtain approval from local authorities before they felled trees, and Ootacamund title deeds included a provision that owners plant a sapling for every tree they removed.[40] However, these regulations do not appear to have been rigorously enforced. Only after midcentury did the forests come under some real measure of protection. In 1852 a European forester and six Indian assistants were appointed to patrol the Nilgiri woodlands and prevent over-cutting.[41] The authorities at Mahabaleshwar established a five-mile forest-conservancy zone around the station in 1853.[42] In 1856 the commissioner of Kumaun, Henry Ramsay, issued an order prohibiting the indiscriminate felling of trees in his district.[43] And in 1865 the trees within a five-mile radius of the center of Darjeeling were protected under new rules.[44] These and other

*and Oudh,* vol. 1 (Allahabad, 1911), 216; and Col. G. B. Mainwaring, *A Grammar of the Rong (Lepcha) Language* (1876; reprint, Delhi, 1985), xviii n.

37. *Selections from the Records of the Government of India (Military Department),* no. 3: *Report on the Extent and Nature of the Sanitary Establishments for European Troops in India* (Calcutta, 1861–62), 98.

38. Annual Report of the Simla Municipality, 1882–83, 17, HPSA.

39. For the background to this conservationist impulse, see Grove's articles "Conserving Eden" and "Colonial Conservation."

40. Capt. Kennedy to Col. Stevenson, 13 May 1831, no. 4, Political Proceedings, Foreign Dept., INA; Francis, *Nilgiris,* 210.

41. Capt. J. Ouchterlony, *Geographical and Statistical Memoir of a Survey of the Neilgherry Mountains* (Madras, 1868), 70; Francis, *Nilgiris,* 210.

42. *Gazetteer of the Bombay Presidency,* vol. 19: *Satara,* 496.

43. A. S. Rawat, "Henry Ramsay: The Uncrowned King of Kumaon," in *Himalaya Frontier in Historical Perspective,* ed. N. R. Ray (Calcutta, 1986), 184.

44. E. C. Dozey, *A Concise History of the Darjeeling District since 1835* (Calcutta, 1922), 165.

local initiatives culminated in an India-wide policy of forest conservancy. The first inspector-general of forests was appointed in 1865, and his powers were broadened with the passage of forestry legislation in 1878, which allowed the state to place extensive tracts of forest under its protection and management.[45] By the end of the century, many hill stations were encircled by belts of protected forest administered either by the Forestry Department or by the stations themselves. In Simla, for example, the municipality assumed management of 2,115 acres of local forest in 1889, and it succeeded in doubling this protected acreage within a decade.[46]

These forest reserves served both aesthetic and practical purposes. The Simla gazetteer explained: "The primary object of management, especially in those parts which are visible from the main roads, is to preserve the beauty of the station by the maintenance of ornamental high forest; while at the same time, and as far as is compatible with that object, the forest must be made to yield as large a supply as possible of timber for municipal works and fuel for the general market."[47] Unlike the great tracts of territory administered by the Forestry Department, which were managed with commercial usage foremost in mind, the forest reserves that lay within the orbits of the hill stations were intended above all to accentuate the picturesque qualities of the surroundings. This goal did not, however, prohibit the carefully regulated sale of grass, firewood, and timber, which provided welcome revenue to the local governments. Nor were the administrators of municipal forests any more responsive to the interests of the indigenous communities than were administrators of other forest reserves: both abrogated peasants' customary rights to fodder, fuel, and other forest products because these rights were said to pose an environmental threat.[48]

Deforestation was so extensive on the slopes surrounding some hill stations that the preservation of surviving stands was not enough—an extensive program of replanting native and new species of trees was necessary to repair the damage and to meet the demand for firewood and building timber. Widely scattered initiatives by amateur horticulturists gradually turned into a full-scale undertaking by government authorities

45. Tucker, "British Colonial System," 164.

46. Annual Reports of the Simla Municipality, 1890–91, xxix, and 1900–1901, 11, HPSA.

47. *Punjab District Gazetteers, Simla District, 1904*, vol. 8A (Lahore, 1908), 77.

48. See Ramachandra Guha and Madhav Gadgil, "State Forestry and Social Conflict in British India," *Past and Present* 123 (May 1989): 141–77; and Ramachandra Guha, *The Unquiet Woods: Ecological Change and Peasant Resistance in the Himalaya* (Berkeley, 1989), chs. 3–5.

that brought profound changes in the landscape. These changes reinforced the effects of the introduction of English garden plants: they made the hill stations even more friendly environments for their expatriate residents.

Perhaps the most dramatic transformation occurred in the Nilgiris. Here the scattered groves, or *sholas,* of native timber were rapidly depleted by the growing demands from Ootacamund and Coonoor, and the shortage of firewood prompted some settlers to introduce trees that would grow rapidly. The most successful of these imports were the Australian blackwood (*Acacia melanoxylon*), wattle (*Acacia dealbata*), and blue gum (*Eucalyptus globulus*). In 1849–50, authorities planted twenty thousand blackwood trees around the lake at Ootacamund; they also established a 1,696-acre blue-gum plantation near the station in 1863 and another near Coonoor that comprised 1,379 acres.[49] Within a few decades these trees had entirely altered the appearance and ecology of the region, covering the rolling hills with dense foliage. As one visitor to the Nilgiris in the late nineteenth century observed, ''The blue gum, or eucalyptus, has been extensively planted, and is to be seen everywhere in clumps and belts. . . . The Australian 'wattle', a kind of mimosa, very like the beautiful tree on the Riviera, spreads like a weed, resisting every effort to restrain it.''[50]

Much the same pattern of replanting occurred at other hill stations. The arboreal imports from Australia spread to most of the southern stations and their surroundings, particularly the Palni and Shevaroy hills. Blue-gum and blackwood plantations like the one established in 1870 to supply the firewood needs of Kodaikanal became widespread.[51] The Australian trees were also introduced to the Himalayas, but success was more mixed: the wattle, for example, gained a substantial foothold in Almora, but attempts to transplant it to Simla failed. Other species did better in the Himalayan stations. Simla had great success with its famed deodar, a sizable cedar tree: large numbers of deodar seedlings, as well as fir, maple, hazel, horse chestnut, and others, were planted by the municipality in the late nineteenth and early twentieth centuries, with more than ten thousand plantings in some years.[52] In Darjeeling, authorities turned to the *Cryptomeria*

49. Price, *Ootacamund,* 35, 122; *Imperial Gazetteer of India, Provincial Series: Madras,* vol. 2 (Calcutta, 1908), 308; P. F. Fyson, *The Flora of the South Indian Hill Stations,* vol. 1 (Madras, 1932), 185–86, 216–17.

50. Mitchell, *In Southern India,* 351.

51. Charlotte Chandler Wyckoff, *Kodaikanal: 1845–1945* (Nagercoil, Travancore, 1945), 13.

52. See Annual Reports of the Simla Municipality, esp. 1885–86, 1886–87, 1890–91, 1907–8, 1908–9, HPSA.

*japonica,* a fast-growing conifer native to Japan, in an effort to restore the denuded ridges, and it soon became one of the predominant species of tree in the region.[53] Similarly, Shillong's slopes were replanted with pine trees in the late nineteenth century, giving the landscape a much more densely wooded appearance than it possessed when the British established their sanitarium there.[54] And in Panchgani "householders have been spending their money unsparingly in planting trees of every variety," with French pines particularly popular.[55] In one hill station after another, the British responded to their own depredations with a conservationist impulse that owed much to the aesthetics of the picturesque landscape.

A parallel process of destruction and reconstruction can be charted in the British response to the fauna of the hill stations. One of the principal attractions that the highlands of India offered early visitors was an abundance of wildlife. The foothills of the Himalayas were home to the tiger, panther, bison, boar, and elephant; the higher elevations were inhabited by antelopes, bears, deer, leopards, jackals, and mountain goats, as well as a great variety of game birds. The highlands of central and southern India were also rich in game. The Nilgiris had a reputation as the best hunting grounds in the south; tigers, leopards, elephants, sloth bears, ibex, various deer and antelopes, hyenas, wild dogs, and wild boars could be found on the slopes and plateau of the region in the early decades of the nineteenth century.

Hunting was a central element of the British imperial ethos, an expression of the "urge to order the world of nature."[56] The thickly wooded, thinly populated highland regions of India were ideal hunting grounds. Simla first came to the attention of the British as a consequence of a hunting expedition; so did Pachmarhi and several other hill stations.[57] "I have scarcely met a single Englishman on these hills, who does not possess a strong propensity for field sports," remarked an early visitor to the Nilgiris.[58] As growing numbers of young bloods came to the hills for recreation, the slaughter of wildlife reached massive proportions. Many species

53. Dozey, *Concise History,* 165.
54. B. C. Allen, *Assam District Gazetteers,* vol. 10: *The Kahsi and Jaintia Hills* (Allahabad, 1906), 96.
55. John Chesson, "Hill Sanitaria of Western India: Panchgunny," *Bombay Miscellany* 4 (1862): 339.
56. John M. MacKenzie, *The Empire of Nature: Hunting, Conservation and British Imperialism* (Manchester, 1988), 36.
57. Pamela Kanwar, *Imperial Simla* (Delhi, 1990), 15; Forsyth, *Highlands of Central India,* ch. 3.
58. Mignan, *Notes Extracted from a Private Journal,* 84–85.

were simply wiped out. An army officer who came to hunt in the Nilgiris in the 1880s found that elephants, bison, boars, and other game "have been destroyed or driven away." Another hunter in the area reported a decade or so later that peafowl and bears had become extinct, and the ibex and sambur deer were nearly so.[59] Much the same pattern of destruction occurred elsewhere.

Once again, the British responded to the consequences of their depredations with preservationist initiatives. In 1877, a group of Ootacamund "sportsmen" who had become alarmed by the diminution of game formed the Nilgiri Game Protection Association, which drafted the Nilgiri Game and Fish Preservation Act (1879), requiring licenses for, and imposing restrictions on, fishing and hunting. This act inspired the Palni Hills Game Association of Kodaikanal to introduce similar measures. Elsewhere, the Darjeeling Shooting and Fishing Club acquired control over hunting and fishing rights in the Darjeeling forests, the Dehra Dun Fish Protection Association did the same for the streams running through government forests near Mussoorie, and the Simla municipality passed game-protection regulations.[60]

John MacKenzie argues that game-preservation laws in Britain and its imperial possessions were intended to restrict access to hunting to an elite who killed for recreation, not food. This certainly appears to have been the case in British India. Fishing regulations in Naini Tal were clearly directed at the Indian "poacher," as he was defined, who "has no sporting instincts to hamper him." The same party was targeted by the Dehra Dun Fish Protection Association's prohibition against the use of nets or poison. The Darjeeling Shooting and Fishing Club employed guards to prevent local inhabitants from poaching in its protected areas.[61] The official historian of Ootacamund observed that the efforts of the Nilgiri Game Protection Association "materially assisted in the elimination of the men who shot for the market and private customers . . . [and] led to the total disappearance of the native who killed game for a livelihood."[62] This outcome was

59. E. F. Burton, *An Indian Olio* (London, 1888), 130; F.W.F. Fletcher, *Sport on the Nilgiris and in Wynaad* (London, 1911), 19.

60. Price, *Ootacamund,* 197–98; Wyckoff, *Kodaikanal,* 23; Arthur Jules Dash, *Bengal District Gazetteers: Darjeeling* (Alipore, 1947), 138; Walton, *Dehra Dun,* 34–35; Annual Report of the Simla Municipality, 1889–90, 1.

61. MacKenzie, *The Empire of Nature,* ch. 1, passim; Neville, *Naini Tal,* 47; Walton, *Dehra Dun,* 34–35; Dash, *Bengal District Gazetteers: Darjeeling,* 138.

62. Price, *Ootacamund,* 198.

facilitated in the forest reserves, which functioned as game preserves, much as did royal and aristocratic parks in Britain, with the rangers operating as gamekeepers on guard against poachers.

The game associations sought not only to protect existing game for their private pleasure but to introduce new species to expand their hunting opportunities. Once again the effort to intervene in the natural world of the hill stations was inextricably tied to the desire to remake that world in the nostalgic image of a rural Britain. The hedged fields and trout streams of England and Scotland provided the model. The Darjeeling Shooting and Fishing Club went to great trouble and expense to introduce trout in local brooks and to breed pheasants for hunting purposes, although both endeavors failed.[63] The Nilgiri Game Protection Association succeeded in introducing woodcock, snipe, and other British game birds to the Nilgiris, as well as the spaniels and other bird dogs used to hunt them. It also attempted to stock Nilgiri streams with trout, a Herculean endeavor subsequently assumed by the Madras government, which imported eggs from Germany, Wales, and New Zealand. Sir Arthur Lawley, the governor, declared the first trout season open in 1911. But the most striking case of the transfer of English sporting traditions to the region was the Ootacamund hunt. The first foxhounds were introduced to Ootacamund as early as 1829, and a regular pack was running by 1845. By the late nineteenth century the Nilgiri variant of the English fox hunt—the jackal hunt—had become fully institutionalized, with a regular "season," a locally bred pack of hounds, and a large and enthusiastic crowd of participants appropriately attired in pink riding outfits. The halls of Fernhill Palace, built for the maharaja of Mysore as his summer home in Ootacamund, are covered with large framed photographs of the opening day of every hunt since the turn of the century: these images are indistinguishable from those on view in the English countryside.[64]

---

The highland environment as the British came to know it was not merely a tangible place where they sought domicile; it was also an intangible space upon which they inscribed meaning.[65] The meaning they inscribed had its

63. Dash, *Bengal District Gazetteers: Darjeeling,* 138.

64. *A Handbook for Travellers in India, Burma and Ceylon,* 10th ed. (London, 1920), 565; *Madras District Gazetteers, Statistical Appendix for the Nilgiri District* (1928), 41–42; Price, *Ootacamund,* ch. 20.

65. This point is made in a much broader context by W.J.T. Mitchell, "Imperial Landscape," in *Landscape and Power,* ed. W.J.T. Mitchell (Chicago, 1994), 5–34.

source in a rigorously bifurcated vision, one that set "the hills" against "the plains." Even though "the plains" had been regarded by late-eighteenth- and early-nineteenth-century officials and travelers as an environment of prodigal variety, possessing many features of interest and beauty, it acquired a less attractive, more monolithic image over the course of the nineteenth century and in the context of the hill stations. From the increasingly accessible vantage point of the hills, the plains seemed a stark, heat-shimmering, monotonously unvarying landscape, teeming with millions of idol-worshipping, disease-ridden people. For those who assumed this perspective, the hills became an antipodal landscape. These lofty lands appeared unsullied by lowland hordes, untouched by their contaminating influence. Instead, they offered an environment so pristine, so free of human admixture, so empty of history that it seemed to invite the British to engrave their own dreams and desires on its unmarked surface. A visitor to Matheran spoke tellingly of its "simplicity, . . . untouched by either history, tradition, or romance; so much so indeed, that when the veil was lifted from this part of Western India, she stood forth pure and uncontaminated by the hands of man."[66] Implicit in these remarks was the understanding that the men, the histories, the traditions, and the romances that Matheran seemed so free from were those of India. This sense of sequestration from the corroding, corrupting influence of oriental civilization supplied the essential appeal of every hill station.

Yet this appeal was riven with paradoxes. The first was the fact that the features that made the highlands so alluring to the British were themselves threatened by the British appearance on the scene. In this social analogue of the Heisenberg principle, the discovery of what the British took to be enclaves undefiled by people entailed an act of intervention that defiled them. Great devastation was wrought on the natural world of the highlands by the entry of ever-increasing numbers of European sojourners and Indian auxiliaries. The demand for food and fuel and water and building materials that accompanied the growth of hill stations placed enormous pressure on the surrounding countryside—pressure that led inexorably to the degradation of the environment. As forests were cut down, as streams were fouled, and as wildlife was exterminated, the British could not avoid acknowledging the destructive consequences of their presence on these mountain retreats.

At the same time, however, the highlands were subject to a different sort of intervention, the purpose of which was to accentuate their picturesque

66. James Douglas, *Bombay and Western India*, vol. 2 (London, 1893), 270.

qualities. From the first officials who established residence in the hills, the British sought to "improve" these landscapes by introducing new plants, engineering alterations in the terrain, and otherwise reshaping the existing environment. These changes pose a second paradox: the more the natural world of the hill station was deliberately altered by the British, the more "natural" it seemed to them. Artificial lakes were taken to be more natural that undammed streams, exotic flowers and trees more natural than indigenous flora, and imported fish and game birds more natural than native wildlife. The conservationist initiatives that arose in the second half of the nineteenth century were not merely attempts to repair the damage the hills had suffered but expressions of the British desire to transform the environment to accord with British images of nature. This underlying intent has been suggestively probed in a book on conservation in Africa. It argues that the colonial roots of conservation can be found in the desire of "Europeans to impose their image of Africa upon the reality of the African landscape." This image "manifested itself in a wish to protect the natural environment as a special kind of 'Eden,'" untouched by the unhappy incursions of civilization.[67] While the conservation movement never achieved the influence in India that it did in Africa, the ethos that motivated it exhibited many of the same characteristics, especially in the rarefied heights of the highlands. The hill station became, in the highly charged words of one visitor, "our Garden of Eden."[68] With this model in mind the British reshaped the world they found, compelling it to conform more closely to the world they wished it to be.

67. David Anderson and Richard Grove, eds., *Conservation in Africa: People, Policies, Practices* (Cambridge, 1987), 4.
68. Lady Wilson, *Letters from India* (1911; reprint, London, 1984), 38.

# 4 Nature's Children

I believe I do not err in assuming our agreement in the conception
of an original ideal state of man, a condition without government and
without force, an unmediated condition as the child of God, in which
there was neither lordship nor service, neither law nor penalty, nor
sin nor relation after the flesh; no distinction of classes, no work, no
property: nothing but equality, brotherhood, and moral perfectitude.
　　　　　　　　　　　—Thomas Mann, *The Magic Mountain*

Where there is so little crime, it may be inferred that the morality
of the inhabitants is the cause; certain it is that there is less
falsehood and theft [among the Paharis of the Simla hills] than
in any quarter of Asia. There is a degree of simplicity too amongst
these people . . . that induces an idea of a certain degree of morality
existing, but when we take into consideration some of the customs
peculiar to them, our belief is shaken. It must be remarked, however,
the people consider them no crime whatever, and in consequence we
ought to view them more leniently. It may not be so much *vice* as
ignorance.
　　　　　—Captain Charles P. Kennedy, political agent for the
　　　　　　　Simla Hill States, quoted in H. Montgomery Hyde,
　　　　　　　　　　　*Simla and the Simla Hill States*
　　　　　　　　　　*under British Protection 1815–1835*

Although the British may have preferred to establish their hill stations
in areas lacking the imprint of Indians, almost all the highland locales where
hill stations arose were already occupied when the first colonial authorities
arrived. The cultivators, herders, and hunter-gatherers who inhabited these
hills posed a problem for the British. How was it possible to claim that these
places stood apart from the rest of India if they were in fact populated by
Indians? The presence of the indigenous hill folk demanded an accounting,
an exegesis that would make them knowable and appropriable to the
peculiar requirements of the hill stations.

In the vast quasi-Linnaean taxonomy that characterized the colonial
ethnographic endeavor in India, the British often placed the peoples of the
highland frontiers under the heading of "martial races," with courage, viril-
ity, and pugnacity among their distinguishing features. The Gurkhas exemplified the type. These were not desirable qualities, however, for peoples

who dwelt within the shadows of the hill stations: it would not do to have British sanctuaries surrounded by fierce warriors. If the highlands were to seem untouched by history and uncontaminated by society, if they were to evoke an Edenic tranquility, then it was essential that their inhabitants be seen to embody a corresponding character, a purity and simplicity that bore some semblance to the qualities exemplified by Adam and Eve. These were the lineaments of the noble savage, and this archetypal creature became the model for representations of the hill stations' aboriginals.

A comparative examination of British representations of the Paharis of Simla, the Lepchas of Darjeeling, and the Todas of Ootacamund reveals just how determined the British were to cast the hill folk as noble savages. These three peoples stood about as far apart from one another as any in British India. The triangulated gap that separated them was measurable not merely in miles but in language, religion, kinship practices, and a great many other standard markers of ethnic identity. Virtually the only feature they shared was the historical contingency of occupying certain highland tracts where the British wished to establish hill stations. Yet such slender grounds of convergence provided the basis for colonial representations of these three peoples in the nineteenth century. The Paharis, Lepchas, and Todas came to be seen in remarkably similar terms, their presumed autochthony lending verity to the claims made for the Edenic qualities of their habitats. The singular importance of hill stations to the expatriate rulers of the raj explains why and how the indigenes of these areas came to be defined, confined, reduced, and ultimately recast.

———

The inhabitants of the hills around Simla were part of a culturally distinct population known as Paharis, who populated the lower Himalayas between Nepal and Kashmir. Although they were Hindus, their customs regarding caste restrictions, the role of women, diet, and certain other matters diverged in significant respects from the "Great Tradition" of Hinduism. In the view of one scholar, the distinctive demands of the highland ecosystem played a determining role in Pahari peasant life, causing it to be more egalitarian and communal in character than was peasant life elsewhere in India.[1]

Early British travelers to Simla and the surrounding hill country were quick to observe that Pahari society and culture were distinctive. They gave

1. Ramachandra Guha, *The Unquiet Woods: Ecological Change and Peasant Resistance in the Himalaya* (Berkeley, 1989), ch. 1. Also see Gerald D. Berreman, *Hindus of the Himalayas* (Berkeley and Los Angeles, 1963).

special attention to what they regarded as especially colorful or unusual practices, such as the lulling of Pahari infants to sleep by placing their heads in cold mountain streams. The quaint temples and exotic festivals, the rumored prevalence of polyandry and infanticide, the limited number of castes and caste prohibitions, and the females' freedom from purdah also attracted interest. These seemingly random observations and judgments were part of a persistent endeavor to contrast the Paharis with the population of the plains, a distinction that was generally meant to advantage the Paharis.

The British, to be sure, were far from enamored with every feature of Pahari society. They were especially offended by the practice of polyandry and its frequent corollary, female infanticide. James Fraser, one of the first British travelers in the region, voiced feelings shared by most subsequent commentators when he pronounced these practices "disgusting." He also dismissed the inhabitants of the lower hills as "contemptible in size, mean in aspect, cringing in address; their intellect appears degraded, and their ignorance almost brutal." However, his views grew more favorable as he trekked further into the interior. He spoke admiringly of the inhabitants of the highlands as modest, able, and hard-working peasants, and he judged them superior in many respects to his own Scottish highland countrymen. These observations led him to suggest that a sort of geographical determinism operated on the native character: "the farther removed from the plains, the heat, and the more accessible parts of the country, the higher does the highlander seem to rise in activity of mind and body."[2] The distinction between high and low, vertical and horizontal, hills and plains was an enduring point of departure for discussions of the people who occupied the slopes around Simla.

For the Victorians, an essential aspect of any ethnographic commentary was an assessment of moral temper, which manifested itself above all in religious belief. Despite the fact that the Paharis shared their faith with their brethren on the plains below, their version of Hinduism was deemed less corrupting. "The religion of the Puharies is a simple form of Hindooism, free from some of its worst features as followed in the plains," explained one observer.[3] The caste-bound inequities and ritual-enmeshed superstitions generally associated with Hindu communities were thought

2. James Baillie Fraser, *Journal of a Tour through Part of the Snowy Range of the Himala Mountains and to the Sources of the Rivers Jumna and Ganges* (London, 1820), 70, 67, 209, 204.

3. "Mountaineer," *A Summer Ramble in the Himalayas* (London, 1860), 187.

not to exist among the Paharis, who were seen as living close to nature in simple egalitarian communities. John Lowrie, the secretary of the Board of Foreign Missions for the Presbyterian Church, attributed what he regarded as the uncommon moral integrity of the inhabitants of the Simla hills to their freedom from "artificial distinctions." He explained:

> In the manners of the Hill people there is a frank and independent bearing, which is much more pleasant than the sycophancy and servility towards superiors so common throughout India. They seem to be very ingenuous. They might be characterized as a simple-minded people, who are little encumbered with artificial distinctions of wealth and rank. Their chiefs have commonly but little power. . . . Hence, there is among them the absence both of the polish of address, and of the specious but deceitful ingenuity of mind, which are found among the subjects of more powerful and wealthy native rulers. This absence of artificial usage may be partly owing, also, to the fact, that there are few persons among them of overgrown wealth.[4]

Lowrie believed that the Paharis' simple social order made them promising candidates for conversion, an expectation destined for disappointment.

Simla's founder, Captain Charles Kennedy, also believed that the rustic simplicity of the Paharis connoted moral innocence. However, rather than wonder about their prospects for conversion, he meditated on the relationship between morality and sexual behavior. In a continuation of the epigraph that opens this chapter, Kennedy observed: "No horror is expressed at the violation of female chastity. Shame hardly exists in some of the remoter States."[5] Edging toward a kind of cultural relativism, he suggested that conduct which elicited opprobrium from civilized Englishmen had more innocent connotations for simple Paharis. Kennedy was not alone in his preoccupation with the sexual morality of the hill folk. "More free in manner than the natives of the plains, they are at the same time far less indolent; and I am persuaded that, however lightly they may weigh the crime and shame of the forfeiture of chastity, their natural tendencies are comparatively pure," professed a priggish Captain George Thomas. "I have seen some beautiful and sinless little hill girls of grace and air so innocent, so pure, so cherub-like, that it seemed impossible that they should become sensual—impossible that they should have within them the seeds of lasciviousness and guilt."[6]

4. John C. Lowrie, *Two Years in Upper India* (New York, 1850), 221.

5. Quoted in H. Montgomery Hyde, *Simla and the Simla Hill States under British Protection 1815–1835* (Lahore, 1961), 23–24.

6. Capt. George Powell Thomas, *Views of Simla* (London, c. 1846), 7.

In the final analysis, however, the quality that the British found most compelling about the Paharis was not their supposed guiltless sexuality nor their inferred receptivity to Christian doctrine but their seemingly placid, peaceful character, which became particularly important after 1857. Despite a scare during the early days of the rebellion, Simla and the surrounding countryside remained tranquil and served as a refuge for British women and children. Consequently, the inhabitants of the area found understandable favor with the British. The *Times* war correspondent William Howard Russell, who came to Simla to recuperate from the rigors of following the military campaign, found the native inhabitants "a very interesting race, with greater intelligence and gentleness than those of the plains."[7] A late-nineteenth-century district gazetteer for Simla described the Pahari as a "simple-minded, orderly people, quiet and peaceful in their pursuits, truthful in character, and submissive to authority." Lest the significance of this final clause be lost on his readers, he added, "They hardly require to be ruled."[8]

Despite some shifts of perspective over time, British representations of the Simla Paharis remained consistent in certain fundamental respects. The predominant theme was that they were an open, naive, harmless populace, perhaps misguided in some of their social practices but graced with the vestiges of a more pristine moral order. Emily Eden expressed this view with characteristic vividness: "I imagine half these people must be a sort of vulgar Adams and Eves—not so refined, but nearly as innocent."[9] Such representations had less to do with ethnographic accuracy than with the evocation of a mythic charter. They reappeared in even sharper form in the commentary on the aboriginal inhabitants of Darjeeling and Ootacamund.

———

The occupants of the slopes around Darjeeling in the eastern Himalayas shared little except the experience of colonial subjugation with their Simla counterparts in the western Himalayas. They were mainly monogamous, not polyandrous; Buddhists, not Hindus; and bound to the legacy of Mongolian Asia, not the plains of the Ganges. But the British portrayed them in much the same terms.

7. William Howard Russell, *My Diary in India*, vol. 2 (London, 1860), 94.
8. Punjab Government, *Gazetteer of the Simla District, 1888–89* (Calcutta, n.d.), 43.
9. Emily Eden, *Up the Country: Letters from India* (1930; reprint, London, 1984), 162.

These mountain dwellers were known as the Lepchas.[10] They quickly acquired a reputation among the British as an honest, happy, gentle, candid people. Despite frequent complaints about their reluctance to wash and to work, many visitors were charmed by their seemingly innocent contentment. The naturalist Joseph Hooker described them as "amiable and obliging, frank, humorous, and polite, without the servility of the Hindoos." "They are a cheerful, and apparently contented people," declared the *Calcutta Review*, "with few wants and little or no anxiety." According to the author of the first gazetteer for the region, the Lepchas were "a fine, frank race, naturally open hearted and free handed," although a subordinate clause added ominously that "they do not seem to improve on being brought into contact with civilization."[11]

Some of the earliest commentaries on the Lepchas were among the most telling. Darjeeling's founding father, Dr. Arthur Campbell, described them in an article for the *Journal of the Asiatic Society of Bengal* as cheerful, curious, honest, and gentle. "The marked contrast in these respects with the listless, uninquiring native of the plains, renders association with them a source of much pleasure to Europeans." The *Bengal Hurkaru* praised them for being "wholly exempted from the prejudices of caste, and that inveteracy in superstitious customs which characterizes Hindoo idolatry."[12] Similarly, a Captain Herbert, who had investigated Darjeeling as a site for a European sanitarium, wrote in the 1830s:

[A]ll who saw them would prefer their open and expressive countenances to the look of cunning, suspicion or apathy that marks the more regular features of the Hindoostanee.... They are the most good humoured, active, curious yet simple people, that [I have] ever met with, ... bold and free in their manners, yet perfectly respectful, curious to a degree characteristic of the Europeans, sociable, obliging, cheerful, and of imperturbable good humour, with the most perfect simplicity, and complete freedom from guile ... being superior in moral character and social qualities to the

10. The most recent studies of the Lepchas are Veena Bhasin, *Ecology, Culture and Change: Tribals of Sikkim Himalayas* (New Delhi, 1989); and R. N. Thakur, *Himalayan Lepchas* (New Delhi, 1988).

11. Joseph Dalton Hooker, *Himalayan Journals*, vol. 1 (London, 1854), 129; *Darjeeling*, pamphlet reprinted from the *Calcutta Review*, no. 55 (1857): 27; W. W. Hunter, *A Statistical Account of Bengal*, vol. 10: *Districts of Darjiling and Jalpaiguri, and State of Kuch Behar* (London, 1876), 47.

12. A. Campbell, "Note on the Lepchas of Sikkim," *Journal of the Asiatic Society of Bengal* 92 (1840): 386; *Bengal Hurkaru*, 1 February 1839, quoted in Fred Pinn, *The Road to Destiny: Darjeeling Letters 1839* (Calcutta, 1986), 32.

people of the plains . . . free from all those degrading superstitions and absurd and injurious prejudices.[13]

Once again a description of hill folk draws its force from a Manichaean
contrast. The natives of Darjeeling, like their analogues in Simla, represented a moral antithesis to the intractable and unfathomable subjects who
occupied the plains.

For many observers, an equally compelling contrast could be drawn
between the Lepchas and their mountain neighbors, the Nepalese and the
Bhutanese. While the Nepalese and Bhutanese were seen as aggressive,
industrious, and warlike, the Lepchas were, in the oft-repeated words of
Hooker, "timid, peaceful, and no brawler[s]."[14] It is quite clear that the
British found much to admire in the "virile" Gurkhas of Nepal and the
Bhutanese, at least after they had been pacified by force of arms. But
the Lepchas, with their supposed "cowardly disposition," were vastly
preferable as neighbors.[15]

The Lepchas were believed to live in intimate accord with their forest
environment, possessing a remarkable knowledge of its flora and fauna, and
they were highly prized as guides into the Himalayan interior. Various
writers described them as "born naturalists." Major L. A. Waddell, who
relied on Lepchas to guide his party through parts of the Himalayas in the
1890s, believed that they "represent the state of primitive man when he
subsisted by hunting, fishing, and gathering wild fruits and digging roots,"
which left them with "absolutely no true conception of private property"
but possessing a rare bond with nature that endowed them with a simple
nobility as "true son[s] of the forest."[16] Samuel Bourne, the great pho-
tographer of mid-nineteenth-century India, took a pair of portraits of two
Lepchas that gave visual expression to this view. The images show a Lepcha
man and woman, each bare-legged and plainly dressed, situated in a rugged
outdoor setting and facing the camera with direct, frank gazes. "Just as
European royalty was often photographed with one foot elevated, resting
on a cushion or stool," observes the Bourne scholar Arthur Ollman, "so
too are these tribal individuals seen, right foot placed on a rock. They sit

13. Quoted in H. V. Bayley, *Dorje-ling* (Calcutta, 1838), 50.

14. Hooker, *Himalayan Journals*, vol. 1, 128.

15. *Newman's Guide to Darjeeling and Neighbourhood*, 6th ed. (Calcutta,
1919), 81.

16. L. A. Waddell, *Among the Himalayas* (1899; reprint, Delhi, 1979), 91–92,
105, 77–78.

at the center of the image, slightly higher than the camera, again adding dignity to their fine posture."[17]

The most fervent advocate of this idealized view of the Lepchas was General George Byres Mainwaring of the Bengal Army, who is said to have married a Lepcha woman. Mainwaring devoted decades of his life to the study of the Lepcha language. He described the Lepchas as "the free sons of the forest, the hearty yeomen of the land, the lords of the soil," who "dwelt in pretty cottages" and "roamed through the forest inhaling health." When he called their homeland "the very garden of Eden," he was not speaking metaphorically. Indeed, the paramount purpose of his linguistic labors was to prove that the Lepcha tongue was the source from which all other languages had derived. "The language . . . is unquestionably far anterior to the Hebrew or Sanskrit. It is preeminently an *Ursprache*, being probably, and I think, I may, without fear of misrepresentation, state it to be, the oldest language extant. . . . [I]t possesses and plainly evinces the principle and motive on which all language is constructed."[18] This weird tributary of Sir William Jones's linguistic genealogy gave Mainwaring a reputation as the leading expert on the Lepchas in the late nineteenth century.[19]

———

Of all the peoples who inhabited the highland sites where hill stations were established, the Todas of the Nilgiris most clearly evoked for the British the primitive and the pristine. One of the earliest reports described them as "a very remarkable people," and this judgment held sway for nearly all subsequent colonial observers.[20] Their intriguing presence inspired a large ethnographic literature, perhaps the earliest and most extensive devoted to any group of Indians in the nineteenth century.[21] Visitors as diverse as the explorer Richard Burton and the theosophist Madame H. P. Blavatsky published accounts of the Todas, and W. H. R. Rivers's weighty book on the

17. Arthur Ollman, *Samuel Bourne: Images of India* (Carmel, Calif., 1983), 20.

18. Col. G. B. Mainwaring, *A Grammar of the Rong (Lepcha) Language* (1876; reprint, Delhi, 1985), xiii, ix, xix–xx.

19. See, for instance, the remarks of Florence Donaldson, *Lepcha Land* (London, 1900), 40.

20. Reginald Orton, "Medical Report on the Nilgherry Mountains," [1821], 92, F/4/711/19407, Board's Collection, IOL.

21. Paul Hockings, *A Bibliography for the Nilgiri Hills of Southern India*, rev. ed., 2 vols. (New Haven, 1978), provides a thorough guide to this literature.

subject is widely regarded as one of the classics of modern anthropological scholarship.[22]

The Todas were pastoralists who grazed their cattle exclusively on the Nilgiri plateau.[23] They practiced polyandry and female infanticide, and they firmly resisted Western efforts to convert them to Christianity and to incorporate them into the colonial economy. These traits might have been enough under other circumstances to condemn them in the eyes of the British, but a special set of factors worked in their favor. The Todas' striking appearance, demeanor, and customs intrigued and attracted visitors to the Nilgiris. They were described as a statuesque people, which supposedly set them apart from other Indians in the south. The Toda men's full beards and the women's long, unbound hair reinforced this reputation for difference. They wore long togalike gowns, lived in dwellings of distinctive half-barrel design, spoke a Dravidian dialect so singular that it was widely thought to be an entirely separate language, and centered their religious life on a novel dairy cult.[24] Although more recent scholarship dismisses the notion, nineteenth-century observers believed that the Todas were "the lords of the soil" and pointed to what they interpreted as the payment of tribute by the other inhabitants of the area as evidence.[25]

Little wonder, then, that speculation arose about the Todas' origins. "The appearance of the Todas . . . is very prepossessing," wrote Captain Henry Harkness in the first book to appear about them. "Generally above the common height, athletic, and well made, their bold bearing, and open and expressive countenances, lead immediately to the conclusion that they

22. Richard F. Burton, *Goa, and the Blue Mountains* (1851; reprint, Berkeley, 1991); H. P. Blavatsky, *The People of the Blue Mountains* (1893; reprint, Wheaton, Ill., 1930); W.H.R. Rivers, *The Todas* (London, 1906). For an interesting assessment of Rivers's work, see R. L. Rooksby, "W.H.R. Rivers and the Todas," *South Asia* 1 (Aug. 1971): 109–21.

23. An excellent study is Anthony R. Walker, *The Toda of South India: A New Look* (Delhi, 1986). An abbreviated version appears as "Toda Society between Tradition and Modernity," in *Blue Mountains: The Ethnography and Biogeography of a South Indian Region,* ed. Paul Hockings (Delhi, 1989), 186–205.

24. The first work to challenge seriously the exceptionalism that characterized most literature on the Todas, restoring them instead to their South Indian context, was James Wilkinson Breeks, *An Account of the Primitive Tribes and Monuments of the Nilagiris* (London, 1873), ch. 2.

25. As far as I have been able to determine, the earliest use of this phrase to describe the Todas' relationship with their neighbors appears in a letter by Evan McPherson, superintendent of the Neilgherry roads, to John Sullivan, 12 June 1820, PP, *Papers Relative to the Formation of a Sanitarium on the Neilgherries for European Troops,* Session 729, XLI, 1850, 4.

must be of a different race to their neighbours of the same hue; and the question naturally arises, who can they be?"[26] Conjecture variously identified them as the descendants of Jews, Arabs, Scythians, Druids, Romans, even Polynesians. Captain John Ouchterlony believed that "their aquiline nose, receding forehead, and rounded profile, combined with their black bushy beards and eyebrows, give them so decidedly Jewish an aspect, that no beholder can fail to be impressed with the idea that they must, in some way, . . . be connected with one of the lost and wandering tribes of the ancient Israelites."[27] Such speculation soon created its own reality, as one early commentator inadvertently discovered:

> The countenances of a few are strikingly Jewish, which is remarked by almost every stranger. I found several of them possessed of Jewish names, and began to flatter myself that I had discovered a colony of the scattered tribes of God's ancient people. But, on communicating my supposed discovery to a friend, I hardly thanked him, at the moment, for dispelling the illusion, by informing me, that *he* had given them these names, as he found it difficult to pronounce the barbarous appellations by which they are called.[28]

Regrettably, the implications of this disclosure did not fully register with the author. He went on to suggest that the Todas were the forgotten remnants of a Roman colony.

With so many amateur ethnographers engaged in madcap postulations, it became increasingly apparent to the more sober students of the Toda that the endeavor to determine these people's past led to the fabrication of fantasies. A full century before academic anthropologists had begun to question the foundations of ethnographic authority, the German missionary Friedrich Metz noted that the Todas "soon detect what information the latter [Europeans] desire to obtain and make their replies accordingly. . . . [I]t is now a matter of difficulty to obtain from them any account of their previous history, upon the truth of which implicit reliance can be placed."[29]

26. Capt. Henry Harkness, *A Description of a Singular Aboriginal Race Inhabiting the Summit of the Neilgherry Hills* (London, 1832), 6–7.

27. Capt. J. Ouchterlony, *Geographical and Statistical Memoir of a Survey of the Neilgherry Mountains* (Madras, 1868), 52. This report was first drafted in 1847, and it is repeated almost verbatim by Duncan MacPherson, *Reports on Mountain and Marine Sanitaria* (Madras, 1862), 24.

28. James Hough, *Letters on the Climate, Inhabitants, Productions, etc. of the Neilgherries, or Blue Mountains of Coimbatoor* (London, 1829), 63.

29. F. Metz, *The Tribes Inhabiting the Neilgherry Hills*, 2d ed. (Mangalore, 1864), 13.

Yet, as several works inform us, ethnography often has as much to do with poetics as it does with science.[30] Poetics played a substantial role in the speculations that the British entertained about the ancestry of the Toda. These speculations supplied a genealogical point of reference, a kind of *Burke's Peerage* for primitives, that certified the high symbolic standing of the Todas in the eyes of the British. References to their nobility and dignity of bearing abounded. The 1880 district gazetteer for the Nilgiris observed that there was "something in the fearless manners and independent bearing of the Todas, which makes them very attractive." A subsequent gazetteer stressed their "attractively dignified and fearless manners when conversing with Europeans." A guidebook to Ootacamund spoke of them as an "aristocracy," and the term "lords of the land" was repeatedly applied to them. Indeed, the first Europeans to reside in the Nilgiris were so taken by the Todas' hereditary claims to the land that they voluntarily paid them compensation for their building stands, while John Sullivan, the founder of Ootacamund, pressed the government (without success) to grant them proprietary rights over virtually the entire expanse of the Nilgiris, even though this advocacy ignored the rights of other inhabitants of the hills, as well as the fact that the Todas did not share British notions of land ownership.[31]

When the British expressed admiration for the noble mien of the Todas, they had in mind a quality so plainly bound to nature and so primitive in its purity that it posed no challenge to their own sense of superiority, vested as it was in the claims of civilization. Thus, commentators moved effortlessly from assertions about the natural dignity of the Todas to avowals of their submissive affection for Europeans. One of the first medical officers to investigate the Nilgiris claimed that his two Toda assistants "became so much attached to Mr. Stoddart and myself that they actually shed tears on our departure."[32] Others offered their assurances that the Todas were a modest and harmless people whose presence merely added an Arcadian flavor to the highland environment.

---

30. See James Clifford and George E. Marcus, eds., *Writing Culture: The Poetics and Politics of Ethnography* (Berkeley and Los Angeles, 1986); and Clifford Geertz, *Works and Lives: The Anthropologist as Author* (Stanford, 1988).

31. H. B. Grigg, *A Manual of the Nilagiri District* (Madras, 1880), 186; W. Francis, *The Nilgiris* (Madras, 1908), 138; Geofry [pseud.], *Ooty and Her Sisters, or Our Hill Stations in South India* (Madras, 1881), 116; Walker, *Toda*, 243, 245. A useful summary of early British policy regarding Toda land rights can be found in *Guide to the Records of the Nilgiris District from 1827 to 1835* (Madras, 1934).

32. Reginald Orton, [1821], 93, in F/4/711/19407, Board's Collection, IOL.

This impression was reinforced by the numerous pictorial representations of the Todas. They repeatedly appeared in the early prints of the Nilgiris as an integral part of the pastoral landscape, noble figures herding their cattle on rolling green slopes. With their full beards, long tresses, and togalike gowns, they took on for the British a classical or biblical appearance. The frontispiece to Harkness's book offers an especially revealing image: a bucolic family group consisting of a toga-draped patriarch standing behind his seated wife and naked child under the shade of a tree. Here the polyandrous Toda family has been transformed into the West's archetypal nuclear household, the Christian holy family of Jesus, Mary, and Joseph (Figure 4). As if to go one better, William Marshall included in his late-nineteenth-century study of the Todas a photograph of an elderly Toda couple with the caption "Adam and Eve."[33]

The main intent of this characterization was to set the Toda in stark contrast to the stereotypical Indian of the plains. "This remarkable race differ in almost every essential respect from the other tribes of the natives of Hindustan," declared Captain Ouchterlony, who stressed that their appearance "attest[s] that they can be sprung from no effeminate eastern race." Reverend James Hough found the Toda "remarkably frank in their deportment; and their entire freedom from Hindoo servility is very engaging to the Englishman, and cannot fail to remind him of the 'bold peasantry' of a still dearer land." Major Walter Campbell's hunting memoirs included a conversation between two English sportsmen about the Todas: "'Are not these a fine race of men?' remarked Mansfield. . . . 'How different is their manner from that of the effeminate Hindoos! You see they are perfectly respectful . . . but there is nothing cringing or timid in their mode of doing so.'"[34]

Various commentators found the Toda women of particular interest. Unconstrained by purdah, they "have no shyness or reserve," remarked Captain Robert Mignan, an early visitor to the Nilgiris. Campbell's sportsmen regarded the Toda female's "easy, natural, yet graceful carriage [as] that of a true child of nature, ignorant of crime, and happy in her ignorance." These women "have a self-possession with strangers quite unknown among

33. William E. Marshall, *A Phrenologist amongst the Todas* (London, 1873), Plate 16. More recently, a reminiscence about Ootacamund included the remark that "the most casual observer cannot fail to be struck by [the Toda's] extraordinary resemblance to the traditional pictures of Christ." J. Chartres Molony, "An Indian Hill Station," *Blackwood's Magazine* 247, no. 1495 (May 1940): 628.

34. Ouchterlony, *Geographical and Statistical Memoir*, 51; Hough, *Letters*, 65; Major Walter Campbell, *The Old Forest Ranger; or, Wild Sports in India* (London, 1863), 42.

Figure 4.   The Toda family portrayed in Henry Harkness's 1832 book bears a striking resemblance to popular representations of the Christian holy family of Jesus, Mary, and Joseph. From Capt. Henry Harkness, *A Description of a Singular Aboriginal Race Inhabiting the Summit of the Neilgherry Hills* (London, 1832).

the Hindus of the plains," observed an American missionary. "They are ready to chat with the stranger, and have smiles almost constantly on their faces." Others also contrasted the frank and friendly demeanor of the Toda women with that of their counterparts on the plains.[35] There was, as we shall see, a sexual subtext to these comments, but their main purpose was to draw a distinction that privileged these hill people.

This discourse tended to pass over the fact that the Todas were not the only nor even the most numerous occupants of the Nilgiris when the British arrived. They lived amid large and important communities of Badagas, Kotas, Kurumbas, and Irulas, and all of these peoples existed in social and economic symbiosis. This relationship was rarely mentioned by the British, who thereby managed to minimize the similarities that Anthony Walker has noted between Nilgiri society and the pattern of multicaste social organization found elsewhere in rural India.[36] Most visitors to the Nilgiris shared the view voiced by a Madras staff corps officer: "The other inhabitants are not interesting, and may be dismissed in very few words."[37] Insofar as the British gave any attention to the Todas' neighbors, they regarded them as rank inferiors to the Todas, markedly lower in the great chain of being, and readily differentiated by distinctive flaws. The Badagas were "gentle and industrious" cultivators "but timid and ignorant" because of their obedience to Hinduism; the Kotas were "intelligent and hardworking" artisans but morally marred by "their filthy custom of eating carrion"; the Kurumbas were "very uncouth, and wild and squalid in appearance"; and the Irulas, who occupied the lower slopes of the plateau, also occupied the moral depths, "but little removed from . . . utter uncivilization."[38] None challenged the social eminence of the Toda. Hence the British persistently mistook Toda traffic with their neighbors as a form of tribute—a misapprehension that aided British efforts to establish the ancient credentials of the Todas.

The Todas, then, took on an especially evocative network of associations in the British mind. Even so, they shared many features with the indi-

35. Capt. Robert Mignan, *Notes Extracted from a Private Journal, Written during a Tour through a Part of Malabar, and among the Neilgherries* (Bombay, 1834), 128; Campbell, *Old Forest Ranger*, 43; Rev. John W. Dulles, *Life in India; or Madras, the Neilgherries, and Calcutta* (Philadelphia, 1855), 446. Also see Harkness, *Description*, 8.

36. Walker, *Toda*, 22.

37. E. F. Burton, *An Indian Olio* (London, 1888), 141.

38. The statements about the Badagas and the Kurumbas come from Grigg, *Manual*, 224, 209; the Kota comment appears in *A Guide to Ootacamund and Its Neighbourhood* (Madras, 1889), 14; and the defamation of the Irula is from Harkness, *Description*, 29. Remarks in this vein are abundant in the literature.

genous peoples of Simla and Darjeeling: all were simple, guileless, noble beings, nurtured in the healthy embrace of nature, untouched by the depravity that pervaded the social and religious life of the Indian masses. These hill dwellers harbored no surprises and posed no threats of the sort that made their counterparts on the plains seem so duplicitous and dangerous. The translucence of their moral purity left them fully exposed to view. The colonizer's gaze could fix upon these people with confidence that its reading of their character and conduct was essentially unimpeded by the encrustations of debased customs. What it saw was what it wished to see—the corporeal embodiment of an Edenic innocence.

———

This romanticized vision of the hill stations' native inhabitants had a further virtue: it allowed most British commentators to view their own effect on these peoples as part of an inexorable evolutionary process. It was the fate of the innocent savage, they thought, to slide into moral and physical decay when brought into contact with the outside world. By attributing the ample evidence of dislocation and decline among the Todas and other hill peoples to the operation of natural law, the British contrived both to affirm the Elysian character of these subjects and to establish themselves as the ineluctable agents of civilization, the unhappy effect of which they regarded with self-conscious diffidence.

As early as the 1820s, Hough saw signs of "the deterioration of [the Todas'] character," citing their adulteration of milk that they sold and "other dishonest expedients." Later observers lamented the prevalence of alcoholism, beggary, prostitution, and venereal disease among the Todas. "Of late years," noted the author of an ethnographic study of the Todas published in 1868, "they have taken to drink Arrack, and most of their women have been debauched by Europeans, who, it is sad to observe, have introduced diseases to which these innocent tribes were at one time perfect strangers, and which, as they have no means of curing, is slowly . . . sapping their once hardy and vigorous constitutions."[39] Burton was even more stinging in his assessment of the impact of the West:

> The "noble unsophisticated Todas," as they were once called have been morally ruined by collision with Europeans and their dissolute attendants. They have lost their honesty: truth is become almost unknown to

39. Hough, *Letters*, 79; John Shortt, *An Account of the Tribes on the Neilgherries* (Madras, 1868), 8. Mignan stated that syphilis was the most prevalent disease among the Todas when he visited the Nilgiris in the early 1830s (*Notes Extracted from a Private Journal*, 131).

them; chastity, sobriety, and temperance, fell flat before the strong temptations of rupees, foreign luxuries, and ardent spirits. Covetousness is now the mountaineer's ruling passion: the Toda is an inveterate, indefatigable beggar, whose cry . . . "give me a present!" no matter what,—money, brandy, cigars, or snuff—will follow you for miles over hill and dale: as a pickpocket, he displays considerable ingenuity; and no Moses or Levi was ever a more confirmed, determined, grasping, usurer. His wife and daughters have become vile as the very refuse of the bazaar. And what can he show in return for the loss of his innocence and happiness? . . . From the slow but sure effects of strange diseases, the race is rapidly deteriorating—few of the giant figures that abound in the remote hills, are to be found near our cantonments—and it is more than probable that, like other wild tribes, which the progress of civilization has swept away from the face of the earth, the Toda will, ere long, cease to have "a local habitation and a name" among the people of the East.[40]

Many shared Burton's pessimistic verdict. Although contradicted by nineteenth-century census figures,[41] the Todas were believed to be a "dying race," disappearing because of the combined effects of alcohol, syphilis, and their own polyandrous practices. "[I]t seems certain," declared Mignan, "that the Todas, like their buffaloes, are destined to disappear from the face of the earth."[42] This conviction accounts for much of the attention the Todas received from British ethnographers. For instance, Marshall, a Bengal Army officer and amateur phrenologist, obtained a furlough from his regiment so that he could study the Todas before they died out.[43]

A similar fate was thought to await the Lepchas. As Darjeeling became a popular resort and the center of a thriving tea industry, it attracted large numbers of laborers from the neighboring mountain states of Nepal and Bhutan, as well as from the plains below. Aggressive in their pursuit of economic opportunity, these immigrants came to be seen as a threat to the indigenous Lepchas. "[B]efore the advance of cultivation and with the disappearance of the forest to make way for crops and cattle the Lepcha is in great danger of dying out, being driven away from his ancestral glades by the prosaic Nepali and other materialistic Himalayan

40. Burton, *Goa*, 351–52.
41. See the data in Walker, *Toda*, app. 2.
42. Mignan, *Notes Extracted from a Private Journal*, 133. Also see Rev. B. Schmid, "Remarks on the Origin and Languages of the Aborigines of the Nilgiris," *Journal of the Bombay Branch of the Royal Asiatic Society* 3, pt. 1, no. 12 (Jan. 1849): 52; Metz, *Tribes*, 15; and *Letters from India and Kashmir* (London, 1874), 49.
43. Marshall, *Phrenologist*, v.

tribes."[44] General Mainwaring argued that what made the depredations of the Nepalese and Bhutanese possible were the actions of the British themselves. "The advent of the Europeans was the first real blow the Lepchas received; their downfall quickly followed." He traced this decline to the imposition of taxation, the demand for labor, and the growth of Darjeeling. In a parallel to the Toda case, the debasement of the Lepcha women was a fatal blow: "The women also, naturally exceedingly gentle and modest, became the victims of the licentious:—the fall of the Lepchas was complete."[45] Various observers worried about an apparent decline in fertility among the Lepchas and lamented their growing practice of intermarriage with immigrants. They are "losing their identity by the extensive absorption of their women into the Bhotiya and Limboo tribes, with whom they freely intermarry," explained Waddell.[46] All of this commentary suggested that the Lepchas, like the Todas, were a "dying race." According to the author of an 1883 guidebook to Darjeeling, they would soon "be as extinct as the Dodo."[47]

The Paharis, with their much more sizable population and territory, never gave cause for concern about their physical survival. Their moral health, however, did worry the British. "I am told that honesty was the distinguishing characteristic in former times of the Paharis," wrote Fanny Parks at midcentury, "but intercourse with civilized Europeans has greatly demoralized the mountaineers."[48] The destructive effects of the West on the inhabitants of the Simla hills preoccupied others, including Rudyard Kipling, who addressed the issue in one of his most poignant short stories, "Lispeth."

The story concerns a beautiful young Pahari girl from the hills near Simla who is raised by Moravian missionaries after her parents die of cholera. Comparing her to "the original Diana of the Romans," with "a

44. Percy Brown, *Tours in Sikhim and the Darjeeling District* (Calcutta, 1917), 4.
45. Mainwaring, *Grammar*, xii, xiii.
46. Waddell, *Among the Himalayas*, 293.
47. R. D. O'Brien, *Darjeeling, the Sanitarium of Bengal; and Its Surroundings* (Calcutta, 1883), 67. A census conducted in 1892 demonstrated "that there is a fallacy in the common idea that the Lepchas are decreasing in number because of British occupation." J. G. Ritchie, "Darjeeling District Census Report," 15 March 1892, 10, in V/15/37, Census Reports, IOL. Despite this evidence, the myth of the Lepchas as a dying race has persisted up to recent times. See comments by K. C. Bhanja, *Wonders of Darjeeling and the Sikkim Himalaya* (n.p., 1943), 29; and John Morris, *Eating the Indian Air* (London, 1968), 261.
48. Fanny Parks, *Wanderings of a Pilgrim, in Search of the Picturesque*, vol. 2 (London, 1850), 259.

pale, ivory colour" and "a Greek face," Kipling evokes the same sort of ancestral associations that surrounded the Todas and Lepchas, and with much the same intent: he seeks to elicit his readers' sympathies by suggesting that Lispeth possesses a pedigree that sets her apart from other Indians. Because she has converted to Christianity, her own people shun her, and when she saves a young Englishman who has fallen from a cliff, she decides that he shall become her husband. In her simplicity and innocence, she cannot comprehend the racial boundaries that mark the colonial order. Thus, when the missionary couple who have raised her conspire with the young man to shatter her hopes of matrimony, Lispeth abandons the mission and returns to the people of her birth, becoming an embittered, abused, alcoholic "creature" whose beauty soon fades. For the chaplain's wife, these events simply demonstrate that "'Lispeth was always at heart an infidel,'" but Kipling clearly intends a different message. He wants Lispeth to be seen as the exemplar of a people sequestered by their hills from the corrupting influences—the sins—of the outside world. The serpent in this garden is the European, specifically the missionary couple whose contradictory impulses to inculcate notions of Christian brotherhood while defending the privileges of their race destroy her. Kipling panders in this story to the British Indian community's widespread distrust of missionaries, who were accused of fostering expectations of equality on the part of indigenous peoples that were bound to cause disappointment and discontent. At the same time, however, he offers a far more sweeping commentary on the relationship between the British and the inhabitants of the hills. Lispeth serves as the symbol of a paradisiacal people who are too simple, too gentle, too fragile to survive the encounter with the West. Their character informs their fate: their destruction is the natural outcome of their role as noble savages.[49]

The British, however, did not merely lament the precipitate destruction of these people. By the late nineteenth century, authorities sought to alleviate the full force of the colonial impact through a policy of protection and preservation that paralleled their efforts to mitigate the havoc wrought on the physical environment of the hills. This enterprise was part of a general drive in the final decades of the century to preserve and revive the vestiges of a supposedly untarnished traditional India, whether it was manifested in an imperiled architecture, craft, custom, or people them-

49. Rudyard Kipling, "Lispeth," in *Plain Tales from the Hills* (London, 1987), 33–37. Lispeth is resurrected by Kipling in *Kim;* now the powerful matriarch of a village, she assists Kim in his efforts to thwart three Russian agents.

selves. John Lockwood Kipling, Rudyard's father, was one of the leading figures in this enterprise, and it is worth noting that he devoted some of his labors to preserve the hill temples and indigenous decorative arts of Simla.[50] The small princely hill states that surrounded Simla provided some measure of protection against the European impact, and British officials in the late nineteenth century made a conscious effort to ensure that they remained reservoirs of traditional Pahari culture. In Darjeeling district, concerns about the survival of the Lepchas led to the passage of a statute that sought to protect them against the dispossession of their last five acres of land, and General Mainwaring undertook his quixotic endeavor to save the Lepcha language. The maharaja of neighboring Sikkim was persuaded to establish within his state a special Lepcha reserve, which became a magnet for anthropologists in search of uncontaminated aboriginals.[51] The most extensive campaign to protect an indigenous people occurred, however, in the Nilgiris, where a system of land reserves was established for the Todas. The government sought to stem the Todas' presumed decline by prohibiting them from selling or leasing these lands, which an 1882 ruling declared to be communally owned. Regulations also controlled land usage, including a ban on cultivation until 1893. In effect, as Walker has observed, British officials attempted to confine the Todas within the boundaries of their traditional pastoral economy, insulating them from all change.[52]

These institutional efforts reflected a larger public interest in what might be termed the picturesque primitive. The growth of tourism in the mid to late nineteenth century propelled this ethnographic curiosity. A popular activity among newcomers to the hill stations was an excursion to view the local inhabitants in their exotic costumes and habitats. The encounter was certified by the purchase of postcards and photographs, handicrafts, and

50. See Thomas R. Metcalf, *An Imperial Vision: Indian Architecture and Britain's Raj* (Berkeley, 1989); and Mahrukh Tarapor, "John Lockwood Kipling and British Art Education in India," *Victorian Studies* 24, no. 1 (autumn 1980): 53–81. For John Lockwood Kipling's interest in the crafts of Simla, see Punjab Government, *Gazetteer of the Simla District, 1888–89*, 69–71.

51. See Geoffrey Gorer, *Himalayan Village: An Account of the Lepchas of Sikkim* (London, 1938); John Morris, *Living with Lepchas* (London, 1938); Bhasin, *Ecology, Culture and Change*.

52. Walker, *Toda*, 245–53. Also see Edgar Thurston, *Anthropology of the Todas and Kotas of the Nilgiri Hills* (Madras, 1896), 183–84; and David G. Mandelbaum, "Culture Change among the Nilgiri Tribes," in *Beyond the Frontier: Social Process and Culture Change*, ed. Paul Bohannan and Fred Plog (Garden City, N.Y., 1967), 203.

other locally manufactured curios (Figure 5). It became obligatory for
tourists in the Nilgiris, for instance, to visit those Toda *munds*, or hamlets,
that stood within easy walking distance of hotels in Ootacamund and its
sister hill station, Coonoor. When dignitaries visited the region, Todas were
often rounded up for inspection. "I have arranged for ten specimen males
and ten females to be at the place where my carriage will await you and
while you are having a little refreshment in a tent you will be able to look
at them," the governor of Madras wrote to Lord Curzon in 1902.[53] In Simla,
it became de rigueur for newcomers to attend the annual Sipi festival, which
the rana of neighboring Koti hosted in a glade at Mahasu, a hamlet several
miles from Simla where some officials had homes. Here visitors could view
Paharis bedecked in their finest costumes and engaged in folk dances,
archery competitions, the sale of handicrafts, and other activities that
reminded Simla's first historian, Edward Buck, of "an old English rural
gathering." Beginning with Lord Mayo, every viceroy made a point of
attending the Sipi festival, which came to be "observed as a public holiday
by the official world of Simla."[54] In Darjeeling, visitors were encouraged
to venture about a mile from their hotels to "a quaint and picturesque
village inhabited by Bhutias and Lepchas." Even more popular with tourists
was Darjeeling's Sunday bazaar, where plenty of Lepchas and other colorful
ethnic "types" could be observed and where local curios such as prayer
wheels, amulets, and skull drums could be purchased.[55] In those hill stations where the native populace was insufficiently colorful, traders from
afar sometimes offered a satisfactory substitute. Although by the late
nineteenth century the population around Mussoorie, for instance, had
little to offer tourists with a taste for the unfamiliar, one visitor there
described her delight when during a stroll she encountered an old Tibetan
woman wearing an unusual necklace, which she persuaded her to sell. "The
natural good manners of these natives are striking," she enthused, in-
stinctively regarding this traveler from Tibet as more "native" than the

53. Quoted in Judith Theresa Kenny, "Constructing an Imperial Hill Station:
The Representation of British Authority in Ootacamund" (Ph.D. diss., Syracuse
University, 1990), 275–76. Also see Sir Mountstuart E. Grant Duff, *Notes of an
Indian Journey* (London, 1876), 204.

54. Edward J. Buck, *Simla Past and Present*, 2d ed. (1925; reprint, Simla, 1989),
244, 243. Also see Raja Bhasin, *Simla: The Summer Capital of British India* (New
Delhi, 1992), 184; and the personal account of the festival by Col. Robert J.
Blackham, *Scalpel, Sword and Stretcher* (London, 1931), 193.

55. See W. S. Caine, *Picturesque India: A Handbook for European Travellers*
(London, 1890), 356; and J. D. Rees, *Lord Connemara's Tours in India* (London,
1892), 216.

Figure 5.    A dignified Lepcha man gazes at the viewer in this photograph from a tourist guidebook. From *Darjeeling and Its Mountain Railway* (Calcutta, 1921).

neglected inhabitants of the region.[56] To visit a Toda *mund*, a Buddhist monastery, or a Hindu hill temple, to dig among the burial "cairns" in the Nilgiris, to attend the village festivals near Simla, or to discover curios in the Darjeeling bazaar became just as much a part of the tourist itinerary as to take in the favored views of snow-capped peaks, heat-shimmering plains, and mist-enshrouded waterfalls.

———

If it is true that representations of the indigenes of Simla, Darjeeling, and Ootacamund were shaped by the special significance these highland sites held for the British, then one would expect the native peoples who inhabited the environs of other hill stations to be represented in similar fashion. A brief review of several other cases confirms this supposition.

The hills around Matheran, a popular sanitarium within easy reach of the residents of Bombay, were inhabited by several tribes—the Thakars, the Katkaris, and the Dhangars. The Dhangars were a pastoral people who, in the view of the British, had many of the same features as the Todas. They were said to possess a similar pride and noble bearing, and to overshadow their highland neighbors much as the Todas overshadowed the Badagas and the Kotas. They were described as "superior in physique to any other forest tribe," and their physiognomy was seen as a physical manifestation of their superiority of character: "their expression is frank and open, the features more refined, the nose more aquiline than is usual in the aborigines of India. The forehead is broad, and the eyes deep set, with a bright good humoured look in them."[57] Their reputations as children of nature made them popular guides for tours through the hills.[58] The Dhangars, in short, became the embodiment of the noble savage.

On the other side of the subcontinent, the Khasi people of Assam took on a similar celebrity in relationship to Shillong. Initially, however, the Khasis' armed resistance to British colonial rule caused them to be cast as "sulky intractable fellows," as Hooker put it.[59] Once pacified, a process completed some time before Shillong was founded in 1864, they acquired

56. Mrs. Robert Moss King, *The Diary of a Civilian's Wife in India 1877–1882*, vol. 1 (London, 1884), 146.

57. Mrs. A. K. Oliver, *The Hill Station of Matheran* (Bombay, 1905), 116. Also see J. Y. Smith, *Matheran Hills: Its People, Plants, and Animals* (Edinburgh, 1871), passim; and Isabel Burton, *AEI: Arabia Egypt India, A Narrative of Travel* (London and Belfast, 1879), 285–89.

58. Grant Duff, *Notes*, 25–26.

59. Hooker, *Himalayan Journals*, vol. 2, 274.

a more attractive reputation. Their Mongoloid appearance, matriarchal institutions, Mon-Khmer language, and other distinguishing characteristics attracted the interest of numerous ethnographers and comparative philologists and set them apart from neighboring peoples. The leading colonial study of the Khasis described them as a "simple and straightforward people" who "are cheerful in disposition, and are light-hearted in nature, and, unlike the plains people, seem to thoroughly appreciate a joke." Moreover, they "are fond of nature," a trait "not found usually in the people of India." Their women "are especially cheerful, and pass the time of day and bandy jokes with passers-by with quite an absence of reserve."[60] These remarks could just as well have referred to the Todas, the Lepchas, or the Paharis, and they established a similarly favorable dichotomy between the Khasis and the peoples of the plains.

It is perhaps less surprising to hear echoes of the commentary about the Simla hill folk in the discourse from other hill stations of the western Himalayas. After all, Paharis populated these places too. But the association between Paharis and a particular body of attributes was not as consistent as might be supposed. The self-styled founder of the hill station at Naini Tal did describe its inhabitants in terms reminiscent of remarks about Simla's indigenes. The "rational simplicity" of Hindu worship among the local hill people, he insisted, "compared with the noise and pomp, the obscenities and abominations of the same religion in the lower provinces, . . . leaves on the mind a pleasing impression of the Brahminical faith." The villages in the region bear "a striking resemblance to the nice cottages of industrious peasants in England," and their occupants possess "habits of industry, cleanliness, and simple pastoral manners."[61] Readers contemplating a visit to Naini Tal could scarcely find a more reassuring assessment of its inhabitants. Yet the adjacent hills also became an important recruiting ground for the military. For many years young Pahari males from the neighboring Tehri Garhwal State and Garhwal district (which was joined with Naini Tal district in the Kumaun division) served with distinction in the famous Gurkha regiments. Their martial reputation led to the creation of a separate Garhwali regiment in 1890, which achieved note as the 39th Garhwal Rifles.[62] This bifocal image of the Paharis of Kumaun—peaceful peasants in one context and fierce warriors in

60. Major P.R.T. Gurdon, *The Khasis* (London, 1907), 8, 4, 5.
61. "Pilgrim" [P. Barron], *Notes of Wanderings in the Himmala* (Agra, 1844), 65, 105.
62. Philip Mason, *A Matter of Honor* (New York, 1974), 384.

another—demonstrates the particularistic processes entailed in the representation of the ethnographic other.

_____

The British characterizations of the Paharis, the Lepchas, the Todas, and the various other peoples who inhabited the environs of hill stations were a particular aspect of the larger ontological endeavor known as orientalism. Its principal purpose was to make the unknown knowable and to use that knowledge with instrumental intent. In a remarkable series of essays, Bernard Cohn has shown how British authorities in India came to construct a knowledge of the peoples they governed that served their imperial purposes. The representation and reification of Indian castes, religions, laws, languages, and rituals were accomplished through census surveys, ethnographic inquiries, and other state-sponsored projects. In their endeavor to classify, codify, and normalize these unfamiliar subjects, the British saw themselves in the role of "curators of a vast outdoor museum."[63] The image calls to mind the museum curator in the opening pages of *Kim*, whose fund of knowledge about the subcontinent left the lama in awe. Like all curators, the British in India were obliged to devise a taxonomy for their bewildering collection. This system drew its inspiration from Europe's intellectual heritage, introducing Western notions of rationality, hierarchy, evolution, race, class, progress, modernity, and much else. It had the consequence, argues Cohn, of appropriating indigenous peoples, practices, and beliefs within the "discursive formation" of the West, "converting Indian forms of knowledge into European objects."[64]

What purposes were served by constructing this great colonial museum of ethnography? Edward Said has insisted that the central object was power, that the orientalists sought the means "for dominating, restructuring, and having authority over the Orient."[65] While there seems little question that the colonial state and its Western servants saw the accumulation of knowl-

63. Bernard S. Cohn, "The Past in the Present: India as Museum of Mankind," unpublished paper, 14. Also see Bernard S. Cohn, "The Command of Language and the Language of Command," in *Subaltern Studies*, vol. 4, ed. Ranajit Guha (Delhi, 1985), 276–329; Bernard S. Cohn, "Law and the Colonial State in India," in *History and Power in the Study of Law*, ed. June Starr and Jane F. Collier (Ithaca, 1989), 131–52; Bernard S. Cohn, "The Census, Social Stratification and Objectification in South Asia," *Folk* 26 (1984): 25–49; and Bernard S. Cohn, "Representing Authority in Victorian India," in *The Invention of Tradition*, ed. Eric Hobsbawm and Terence Ranger (Cambridge, 1982), 165–209.
64. Cohn, "The Command of Language and the Language of Command," 283.
65. Edward W. Said, *Orientalism* (New York, 1979), 3.

edge about India as vital to the maintenance of authority, a different set of preoccupations were operative as well. Ronald Inden has identified two schools of Indian orientalism, or Indology: both posed India as Europe's opposite, but one emphasized the positivist, empiricist, materialist concerns relevant to matters of power, while the other stressed romantic, spiritualist, and idealist considerations. A distinguishing characteristic of the romantic school, as works on ethnographic photography in British India and Western representations of Tibet have demonstrated, has been the projection of European dreams and desires onto an idealized object often existing at the furthest reaches of the Orient.[66] British representations of the indigenous inhabitants of the hill stations arose within this idealist context.

The recurrent emphasis given to the gulf between the hills and the plains was essential to the ethnographic image of the peoples who inhabited the hills. This binary opposition was part of what Said has termed the "imaginative geography" of orientalism.[67] Boundaries were drawn that assured the officials and others who patronized the hill stations that these enclaves and their aboriginals were a world apart from the harrying subcontinent with its confusing, contentious, and subversive hordes. The tropes that accrued around the Todas, the Lepchas, and their counterparts elsewhere stressed the moral innocence of the noble savage, the rustic simplicity of the pastoral life, the primitive egalitarianism of the peasant village, and the legitimizing aura of a classical or biblical genealogy. The purpose of these tropes was clear—to fashion an image of these peoples as the noble guardians of Edenic sanctuaries.

66. Ronald Inden, "Orientalist Constructions of India," *Modern Asian Studies* 20, no. 3 (July 1986): 401–46; Christopher Pinney, "Classification and Fantasy in the Photographic Construction of Caste and Tribe," *Visual Anthropology* 3 (1990): 259–88; Peter Bishop, *The Myth of Shangri-La: Tibet, Travel Writing and the Western Creation of Sacred Landscape* (Berkeley and Los Angeles, 1989).
67. Said, *Orientalism*, 49–73.

# 5 Home in the Hills

We practice a pretty high degree of retirement from the world, we
up here.

—Thomas Mann, *The Magic Mountain*

Simla is in a peculiar sense not merely the official residence of the
Viceroy during the hot weather, but his country home. For here he
divests himself if not of the cares of office—this is I fear never
possible in India—at least of some of the trappings of State; and
amid your beautiful mountains he may almost succeed in mistaking
himself for an Anglo-Indian Horace retiring from the noise and
smoke of Rome to the peace of the Tiburine hills.

—Lord Curzon, speech to the Simla Municipal Committee,
6 April 1899, Simla Municipal Proceedings, vol. 10, 1899, HPSA

The appeal of hill stations was rooted in their promise of escape from the
refractory world of colonial India. While British representations of the
climate, the landscape, and the inhabitants of these highland sites hinged
on this oppositional relationship to the plains, its lines of demarcation
were delineated in the very fabric of social life in the hill stations. The
sheer remoteness of the highlands guaranteed that the British in India
could construct there a community that resembled the one whence they
had come. In the hill stations they were not obliged to assume the official
guises or to follow the codes that regulated their behavior among a colonized population. Instead they could shed their imperial mien and stretch
their psychic limbs in the comforting familiarity of an environment that
replicated the social institutions and the cultural norms of their homeland.
The hill stations afforded a public site for the pursuit of private interests,
a site where the British could re-create some semblance of a bourgeois
civic life.

The creation of hill stations was therefore as much a matter of memories
and desires as of bricks and mortar. If these communities were made from
roads and railways, shops and markets, houses and hotels, they were also
born of words and patterns and intentions, of the names and designs that
gave meaning to the physical features of the built environment, of the
habits and customs that characterized the daily workings of the social

environment, of the manifold means by which the men and women who came together in them sought to infuse their habitat with significance.

———

Most firsthand accounts of visits to hill stations begin with the journey from the plains. This journey often had some of the emotional resonance of a religious pilgrimage, and, indeed, it was oddly analogous to Hindu pilgrimages to Hardwar and other holy sites in the Himalayas. The author of the first book to advertised the charms of Naini Tal as a hill sanitarium wrote under the telling pseudonym "Pilgrim." "As we ascend," wrote a missionary, "we seem to find the air purer and purer. . . . So, we thought, our souls may climb height after height."[1] Travelers detailed their elaborate logistical preparations, their various misadventures on the road, their nervous passages through the dense malarial forests that ran along the base of the hills, and their breathless ascents into the clouds, with every bend in the trail marked, or so it seemed, by changes of terrain, of flora, and of perspective: "Every step taken, every corner passed, every fresh altitude attained, unfolds to the astonished eye fresh beauties and marvels of nature."[2] Above all, the rise in elevation brought with it a fall in temperature. "I don't think there is anything in life," remarked one Englishman in India, "which is such a relief and such a physical delight as going from the heat of the plains in the hot weather up into the mountains, gradually feeling it getting cooler." Kipling captured the change with characteristic vividness. "[The journey] began in heat and discomfort, by rail and road. It ended in the cool evening, with a wood fire in one's bedroom."[3] The British signaled the shift from one realm to another by exchanging their light tropical attire for the warm woolens of their homeland.

The inaccessibility of most hill sites contributed to their allure as retreats from the trials of the colonial experience. Until the second half of the nineteenth century, hill stations could be reached only by a long, arduous journey accomplished entirely by means of human and animal labor. Invalids and other visitors had to travel hundreds of miles by horse, cart

1. "Pilgrim" [P. Barron], *Notes of Wanderings in the Himmala* (Agra, 1844); Margaret B. Denning, *Mosaics from India* (Chicago, 1902), 198.

2. F. Drew Gay, *The Prince of Wales; or, From Pall Mall to the Punjaub* (Detroit, 1878), 357, describing the journey to Simla.

3. Quoted in Charles Allen, *Plain Tales from the Raj* (London, 1976), 152; Rudyard Kipling, *Something of Myself and Other Autobiographical Writings*, ed. Thomas Pinney (Cambridge, 1990), 35.

(known as a tonga or gharry), or boat where possible, then wind their way up the mountain slopes on the backs of ponies or bearers (commonly referred to as coolies), who carried their charges in conveyances known as doolies (litters), jampans (sedan chairs), and palanquins (which Richard Burton aptly described as a kind of coffin suspended on poles). The mountain roads were often little more than bridle paths that washed out in the monsoon rains. It took one early visitor more than a month to get to Darjeeling from Benares, and many of his Indian bearers fled along the way. By the mid-1840s, however, it was possible to reach Darjeeling from Calcutta in five days of hard travel.[4] The Nilgiris were at least four days' journey from Madras in the same period—an improvement over the week it took Thomas Macaulay to make the same journey in 1834.[5] Mahabaleshwar, favored by Bombay residents for its accessibility, required a seventy-mile voyage down the coast, another thirty miles upriver, then thirty-five miles of slow slogging by land, or a shorter sea voyage followed by a seventy-six-mile land journey.[6] The most daunting journey of all, however, was the epic march by the governor-general and his staff from the government house in Calcutta to the summer residence at Simla, which covered over a thousand miles, took more than a month, and involved an army of Indian retainers.[7]

The hill stations became more accessible with the railway-construction boom that started in the 1850s. The opening of the rail line from Calcutta to Raniganj in 1855 reduced the laborious cart journey to Darjeeling by 120 miles, and the East Bengal State Railway pushed steadily northward in the following decades. Even so, an 1873 trip to Darjeeling was an eight-day ordeal for the artist Edward Lear, whose cart broke down and whose coolies fled.[8] By 1881, however, a narrow-gauge rail line had reached Darjeeling itself, making it the first hill station to become directly linked by rail to the plains. As a result, a Calcutta resident could arrive in Darjeeling in as little as twenty-one hours by the end of the century and in less than fourteen hours by the 1940s.

4. J. T. Pearson, "A Note on Darjeeling," 1839, reprinted in Fred Pinn, *The Road to Destiny: Darjeeling Letters 1839* (Calcutta: Oxford University Press, 1986), 1–4; *The Dorjeeling Guide* (Calcutta, 1845), 14.

5. W. Francis, *The Nilgiris* (Madras, 1908), 228–29; Thomas Babington Macaulay, *Letters*, ed. Thomas Pinney, vol. 3 (Cambridge, 1976), 44–45.

6. *Mahableshwur Guide* (Bombay, 1875), 11.

7. See the description of this journey by Emily Eden, *Up the Country: Letters from India* (1930; reprint, London, 1984).

8. Edward Lear, *Indian Journal*, ed. Ray Murphy (London, 1953), 56–62.

The railway shortened the journey to Simla and other western Himalayan stations as well. From 1869 travelers were able to take a train to Ambala junction, where they caught a coach for a thirty-eight-mile journey to Kalka, a dusty village at the foot of the hills, and then transferred to pony or jampan for the winding fifty-six-mile journey up to the station. The railroad reached Kalka in 1891, and after a decade-long endeavor that involved cutting over a hundred tunnels through the hills, it came to Simla in 1903. Elsewhere in the region, the completion of a branch line to Kathgodam in 1881 reduced to twenty-two miles the cart journey to Naini Tal, and the opening of the Hardwar-Dehra Dun Railway in 1900 made Mussoorie "perhaps the most accessible hill station in Northern India"—at least until the line to Simla was completed several years later.[9] Perhaps the least accessible station in the northwest was Dalhousie, which was located 117 miles from the nearest rail line.

In southern India, the railhead at Mettupalayam, at the foot of the Nilgiris, reduced travel from Madras to Ootacamund to little more than two days by the 1860s. The journey was shortened even further by the construction of a narrow-gauge line from Mettupalayam to Coonoor in 1899; it was extended to Ootacamund a few years later. In the Bombay region, the Great Indian Peninsular Railway came within seven miles of Matheran as early as 1854, and Sir Adamji Peerbhoy personally financed the construction of a light rail across the intervening distance in 1907. Mahabaleshwar remained a good deal more difficult to reach, but by the mid-1880s visitors could take the West Deccan Railway from Poona to Wather junction, which reduced to thirty-nine miles the trek by cart or horse.

Nearly every hill station in India was within fifty miles of a railway junction by the end of the century. These improvements in transportation inevitably brought an increase in visitors and residents. Hill stations consisted of relatively small, intimate communities through the first half of the nineteenth century. Even Simla, Mussoorie, and Ootacamund, the largest of the hill stations with the widest range of patrons, had little more than a hundred European dwellings each in the early 1840s, while Darjeeling had just thirty or so and Mahabaleshwar perhaps a dozen. The advent of the railway, as some contemporaries anticipated, emphatically quickened the pace of development.[10] In Darjeeling, the number of

9. Resolution, 28 December 1905, Municipal Department, Proceedings of the Government of the United Provinces, IOL.

10. See, for instance, Hyde Clarke, *Colonization, Defence and Railways in Our Indian Empire* (London, 1857), esp. ch. 1.

European houses more than doubled within three years of the opening of the Darjeeling-Himalayan Railway.[11] Simla's housing figures grew to 290 in 1866, 350 in 1870, and, with the completion of the Ambala-Kalka line, 550 in 1898. Ootacamund's numbers rose to 230 in 1868 and 328 in 1897; Mahabaleshwar's climbed from 48 in 1860 to 81 in 1875 to 98 in 1884; Mussoorie's leaped from 141 in 1862 to 354 in 1881.[12]

Before the railways were built, sojourns in hill stations were restricted almost entirely to residents of nearby districts or to those who were able to leave their permanent posts for six months or more for either official or medical reasons. The railway, by substantially reducing both the time and the cost of travel, opened the way to a significant increase in the number of people who spent three months or less in a hill station. One measure of this development was the growth in short-term accommodations: in Ootacamund, for instance, the number of hotels and boarding houses increased from two in 1857 to eleven in 1886.[13]

Statistical data about summer visitors are limited since the imperial census was conducted in February, when hill-station populations were at their lowest. Simla, however, conducted its own summer census at irregular intervals, and the juxtaposition to winter-census figures is illuminating. The imperial census of 1881 gave the total population of Simla as 13,258, a 53 percent increase over the 8,672 counted in an 1875 census. A summer census for 1878, however, found 17,440 inhabitants, 32 percent higher than the winter count of 1881. The winter population actually declined in 1891 and did not grow again until after the turn of the century: the figures were 13,034 for 1891, 13,960 for 1901, 18,934 for 1911, and 26,149 for 1921. The summer population, however, grew steadily from 24,179 in 1889 to 33,174 in 1898, 36,002 in 1911, and 45,510 in 1921. These figures ranged from 74

11. R. D. O'Brien, *Darjeeling, the Sanitarium of Bengal; and Its Surroundings* (Calcutta, 1883), 25.

12. The figures for Simla come from Punjab Government, *Gazetteer of the Simla District, 1888–89* (Calcutta, n.d.), 108; W. H. Carey, *A Guide to Simla with a Descriptive Account of the Neighbouring Sanitaria* (Calcutta, 1870), 34–41; and *Report of the Simla Extension Committee, 1898* (Simla, 1898), list of houses accompanying Map 3. For Ootacamund, see Sir Frederick Price, *Ootacamund: A History* (Madras, 1908), app. C; Capt. J. Ouchterlony, *Geographical and Statistical Memoir of a Survey of the Neilgherry Mountains* (Madras, 1868), 51; and *The Visitors' Handbook of the Nilgiris* (Madras, 1897), 74–78. For Mussoorie, Edwin T. Atkinson, *The Himalayan Gazetteer* (1882; reprint, Delhi, 1973), 598. For Mahabaleshwar, *Gazetteer of the Bombay Presidency*, vol. 19: *Satara* (Bombay, 1885), 502; and *Mahableshwur Guide*, 12.

13. Robert Baikie, *The Neilgherries*, 2d ed. (Calcutta, 1857), 29; *A Guide to the Neilgherries* (Madras, 1886), 80–81.

percent to 137 percent higher than equivalent winter figures. The overwhelming majority of these people were, of course, Indians. An analysis
limited to the European population is complicated by the fact that the
imperial census, unlike the summer census, counted Christians, a somewhat larger figure than the number of Europeans. Even so, the disparity
was striking. The summer census of 1889 counted 3,400 Europeans, compared with 1,484 Christians in the 1891 imperial census. Simla had 4,126
Europeans in the summer of 1898 versus 1,471 Christians in the winter of
1901, 4,153 versus 2,415 in 1911, and 5,126 versus 3,181 in 1921.[14] No
other hill station has such an extensive run of census information, but those
pockets of data available elsewhere suggest that the disparity between
summer and winter figures for other stations was even greater than it was
for Simla, which enjoyed a substantial year-round bureaucratic presence.[15]

Proximity to a railroad, however, was not sufficient in and of itself to
account for the growth of a hill station. Panchgani was eleven miles closer
to the West Deccan Railway than Mahabaleshwar, and it had better
weather, yet it remained a satellite station with far fewer inhabitants than
its neighbor. In fact, virtually every hill station in the Bombay presidency
had better access to rail transportation than Mahabaleshwar, but only
Matheran approached it in size and popularity. Similar incongruities can
be found elsewhere. Yercaud, for instance, remained a small and sleepy
hamlet in the Shevaroy Hills even after the railway came within fourteen
miles of it. The point, then, is that even though a railway provided the
means for a hill station to increase substantially in size, other factors
mediated this effect.

Some hill stations benefited from the development of a European-
managed agricultural sector in their vicinity. For Darjeeling, the introduction of tea in the 1850s provided an enormous boost to development.
By 1895, 186 tea estates covered 48,692 acres across the district, injecting
large amounts of capital into Darjeeling as well as into its neighbors
Kurseong and Kalimpong. Planters became important parts of the European

14. These statistics are drawn from Punjab Government, *Gazetteer of the Simla
District, 1888–89*, 108; *Punjab District Gazetteers, Simla District Statistical Tables,
1936*, vol. 6B (Lahore, 1936), Table 7; Annual Reports of the Simla Municipality,
1889–90 and 1911–12, and Simla Municipal Corporation Records, 179/1933/123/
1921/II, HPSA.

15. For example, a summer census conducted in Dalhousie and Murree in 1911
showed that the summer population of Dalhousie was five times as large as its
winter population, while the population of Murree was ten times as large! See
*Report on the Summer Census of Dalhousie, 1911* (Lahore, 1912); and *Report on
the Summer Census of Murree, 1911* (Lahore, 1912).

communities in each of these hill stations.[16] A further economic stimulus for the region came with the introduction of cinchona, the South American tree or shrub from whose bark the antimalarial drug quinine was extracted. The colonial state established the first cinchona plantation in the early 1860s, and its success prompted a rapid expansion in production in subsequent decades.

Coffee and cinchona estates, followed by tea toward the end of the century, played a similar role in Ootacamund and its satellites in the Nilgiris. The first coffee plantation was established at Coonoor in 1838, and the industry reached its peak in 1879 with twenty-five thousand acres in production. As disease and international competition undermined the coffee market toward the end of the nineteenth century, many planters turned to tea, which increased from about three or four thousand acres in 1897 to twenty-two thousand acres by 1940. The government was again responsible for getting the cinchona industry started; by 1891 it had planted 1,800,000 cinchona trees. But a significant number of private planters also took up the crop. An 1886 directory listed well over three hundred estates in the Nilgiris engaged in the production of coffee, tea, cinchona, and other products.[17] Further south, Kodaikanal became an entrepot for coffee and plantain growers, and the tea gardens of Assam provided an important boost to the economy of Shillong. Some of the smaller hill stations, notably Munnar, Ponmudi, and Yercaud, owed virtually their entire existence to the presence of planters.

Other hill stations, however, had little or no agricultural industry to sustain them, particularly those resorts located in the western Himalayas and the Bombay presidency. Efforts were made to introduce tea and sericulture to the areas around Mussoorie, Almora, Naini Tal, and Dharamsala, but most of these ventures did not flourish. Sal and other trees located in the foothills of the Himalayas became targets for commercial exploitation, especially to supply railway sleeper ties and charcoal, but the ruthless clear-cutting of these nonrenewable resources provided little in the way of economic gain to the stations of the western Himalayas. What would later

16. Arthur Jules Dash, *Bengal District Gazetteers: Darjeeling* (Alipore, 1947), 114.

17. *A Guide to the Neilgherries*, 36–53. Concerning plantation agriculture in the Nilgiris, see Francis, *The Nilgiris*, ch. 4; Kaku J. Tanna, *Plantations in the Nilgiris: A Synoptic History* (n.p., c. 1969), passim; and Lucile H. Brockway, *Science and Colonial Expansion: The Role of the British Royal Botanic Gardens* (New York, 1979), 114–21.

become a successful fruit industry in the region was still in its infancy in the nineteenth century. The hill stations around Bombay and through most of central India also lacked natural conditions suited to commercial agriculture. Government efforts to establish cinchona plantations in the vicinities of Mahabaleshwar and Pachmarhi failed miserably, and scarcely any private planters were to be found in these areas. Hill stations could sometimes count on local peasant production. Most highland peasants, however, were engaged in little more than subsistence farming when the British arrived, and even though they often responded to the demands of the European enclaves in their midst, the scale of their enterprise prohibited it from being a significant impetus to the growth of these enclaves. And, apart from agriculture, the only productive enterprise that arose in association with the hill stations was brewing. The cool temperatures, clean water, and captive market provided by British troops in hill cantonments prompted the establishment of fifteen or more breweries in highland locations across India. Yet only the smallest hill stations gained any measurable boost from these enterprises.

Most hill stations were economically parasitic.[18] They drew upon two main sources of subsistence: state support and private investment. Without the willingness of the British raj to grant annual subsidies to the hill stations and to transfer much of the machinery of government to their precincts, many of them could never have grown as they did. The leading example is Simla, which depended profoundly on its role as the summer capital of India, as Pamela Kanwar has amply demonstrated.[19] Apart from its attractions to those with the freedom to escape the summer heat of the plains, who came as often for its heady social and political climate as for its natural one, Simla had no raison d'être. The same was true of Mahabaleshwar, Mount Abu, Naini Tal, and several other summer headquarters for officialdom. In fact, the essential impetus to the development even of those hill stations that operated as important entrepots of agricultural production, such as Darjeeling, Ootacamund, and Shillong, was their political standing. The hill stations whose survival was most fully dependent on the state, however, were those that served primarily as cantonments for British troops: without the military presence, most of them might never have come into being at all.

18. This point has been made by S. Robert Aiken, "Early Penang Hill Station," *Geographical Review* 77, no. 4 (Oct. 1987), 434; and Anthony D. King, *Colonial Urban Development: Culture, Social Power and Environment* (London, 1976), 158.
19. Pamela Kanwar, *Imperial Simla* (Delhi, 1990).

Even those hill stations that had no official purpose usually received financial subsidies from the colonial state. In 1861, for example, the government of India approved annual grants both for Bombay's summer headquarters, Mahabaleshwar, and for the entirely unofficial Matheran.[20] While the size of these subsidies varied over time and from place to place, nearly all hill stations received some form of state assistance for municipal improvements and other needs.

For most hill stations, however, and particularly for the unofficial ones like Mussoorie, Matheran, and Kodaikanal, the most important source of revenue was the residents themselves. Once hill stations became legally recognized municipalities, which Mussoorie did in 1842, followed by Darjeeling in 1850, Simla in 1852, Mahabaleshwar in 1865, and Ootacamund in 1866, they could levy fees and taxes, which they did with alacrity. They instituted taxes on houses and other buildings, taxes on land, taxes on market stalls, taxes on servants, taxes on rickshaws, carts, and other vehicles, taxes on horses, mules, cows, and dogs, taxes on slaughtered animals, conservancy taxes, fees for gathering firewood and grasses in municipal forests, fines for breaking municipal ordinances, and levies (known as octroi) on goods entering municipal boundaries. Simla and the other large hill stations were among the most heavily taxed municipalities in India.[21] The revenues collected were used to maintain water supplies, roads, and other public services, to inspect and regulate housing and sanitary conditions in the overcrowded bazaars, to construct town halls and other public facilities, and in general to provide the civic amenities that made the hill stations so attractive.

The visitors drawn by those amenities accounted for much of the prosperity of the hill stations. They injected an incalculable supply of capital into the local economies. Their investments in land and houses accelerated the pace of private construction. Their expenditures on provisions and accommodations supported a vast entourage of shopkeepers, servants, and others. The seasonal influx of these visitors supplied the economic life blood of the hill stations.

From the start, station property was recognized as an attractive investment. Authorities were frequently unprepared to control the initial scramble for land, leaving the indigenous inhabitants easy marks for theft and extortion. Some of the first Englishmen to occupy Mussoorie used their

20. Mahabaleshwar received Rs. 10,000 per annum and Matheran Rs. 5,000. *Times of India*, 10 October 1861, p. 3.
21. Kanwar, *Imperial Simla*, 125.

servants as intermediaries to coerce villagers into alienating their land. An early promoter of Naini Tal tempted a local headman onto his boat, took him to the middle of the lake, and threatened to throw him overboard unless he signed a deed handing over rights to the land.[22] The government of Madras received numerous reports in the 1820s and 1830s of Europeans grabbing land in the Nilgiris without compensating indigenous inhabitants. While John Sullivan, the collector for Coimbatore, took up the cause of the Todas, whose property rights he held to be primordial, he also managed by 1829 to accumulate five times as much land around Ootacamund as all other European proprietors put together.[23]

Sooner or later, authorities intervened in this free-for-all, although the local peasantry seldom benefited. Tentatively, and with a good many detours along the way, the colonial state established policies to supervise land alienation, regularize the size of building plots, and impose annual quit rents.[24] This codification of the property market did nothing to depress it. As the demand for accommodations increased, individuals with the capital to build or buy houses for the rental market often made handsome profits. What one contemporary observed in Mussoorie was true elsewhere: "nearly all the houses belong[ed] to officers in the civil and military service" who acted as absentee landlords, relying on local estate agents to lease and manage their properties.[25] A report on the Nilgiris complained that "the only permanent Europeans who could conveniently have rendered any service to the public by encouraging agriculture . . . have found it so much more profitable to build houses to let to Invalids."[26] Particularly

22. F. J. Shore, assistant commissioner, Dehra Dun, to Adjutant General of Army, 4 August 1828, Municipal Department, Jan. 1905-A, Proceedings of the Government of the United Provinces, IOL; "Pilgrim," *Notes of Wanderings,* quoted in Gillian Wright, *The Hill Stations of India* (Lincolnwood, Ill., 1991), 131–32.

23. Price, *Ootacamund,* 23. A summary of the correspondence on the alienation of Nilgiri land to Europeans can be found in *Guide to the Records of the Nilgiris District from 1827 to 1835* (Madras, 1934), vol. 4183.

24. In both Darjeeling and Ootacamund, however, efforts to restrict the size of building plots—to one hundred square yards in Darjeeling and two square acres in Ootacamund—succumbed to pressures from local speculators. See E/4/773, 1 March 1843, India and Bengal Dispatches, IOL; and Judith Theresa Kenny, "Constructing an Imperial Hill Station: The Representation of British Authority in Ootacamund" (Ph.D. diss., Syracuse University, 1990), 128. The vagaries of land-tenure policies in the Nilgiris are detailed by H. B. Grigg, *A Manual of the Nilagiri District* (Madras, 1880), 344–60.

25. "Mountaineer," *A Summer Ramble in the Himalayas* (London, 1860), 14–15.

26. E/4/939, 10 November 1830, Madras Dispatches, IOL.

in the early years, some investors acquired extensive holdings in hill stations. An 1829 map of Ootacamund showed that two army captains owned a third of the station properties. In Darjeeling, a single individual had acquired thirty-two of the eighty-one building plots sold by 1848. At about this time, a Major S. B. Goad owned thirty-three houses in Simla, and two other officers owned at least fifteen each. An 1883 guide to Murree, a station founded at midcentury, showed that 42 of its 164 houses were in the hands of a single person.[27] Like any form of speculation, these investments were subject to risk. In the early years of Yercaud, "land was greedily bought up for building sites, the then would-be residents making pretty sure that there were grand days of development in store for Yercaud; but alas! through the cart road being doomed, the brilliant prospects of this charming place were blighted."[28] Despite such setbacks, the market in highland properties was usually bullish. The steady growth in the number of visitors to hill stations meant that the demand for accommodations was more often than not greater than the supply, which pushed rents and prices to ever higher levels and pumped capital through the local economy at ever accelerating rates.

To generalize about the economic growth of the hill stations is a risky business given the wide variations from place to place. Some stations had easy railway connections to the plains, while others remained hard to reach. Some became successful entrepots for plantation agriculture, while others had little commercial connection with the area around them. Some relied heavily on the subsidies that came from their positions as official head-quarters, while others existed entirely independently of the state. For all of them, however, the principal impetus for development came not from the resources of their immediate surroundings but from the resources introduced from the plains through the patronage of the British, in both their public and their private capacities. Thus, these highland havens arose for reasons that were intimately connected with the rest of India. They were bound up with the responsibilities and the risks that the British shouldered as members of an elite ruling over an alien land. To use the terminology of immigration historians, the "push" of the plains was more important than the "pull" of the hills in accounting for the rise of the hill stations.

27. Price, *Ootacamund,* map between 222 and 223; Clarke, *Colonization,* 40–42; Carey, *A Guide to Simla;* E. B. Peacock, *A Guide to Murree and Its Neighbourhood* (Lahore, 1883).

28. Francesca H. Wilson, *The Shevaroys* (Madras, 1888), 29.

This impetus had a strikingly antipodal influence on the physical and social forms that would come to distinguish these highland resorts.

———————

An American visitor to Ootacamund in the late nineteenth century found it to be "the least like a town of any I ever saw or heard of, for it is so effectually scattered, over so many hills, that as a town it has no individuality whatever."[29] Like the other hill stations of British India, Ootacamund grew in a highly irregular way, with its houses and shops springing up in seemingly random fashion along a maze of lanes. This pattern contrasts with the carefully planned and tightly regulated spatial environment that Anthony King identifies as the distinguishing feature of colonial urbanism.[30] The typical European sector of a colonial city, according to King, was composed of a geometric network of large, closed compounds; this arrangement created an enclave that discouraged penetration by and interaction with the indigenous inhabitants of the city. These purposes were not germane to the hill stations in their early years. For this reason, as much as because of the irregularity of the terrain and because of the many private interests engaged in the construction of houses, they did not follow the normal pattern of colonial urbanism in India. Some measure of planning can be discerned in the separation of European and Indian residential areas (evident in the terminological distinction between "wards" and "bazaars"), but until the late nineteenth century this separation often had less to do with official edicts than with economic forces and ethnic instincts, and it was in any case widely contravened by the persistence of Indian bazaars at the geographical heart of many hill stations. Because the hill stations seemed so far removed from the colonial experience, the British simply felt less need to impose the rigid spatial order that distinguished urbanism on the plains.

This lack of order should not be taken to mean, however, that hill stations lacked civic coherence. From their improvised origins a subtle pattern of development emerged, and its model was the English village. The sinuous lines and simple organization of the home country's rustic villages, venerated as cradles of the nation's virtues, were replicated in the hill stations. At the symbolic center of nearly every English village stood the

29. William T. Hornaday, *Two Years in the Jungle: The Experience of a Hunter and Naturalist in India, Ceylon, the Malay Peninsula and Borneo* (New York, 1908), 96.
30. King, *Colonial Urban Development*.

Figure 6.   St. Stephen's Church, Ootacamund. From Sir Frederick Price, *Oota-camund: A History* (Madras, 1908).

Anglican church, and so it did in nearly every Indian hill station. The Victorian Gothic solidity of these sanctified structures, situated on prominent sites in each station, bespoke the shared values that bound European residents and visitors together. "A beautiful Gothic church is one of the first picturesque objects that greets the eye of the traveller who visits the Neilgherries," declared an early publicist for Ootacamund, where St. Stephen's Church was constructed in 1831 (Figure 6). "The church at Simla is the central point at which all diverging lines seem to meet," wrote the novelist Constance Cumming, who added a telling detail: "here for once mosques and temples have retired into the background."[31] Simla's Anglican house of worship was Christ Church (founded 1844–52), a name that also graced its counterparts in Mussoorie (1836) and Mahabaleshwar (1842). In Darjeeling, the Anglican church was known as St. Andrew's

31. Major William Murray, *An Account of the Neilgherries, or, Blue Mountains of Coimbatore, in Southern India* (London, 1834), 10; Constance F. Gordon Cumming, *From the Hebrides to the Himalayas*, vol. 2 (London, 1876), 121.

(1843, rebuilt 1882); in Naini Tal and Dharamsala, St. John-in-the-Wilderness (1846 and 1852, respectively); in Coonoor and Shillong, All Saints (1851 and date unknown). In Matheran, it was christened St. Paul's (1858–60), and like many of its sister institutions, its site was "one of the highest and most central on the hill."[32] There were exceptions: Kodai-kanal was founded by American missionaries, and the Anglican church arose belatedly and therefore at a rather peripheral location. In most hill stations, however, the Anglican church was the first and foremost civic structure to appear, and it served as the moral and morphological hub of the community.

The hill station's central avenue invariably emanated from the Anglican church. Government buildings such as the postal and telegraph office, the collector's office, and the civil court tended to be located along this thoroughfare, as were banks and other prominent businesses. Particularly in the Himalayan hill stations, where the terrain restrained vehicular traffic, this main street was known as the "Mall," a distinctive term that both suggested its pedestrian nature and evoked associations with elegant precincts at home (Figure 7). Intersecting the Mall at various points were a bewildering array of other lanes that snaked their way across the undulating topography of the station. Rarely were these lanes identified by name since inhabitants were presumed to possess the same cozy familiarity with their surroundings that the village folk at home did. This practice frequently created problems for newcomers to the larger hill stations. Ootacamund's municipal council felt obliged in 1894 to put up street signs on major intersections to orient visitors. In Simla, however, a tourist guide published in 1925 complained that "one of the chief shortcomings in the administration of the town . . . [is] the almost entire absence of street and road names."[33] Other than the Mall or its equivalent, the only route familiar to everyone was the Cart Road, a utilitarian name for a utilitarian road that served as the main artery for people and goods going to and from the station. The Cart Road usually was located at the lower reaches of the hill station, where its constant din would not disturb the serenity of British householders.

32. A. F. Bellasis, *An Account of the Hill Station of Matheran, near Bombay* (Bombay, 1869), 13.

33. Ootacamund Municipal Report for 1893–94, 11, Municipal G.O. #1244, TNSA; F. Beresford Harrop, *Thacker's New Guide to Simla* (Simla, 1925), 57. Also see Pamela Kanwar, "The Changing Image of Simla," Urban History Association Occasional Papers Series 10, 1989, 4.

Figure 7.   The Mall at Simla, with the General Post Office in the background. Courtesy of the British Library, Oriental and India Office Collections.

The same motive that caused most of the stations' lanes to go unnamed led to a profusion of typically English names for the dwellings to which they gave access. William Howard Russell, the *Times* war correspondent, noticed the "English bungalows, with names painted on the gateways, 'Laburnum Lodge,' 'Prospect,' 'The Elms,' and such like home reminiscences" as he passed through the satellite station of Kasauli on his way to Simla, where he again noted the phenomenon. Far to the south, a Madras staff corp officer observed that the houses in Coonoor and Ootacamund had "villa names, such as 'Sunnyside,' 'Rosebank,' 'Fairlawns,' etc."[34] In every hill station, residents posted signboards to identify and personalize their houses, half-hidden behind the transplanted foliage. To christen dwellings invested them "with social and cultural meaning," King observes.[35] The sorts of names

34. William Howard Russell, *My Diary in India*, vol. 2 (London, 1860), 88, 92; E. F. Burton, *An Indian Olio* (London, 1888), 129.

35. Anthony D. King, "Culture, Social Power and Environment: The Hill Station in Colonial Urban Development," *Social Action* 26, no. 3 (July-Sept. 1976): 208–9.

applied to hill-station residences evoked images of the quiet comfort of English country life, with its distinctive vegetation (Apple Lodge, Fernwood, Myrtle Cottage), familiar landmarks (Blackheath, Hampton Villa, Glenrock), and time-worn institutions (the Manor, the Priory, Kenilworth Hall). Equally revealing was the widespread practice of referring to these places in general terms as "cottages" rather than "bungalows." Whereas *bungalow*, a hybrid term of Bengali origin, was the standard word for European houses virtually everywhere else in India, *cottage* was the preferred term in hill stations precisely because it had no colonial associations and suggested instead the quaint abodes of rural England.[36]

The hill-station cottage differed from the plains bungalow not just in name but in form. Although the simple rectangular bungalow with its single story and verandah skirt was transposed to the hills in the early years, it soon lost favor. The rugged terrain of the highlands inhibited the lavish use of level space, and the cool climate negated its environmental appeal. Richard Burton, who visited Ootacamund in 1847, regarded the bungalow, "surrounded by a long low verandah, perfectly useless in such a climate, and only calculated to render the interior of the domiciles as dim and gloomy as can be conceived." Where the bungalow continued to exist, as it did in Mussoorie, it was a frequent object of scorn. "Most houses [in Mussoorie] are planned on the type of the plains bungalow which is for the hills a most unsuitable type," admonished the district gazetteer. It was not, however, simply aesthetic or climatic considerations that made bungalows unsuitable for the hills: their spatial structure was designed to segregate residents from the surrounding environment, with the ubiquitous verandah serving as the boundary between the interior world of the European and the exterior world of India. The bungalow, in effect, was an expression of the colonial condition, and most observers did not consider it appropriate for the different social environment the British sought to create in the hill stations.[37]

36. For the importance of the cottage to Victorian aesthetics, see George H. Ford, "Felicitous Space: The Cottage Controversy," in *Nature and the Victorian Imagination*, ed. U. C. Knoepflmacher and G. B. Tennyson (Berkeley, 1977), 29–48. The bungalow's Indian origin is examined in Anthony D. King, *The Bungalow: The Production of a Global Culture* (London, 1984), ch. 1.

37. Richard F. Burton, *Goa, and the Blue Mountains* (1851; reprint, Berkeley, 1991), 288; H. G. Walton, *Dehra Dun: A Gazetteer, District Gazetteers of the United Provinces of Agra and Oudh*, vol. 1 (Allahabad, 1911), 245. My analysis of the bungalow is drawn from King, *The Bungalow*, ch. 1; and King, *Colonial Urban Development*, 132–48. The absence of verandahs in Simla is noted by Dennis Kincaid, *British Social Life in India 1608–1937* (London, 1938), 232.

The cottage was considered appropriate for the hill station because it replicated the general features of the English country home. Those features were easily recognized by visitors to the hills. "With their small windows, sloping roofs, and many chimneys," applauded one writer, "[hill-station houses] put one in mind of English cottages." Another sketched the scene at Yercaud: "On the summits, . . . amid pretty clumps of trees which the woodman's axe has spared, are scattered cottages very English in appearance, with tile or zinc-covered roofs, and walls overgrown with beautiful many-coloured creepers and blushing fuchsias." On a grander level, the Simla residence of Lord Auckland, the governor-general, was described by his sister, Emily Eden, as "a cheerful middle-size English country-house."[38] The emotional impact of these evocative highland dwellings is apparent in Lady Wilson's remarks about her arrival at the small hill station of Sakesar in Sind:

> Blessings on the man who dreamt of Sakesar and made it an English home. . . . You can't imagine the kind of material pleasure one has in material things that simply look English. The roof of this house enchants me, merely because it slants instead of being flat: the ceilings, because they are much lower than those at Shahpur and are plastered. . . . The woodwork is actually varnished: the bow windows are really windows, not doors: the fireplaces are all in the right place; . . . we are as cosy as cosy could be.[39]

"It was in the hill-stations," Jan Morris believes, "that the British in India achieved the most distinctive of their vernacular styles."[40] With private rather that public initiative driving the construction of houses in the hills, the architectural designs of these dwellings reflected the personal fancies of their builders. And what fancies they were! "Himalayan Swiss-Gothic" is Morris's term for the style that came to predominate in the Himalayan stations by the mid-nineteenth century. It was distinguished by multistoried structures with chimneys thrusting up from steep roof lines, numerous gables and terraces cutting against the vertical grain, and ornately carved fretwork framing the eaves, windows, and doors; the result

38. Edmund C. P. Hull, *The European in India; or, Anglo-Indian's Vade-Mecum* (London, 1872), 58; Burton, *An Indian Olio*, 118; Eden, *Up the Country*, 128.

39. Lady Wilson, *Letters from India* (1911; reprint, London, 1984), 46.

40. Jan Morris with Simon Winchester, *Stones of Empire: The Buildings of the Raj* (Oxford, 1983), 52. Hill-station architecture is also discussed by Philip Davies, *Splendours of the Raj: British Architecture in India 1660–1947* (Harmondsworth, 1987), ch. 5; and Mark Bence-Jones, *Palaces of the Raj* (London, 1973), chs. 8, 11.

looked like a cross between a Victorian garden villa and a Swiss chalet. Joseph Hooker's disparagement of a rest house near Darjeeling for its "miserable attempt to unite the Swiss cottage with the suburban gothic" was exceptional. Most visitors admired the style. The *Calcutta Review* praised the "Swiss-cottage-like houses . . . with their well-trimmed gardens" gracing the ridges of Darjeeling. Cumming was charmed by Simla residences, which "are a good deal like Swiss *chalets*, having verandahs upstairs and down. Moreover, they are generally two storeys high; a style of building which, as we had hardly seen a staircase since leaving Calcutta, astonished the servants considerably." The chalet style also spread to the hill stations of central and southern India. It "pervades much of the architecture of Ootacamund," an architectural historian has noted, and a missionary visitor described Coonoor as "crowned with the prettiest Swiss-looking houses."[41] The hill stations in the south, however, remained wedded to the single-storied structure to a far greater extent than their Himalayan counterparts—perhaps because the terrain tended to be less precipitous—and the pediments and columns of classicism played a larger role. A prominent example is the long, low house with its classical facade that Sir William Rumbold built in 1830 and that the Ootacamund Club later occupied, expanded, and remodeled. Other European influences infiltrated hill stations as well, notably the somber Scottish baronial, best exemplified by the Viceregal Lodge in Simla, and the half-timbered Tudor style, which became especially popular in Shillong after the devastating earthquake of 1897 demonstrated the dangers of masonry structures. Still, Swiss Gothic remained the dominant motif for hill-station architecture.

What was the significance of this architectural eclecticism? A distinguishing feature of Victorian architecture in Britain was its taste for the Gothic, Tudor, Scottish baronial, and other historically resonant styles, and it is not surprising that the same taste constituted part of the cultural baggage the British brought with them to the hill stations, where they added the similarly transplanted Swiss chalet style to their repertoire. But the contrast with architectural practices elsewhere in British India suggests that this importation of European designs was not entirely instinctive and indiscriminate. As we have seen, the Bengali bungalow was widely adopted and modified by the British for their residential use on the Indian plains.

41. Joseph Dalton Hooker, *Himalayan Journals*, vol. 1 (London, 1854), 11; *Darjeeling,* pamphlet reprinted from *Calcutta Review,* no. 55 (1857): 5; Cumming, *From the Hebrides,* vol. 1, 114; Davies, *Splendours of the Raj,* 130; Mrs. Murray Mitchell, *In Southern India* (London, 1885), 347.

Moreover, even though the public buildings of the raj emulated the architecture in the metropole through the mid-nineteenth century, this practice began to change with the spread of the hybrid Indo-Saracenic style, which incorporated Islamic influences into a distinctively imperial architecture.[42] In the hill stations, however, this traffic with exotic traditions was intentionally shunned. The British turned exclusively to European models when they erected and embellished their highland cottages, and they did so not only to re-create something of the physical appearance of their homeland but to recover elements of its moral meaning as well. What is sometimes seen as the aesthetic failure of Victorian architecture—its melange of Gothic and other revivalist styles—had a deliberate, didactic intent: it sought to improve the character and conduct of society by creating structures that communicated through their lineage and design certain ethical and social messages.[43] The same purpose informed the architectural choices made in the hill stations. The Swiss Gothic, in particular, combined a Christian sense of virtue and steadfastness with alpine allusions to aloofness and the sublime. Furthermore, the architectural eclecticism of highland cottages helped to restore to seasonal residents a sense of their individual identities, which the colonial pressures for solidarity tended to submerge elsewhere in India. Edward J. Buck and Sir Frederick Price, the colonial historians of Simla and of Ootacamund, devoted large parts of their works to the histories of particular houses—their origins, their owners, their designs, their renovations—in effect, everything that set them apart and made them unique. Embedded in the contrast between the highly individuated cottages that lay scattered along the ridges of the hill stations and the uniform Public Works Department bungalows that sat in their serried rows on the plains was a world of social meaning.

––––––––

Many of the leading hill stations and some of the lesser ones claimed a founding father, a prominent individual whose foresight and initiative were credited with setting the community on a stable footing. John Sullivan was recognized as the central figure in the establishment of Ootacamund; Captain Charles Kennedy and Dr. Arthur Campbell acquired similar reputations in Simla and Darjeeling. Others included Dr. James Murray of

42. The role of Indo-Saracenic architecture is examined by Thomas R. Metcalf, *An Imperial Vision: Indian Architecture and Britain's Raj* (Berkeley, 1989).

43. See James A. Schmiechen, "The Victorians, the Historians, and the Idea of Modernism," *American Historical Review* 93, no. 2 (April 1988): 287–316.

Mahabaleshwar, Hugh Malet of Matheran, John Chesson of Panchgani, and Vere Leving of Kodaikanal. Each was a functionary of the colonial state, but their role in the hill stations seemed rather more like that of the amiable country squire. Their doors were always open to guests, and they formed a proprietary interest in the land, its people, its wildlife, and its potential for agricultural development. Captain Kennedy was celebrated for his bounteous table. The French traveler Victor Jacquemont described huge dinners accompanied by hock, claret, champagne, port, sherry, and madeira: "I do not recollect having tasted water for the last seven days," he purred.[44] Kennedy also exhibited a paternalistic interest in the Paharis who cultivated the land around Simla, introducing to them potatoes and other unfamiliar crops. An equally imposing presence was Ootacamund's Sullivan, who sought to protect the land rights of the Toda peoples and foster the agricultural prospects of the Nilgiris. He owned a two hundred–acre experimental farm, where he is said to have introduced oats, wheat, barley, beets, turnips, radishes, cabbages, potatoes, strawberries, peaches, apples, roses, violets, and other plants to the region.[45] Similarly, Dr. Campbell was an active horticulturist who made the Lloyd Botanical Garden an important institution and who is credited with establishing the tea industry in Darjeeling. He also published the first ethnographic report on the native Lepchas. A contemporary's assessment of his contribution to the creation of Darjeeling conveys something of the reputation that each of these founding fathers achieved: "Whatever has been done here has been done by Dr. Campbell alone. He found Darjeeling an inaccessible tract of forest, with a very scanty population; by his exertions an excellent sanitarium has been established."[46] This imperialist panegyric, while it ignores the many other figures and forces that played roles in the rise of particular hill stations, does point to the fact that the enlightened paternalism of men like Kennedy and Sullivan and Campbell provided their fledgling communities with the social gravity that attracted people and stimulated production.

Even after these providential patriarchs had died or departed, their hill stations retained some of the quiet country flavor they had created. The

44. Victor Jacquemont, *Letters from India*, vol. 1 (London, 1834), 228.

45. Paul Hockings, "John Sullivan of Ootacamund," *Journal of Indian History Golden Jubilee Volume*, ed. T. K. Ravindran (Trivandrum, 1973), 867. Also see Paul Hockings, "British Society in the Company, Crown and Congress Eras," in *Blue Mountains: The Ethnography and Biogeography of a South Indian Region*, ed. Paul Hockings (Delhi, 1989), 338.

46. *Selections from the Records of the Bengal Government*, no. 17: *Report on Darjeeling*, by W. B. Jackson (Calcutta, 1854), 7–8.

most popular pastimes during the early years were horticulture and hunt-ing, and those visitors who cared for neither activity often found the days exceedingly long. "I was never so dull in my life," groaned Macaulay as he entered the fourth month of his stay in Ootacamund in 1834. His sentiments were echoed thirteen years later by the splenetic Burton, who came to Ootacamund to recuperate from an apparent bout with cholera: "You dress like an Englishman, and lead a quiet gentlemanly life—doing nothing."[47] For others, however, the simple, rustic, tranquil atmosphere was irresistible.

As hill stations attracted larger, more restless populations in the wake of the railway, they developed more lively and labyrinthine social traits. Visitors in the late nineteenth century were often struck by the highly ritualized character of social life in the hill stations. An elaborate code of etiquette governed everything from forms of introduction to rules of seating at dinner parties. Only in the great port cities of Calcutta, Madras, and Bombay and a few of the larger civil stations in the interior did social conventions ever approach this level of punctiliousness: for residents of civil stations and cantonments elsewhere in India the rules of deportment was far less mannered. One feature of hill-station life that was frequently mentioned by visitors was the custom of calling. Within a few days of their arrival, newcomers to the community were expected to place their cards in the "not-at-home" boxes posted at the front of houses; but they were not to call on the residents themselves, who thereby retained the freedom to invite those callers they wished to meet.[48] The model for this practice could be found in Victorian high society; Leonore Davidoff has shown that its primary purpose in Britain was to provide a mechanism for facilitating introductions and regulating interactions among an increasingly large and mobile urban elite.[49] Although the social circumstances in colonial India were certainly different, the objectives underlying the etiquette of calling were much the same. The custom lubricated the process by which a highly transitory population was transformed into a cohesive yet hierarchically

47. Macaulay, *Letters*, 76; Burton, *Goa*, 289. Burton went on to complain about the absence of a hunt, a race course, a theater, a concert room, a tennis court, or a decent library. Nearly all these deficiencies would be rectified in later years.

48. See the descriptions by Kate Platt, *The Home and Health in India and the Tropical Colonies* (London, 1923), 52; Hull, *The European in India*, 174; Russell, *My Diary in India*, vol. 2, 128; and Wilson, *Letters from India*, 80.

49. Leonore Davidoff, *The Best Circles: Women and Society in Victorian England* (Totowa, N.J., 1973), ch. 3. The transfer of calling and other social rituals to the colonial sphere is briefly but perceptively considered by Margaret Strobel, *European Women and the Second British Empire* (Bloomington, 1991), 9–15.

differentiated community. In short, calling was a remarkably functional means for residents of hill stations to welcome new arrivals and steer them into the social circles regarded as appropriate to their background and status.

Almost as soon as they arrived, newcomers were drawn into a network of organizations that enlarged their circle of acquaintances and deepened their sense of civic identity. Religious institutions provided one element of this identity; and it was observed that the churches in hill stations were better attended than those elsewhere in the subcontinent.[50] In addition to the Church of England, Catholic and nonconformist denominations provided their laity with places to worship. Religion, however, was a less pivotal preoccupation for most visitors to the hills than recreation. The hill stations provided their clients with a wide array of social institutions to keep them entertained. These included assembly halls, residential clubs, gymkhanas, subscription libraries, Masonic lodges, sports and recreational clubs, and, in several of the larger stations, theaters. Ootacamund was renowned by the latter part of the nineteenth century as a center of sociality—a renown that rested on the presence of the venerable Ootacamund Club, the later and less exclusive Nilgiri Club, the Gymkhana Club (which was preceded by separate clubs for boating, polo, cricket, golf, and trap, as well as archery, badminton, and croquet—the ABC Club), the Ootacamund Hunt Club (which hosted the largest gathering of horses and hounds in India), Hobart Park (the site of annual horse races), the Nilgiri Library (housed in a handsome Gothic building), the magnificent Botanical Gardens, the Assembly Rooms (for balls and amateur theatricals), and a Freemason lodge. Another hill station that acquired renown for its recreational activities was Gulmarg in Kashmir. By the early twentieth century, little more than a few decades after its founding, Gulmarg was attracting six to seven hundred summer visitors, who had access to a club, theater, ballroom, golf course, two polo grounds, cricket ground, four tennis courts, and two croquet grounds.[51] Even the smallest hill stations were usually able to boast of a club, a library, and some form of organized sport. It was the larger stations, however, that were most heavily dependent upon clubs and other institutional mechanisms to weave newcomers into their social fabric.

The daily pattern of life in the civil hill stations acquired a character very different from that found elsewhere in the subcontinent. As contemporary

50. "Kumaon and Its Hill-Stations," *Calcutta Review* 26 (Jan.-June 1856), 396.
51. Sir Francis Younghusband, *Kashmir* (London, 1911), 98.

prints and photographs show, hill-station sojourners usually exchanged their tropical attire for wardrobes from "home." Heavy woolens and flannels replaced light cottons; top hats and bowlers and bonnets replaced the otherwise ubiquitous solar topis. Residents also reverted to the meal-times observed by the upper-middle class in England.[52] Rather than rise at dawn or even earlier to enjoy the cool of the morning and conduct the bulk of the day's business, as the British were wont to do on the plains, they tended to start the day at midmorning and, with the exception of those who had bureaucratic duties to fulfill, looked forward to uninterrupted leisure during their waking hours. From around noon until 2 P.M., they made social calls or hosted "at homes," an activity that elsewhere in India was reserved for the cool morning hours. They devoted the latter part of the afternoon to quiet relaxation indoors or visits to nearby sites, such as viewpoints and waterfalls, where picnics were popular. At dusk, residents gathered at the Mall to "take the air" and exchange greetings. In the larger stations, at least, evenings were the busiest times, bringing dinner parties, balls, the-atrical performances, and other social gatherings that continued until the early hours of the morning.

As a result, hill stations acquired a reputation for merriment and fel-lowship unmatched in British India. Even the small stations, with their sedate and informal atmospheres, had a surprisingly rich array of social events. In Yercaud's "sociable" small community, activities included "breakfasts, luncheons, pic-nics on an extensive scale, and afternoon tea parties. Sometimes a dinner party, dance, or 'variety entertainments' varies the programme of such amusements."[53] However, the large, multipurpose stations acquired the grandest reputations and the liveliest societies, with Simla again at the forefront. "All are bent on enjoying themselves, and champagne flows on every side," remarked the artist Val Prinsep, who stayed at Simla during the 1876–77 season. A major reason the social atmosphere of this modern Capua, as it was sometimes called, reached such a fevered pitch was the presence of the viceroy and his retinue. During one season at Simla in the 1880s, Lord and Lady Dufferin hosted twelve large dinners (each for as many as fifty people), twenty-nine small dinners (with six to fifteen people each), a state ball, a fancy ball, a children's fancy ball, six dances (some 250 people each), two garden parties, two evening parties, and a charity fete. In addition, they attended innumerable races, dinners, balls, fairs, concerts, and theatrical performances. When Lady Dufferin

52. Platt, *Home and Health in India*, 47.
53. Wilson, *The Shevaroys*, 74.

concluded that "the atmosphere of the place is one of pleasure-seeking," she spoke from experience.[54] The Dufferins' social calendar was scarcely distinguishable from that of other viceregal couples. The pace became so frenetic that the viceroys of the late nineteenth and twentieth centuries sought occasional respite at a weekend chateau at Mashobra, a suburb six miles from the center of Simla.

For most contemporaries, the closest parallel to the hill stations seemed to be the "watering places" of England: spa towns like Bath, Buxton, Cheltenham, Tunbridge Wells, and Malvern, and seaside resorts like Brighton, Margate, Scarborough, and Weymouth.[55] The British in India frequently compared the hill stations to these domestic resort towns. When the decision about whether to establish a sanitarium in Darjeeling hung in the balance in 1839, a Calcutta newspaper proclaimed: "Dorjeling MUST and WILL be our Brighton." Similarly, the earliest advocate of a sanitarium at Mahabaleshwar underscored his case by observing that "we have no Bath or Cheltenham, as at home, where freedom from care and enjoyment of a large and gay society generally performs those cures which are attributed to the virtues of their far famed springs."[56] Evocations of these domestic resorts recurred as succeeding generations of English men and women visited the hill stations. Macaulay thought Ootacamund "has now very much the look of a rising English watering place"; a visitor to Murree remarked on its resemblance to "an English watering-place"; and Prinsep witheringly termed Simla "an English watering-place gone mad." Others were more specific with their comparisons. Mussoorie, according to a veteran of the Indian Army medical service, was "known as the Margate

54. Val C. Prinsep, *Imperial India: An Artist's Journals*, 2d ed. (London, 1879), 261; Marchioness of Dufferin and Ava, *Our Viceregal Life in India: Selections from My Journal 1884–1888* (London, 1890), 99, 305, passim.

55. For a sampling of the literature on this subject, see Edmund W. Gilbert, "The Growth of Inland and Seaside Health Resorts in England," *Scottish Geographical Magazine* 55, no. 1 (Jan. 1939): 16–35; Edmund W. Gilbert, *Brighton: Old Ocean's Bauble* (London, 1954); Simona Pakenham, *Cheltenham* (London, 1971); David Gadd, *Georgian Summer: Bath in the Eighteenth Century* (Ridge Park, N.J., 1972); P. J. Corfield, *The Impact of English Towns 1700–1800* (Oxford, 1982), ch. 4; and Phyllis Hembry, *The English Spa 1560–1815* (Rutherford, N.J., 1990).

56. *Bengal Hurkaru*, 12 September 1839, reprinted in Fred Pinn, *The Road to Destiny: Darjeeling Letters 1839* (Calcutta, 1986), 215; Peter Lodwick, letter to the *Bombay Courier*, 1 May 1824, reprinted in Perin Bharucha, *Mahabaleswar: The Club 1881–1981* (Bombay, c. 1981), app. A. The *Bengal Hurkaru* article went on to state that Darjeeling's "air will be like that of Brighton, remove or lessen 'the ills that flesh is heir to'—Doubtless a Viceregal Pavilion will soon be erected at the 'Bright Spot,' and fashion gather round it."

of the Himalayas"; Coonoor was described by Lear as "not unlike Bourne-mouth"; and Cumming thought Simla bore "much the same relation . . . to Calcutta that Brighton does to London."[57]

This comparison bears further scrutiny, for hill stations fulfilled many of the social functions that the seaside resorts and spa towns served in Britain. Both originated as health sanitaria, offering therapeutic benefits to invalids. Both became popular centers of rest and recreation, attracting a large number of the social elite. Both operated on a seasonal basis, their greatest influx occurring in the summer months. Both offered an abundance of recreational facilities (assembly rooms, libraries, clubs, theaters) and activities (dinners, balls, promenades, races) to lubricate the wheels of social intercourse. Both attracted, among others, young men on the make, young women in search of marriage partners, widows and pensioners, and children attending boarding schools.

A particularly intriguing parallel derives from the role played by heads of state. Most of the great English watering places acquired their reputations as a result of visits by members of the royal family, whose appearance, especially if it became a regular event, served as an endorsement of the spa or seaside resort.[58] For the British in India, the closest thing to royalty were the governors-general and governors, and their actions similarly affected the fortunes of hill stations. "No private family can form a sanitarium," observed Isabel Burton, who visited Matheran and Mahabaleshwar with her husband, Richard, in 1876. "Some great official must go there with all his staff; then bungalows, and inns, and necessaries, and lastly comforts, begin to grow."[59] This observation was not entirely accurate: heads of state visited hill stations only after their establishment, and some stations never saw a governor or other great official. But it is true that the reputation of virtually every prominent hill station was boosted by the early appearance of a head of state. (Darjeeling, at risk from hostile neighbors until 1866, was the main exception.) Ootacamund hosted a visit by the governor of Madras, Sir Thomas Munro, in 1826; Simla welcomed the governor-general of India, Lord Amherst, in 1827; Mahabaleshwar did the same for

57. Macaulay, *Letters*, 59; *Letters from India and Kashmir* (London, 1874), 213; Prinsep, *Imperial India*, 262; Col. Robert J. Blackham, *Scalpel, Sword and Stretcher* (London, 1931), 87; Lear, *Indian Journal*, 195; Cumming, *From the Hebrides*, vol. 2, 119.

58. Gilbert, "The Growth of . . . Health Resorts," 27; P. J. Waller, *Town, City, and Nation: England 1850–1914* (Oxford, 1983), 133.

59. Isabel Burton, *AEI: Arabia Egypt India, A Narrative of Travel* (London and Belfast, 1879), 279.

the governor of Bombay, Sir John Malcolm, in 1828. In each case, the position of the sanitarium was significantly enhanced. These initial state visitors translated their enthusiasm for the place into government support, and the continuance of that support was ensured by visits to the stations by subsequent heads of state. Moreover, they acted as magnets for others, who were drawn by the social and political resonance of these quasi-royal courts. By contrast, those hill stations that seldom if ever received heads of states tended to languish in obscurity.

The influence wielded by heads of state highlights an important feature of hill-station society—its replication of the hierarchical order within British Indian society. Although all hill stations fulfilled the same general role as enclaves for Europeans in search of rest and recreation, they attracted different clientele and acquired different reputations. The broadest line of division lay between civil and military stations. Those that served primarily as cantonments for British troops had a different social character from those that attracted a substantial civilian population. The predominance of a lower-class, largely Celtic, exclusively male soldiery, housed in barracks and subject to army discipline, set the cantonments a world apart from the civil stations, and it should come as no surprise that the social chasm between them was nearly always reinforced by physical distance. The only notable exception to this rule was Landour, a military station founded in 1827 a mere mile from Mussoorie (and five hundred feet above it): the growth of the two communities soon obliterated the distance between them, creating the hyphenated Mussoorie-Landour. Thereafter, the British took care to chose sites for hill cantonments that were some distance from existing civil stations and usually at lower elevations. The most striking example is the string of military stations (Kasauli, Dagshai, Sabathu, Solon, Jutogh) that guarded the route from the plains to Simla. Except for places like Dalhousie and Murree, which began as cantonments but attracted a significant civilian population as well, the military hill stations had much the same social status relative to the civil ones as British soldiers did relative to British civilians in India. They ranked among the least desirable of the hill stations, their appeal limited by their function.[60]

A second fracture point ran between those large hill stations that attracted a regional or even imperial range of patrons and the small stations that served a particular clientele or simply drew their visitors from the

60. Bakloh, a hill cantonment that served as the regimental headquarters for the 4th Gurkha Rifles, is vividly described by John Masters, an officer with the regiment, in his autobiography, *Bugles and a Tiger* (New York, 1968).

immediate surroundings. Among the many hill stations that operated in
relative obscurity were Nandi Hill, a summer retreat for officials from
Bangalore; Lonavala, a sanitarium in the Bombay area for employees of the
Great Indian Peninsular Railway; Dharmkot, a small station near Dalhousie
that served as the summer headquarters of the American United Presbyterian Mission; and Yercaud, inhabited by a miscellany of local planters,
missionaries, and officials from Salem district. By contrast, even in their
early years Simla and Mussoorie attracted sojourners from northern India,
and Ootacamund did the same for the peninsular region. By the late
nineteenth century, the drawing power of these three stations extended
across the subcontinent and beyond, while Mahabaleshwar, Naini Tal, and
particularly Darjeeling had become nearly as popular. Mount Abu,
Coonoor, Dalhousie, Kodaikanal, Matheran, Murree, and Shillong made up
a second tier of stations whose reputations began to spread across their
regions in the latter part of the century. The wider their compass of visitors,
the more spirited and cosmopolitan their social life, which set them ever
further apart from the tranquil provincialism of the smaller stations. The
contrast was implicit in a guidebook's description of Dharamsala as "a quiet
station. . . . There is no unhealthy excitement; the very atmosphere is one
of calm; no scandal, and no dissipation stronger than black coffee and
milk-punch."[61] Embedded in these differences in social behavior lay differences in social rank. The less affluent elements of the British population
in India were seldom able to afford the travel fares, the high rents, and the
other costs connected with visits to renowned but distant hill stations. A
report published in 1870 described Darjeeling as "a sealed book" for
Calcutta residents with small to moderate means, which were defined as Rs.
500–600 or less a month.[62] It was estimated at the end of the nineteenth
century that an income of Rs. 1,500 a month was required to stay in Simla,
placing it beyond the means of most nonofficials.[63] The cost of living
created an effective barrier against the influx of people of lesser rank to
other large stations as well. They turned instead to smaller stations within
their vicinity or did without a stay in a hill station altogether.

Finally, a social schism existed between those large hill stations that had
a significant official presence and those that did not. Simla's role as the

61. J. Fitzgerald-Lee, *Guide to Dharmsala and the Kangra Valley* (Lahore, 1899), 14.
62. C. Palmer, W. G. Murray, and V. Ball, *Report on the Hill of Mahendragiri* (Calcutta, 1870), 1–2.
63. Kanwar, *Imperial Simla*, 4.

summer capital of India gave it a reputation as the "home of the heaven-born," "the abode of the little tin gods," a place so overladen with offi-cialdom that it left little room for people seeking a simple summer of leisure.[64] Its main rival among the hill stations of the northwest was Mussoorie, which drew much of its appeal from the fact that it was "a purely civil station. . . . There are no 'brass hats' to interfere with the young officer on pleasure bent."[65] A similar split existed between Mahabaleshwar and Matheran. "Matheran is not fashionable," Isabel Burton observed. "It is affected by the commercial classes from Saturday till Monday. It is Margate, whilst Mahabaleshwar . . . [is] Brighton." There, she complained, "society is always on duty." In the opinion of another visitor, "One of [Matheran's] great charms is the absence of officialdom."[66] Further south, Ootacamund's status as the summer headquarters of the Madras govern-ment gave it a reputation as "snooty Ooty." Those uncomfortable with its official character patronized nearby Coonoor. The social relationship be-tween the two hill stations was evident in their exchange of insults: "Coonoor calls Ooty stiff, and Ooty calls Coonoor vulgar."[67] At the heart of these rivalries lay the intensifying tensions between the official and nonofficial halves of the British population in India, tensions that broke into the open with the controversy over the Ilbert bill in 1882 and the subse-quent formation of the European and Anglo-Indian Defence Association.[68] The social fissures that separated Britons from one another in India could be seen in the different clientele of different hill stations. Widely known distinctions among stations' reputations demonstrated that both class and race were among the criteria for acceptance in these highland communities.

———

Recalling the days he spent in Simla as an official of the imperial gov-ernment, Sir Walter Lawrence remarked that, "delightful as it was, it was

64. Edward J. Buck, *Simla Past and Present*, 2d ed. (1925; reprint, Simla, 1989), 94.
65. Blackham, *Scalpel*, 87. Also see the remarks in *Guide to Mussoorie* (Mus-soorie, c. 1907), 1; and John Lang, *Wanderings in India: And Other Sketches of Life in Hindostan* (London, 1859), 402.
66. Isabel Burton, *The Life of Captain Sir Richard F. Burton*, vol. 2 (London, 1893), 82; Burton, *AEI*, 285; Francesca H. Wilson, *My Trip to Matheran* (Madras, 1888), 34.
67. "Civilian," *The Civilian's South India* (London, 1921), 168.
68. See Raymond K. Renford, *The Non-official British in India to 1920* (Delhi, 1987), esp. ch. 5.

not India."[69] There can be little doubt that this opinion was widely shared by Britons who patronized the hill stations. They had good reasons for insisting that these places were "not India." Not only were they physically removed from the rest of the subcontinent in their rugged mountain settings; they were socially and culturally aloof from it as well. The British did their best to re-create some of the favored features of their homeland in these highland retreats. From their villagelike morphologies, with quaint cottages scattered along the maze of lanes that converged at a point graced by the Gothic eminence of an Anglican church, to their spalike societies, with the protocol of calls and balls and other customs imposing a framework within which a floating population of visitors devoted themselves to the pursuit of leisure, the hill stations came to bear a striking resemblance to those aspects of metropolitan culture their patrons found especially comforting in their exile. In short, hill stations exuded a heady nostalgia. For those who inhaled this hallucinogen, the effect was immediately enticing.

There is no reason, however, for scholars to be overcome by this nostalgic atmosphere. The purpose of nostalgia is to shift attention away from the circumstances that give rise to it. In the case that concerns us, those circumstances were the experiences of our subjects in India, not their memories of Britain. They came to the hills because of the dangers and the dilemmas they faced on the plains as the rulers of an alien land and people, and they sought to make the hill stations special enclaves set apart from the "real" India. Our task is to reclaim these stations for the colonial experience. By recognizing nostalgia for what it was—an attempt to restore to visitors the sense of cultural identity and common purpose that extended immersion in the alien environment of the plains tended to erode—we can move toward a fuller appreciation of how integral hill stations were to the British endeavor in India.

69. Sir Walter Roper Lawrence, *The India We Served* (London, 1928), 83.

# 6 Nurseries of the Ruling Race

All educational organizations worthy of the name have always recognized what must be the ultimate and significant principle of peda-
gogy: namely the absolute mandate, the iron bond, discipline, sacrifice, the renunciation of the ego, the curbing of the personality.
            —Thomas Mann, *The Magic Mountain*

[The Nilgiris] might prove a nursery for future Indian statesmen,
political residents, counsellors, and governors.
            —Major William Murray, *An Account of the Neilgherries,*
                *or, Blue Mountains of Coimbatore, in Southern India*

No elements of the British colonial community were more closely identified with hill stations than women and children. While in India as a whole
the overwhelming majority of the British were adult males, this was
emphatically not the case in the hill stations. From the early decades of the
nineteenth century, officials took their families to hill stations to protect
them from the physical toll of the tropics. They did so with the endorsement of doctors, who warned that women and children were less suited to
the harsh climate of India than men and more needful of the therapeutic
benefits of the higher elevations. As the advance of the railway made travel
faster and easier, increasing numbers of women took to the hills for the
summer. Some of these women were accompanied by their spouses and
children; others were "grass widows," whose husbands remained at their
posts in the plains; still others were genuine widows and young unmarried
women. A growing number of children also came to the hill stations to
attend the boarding schools that began to spring up in the latter half of the
nineteenth century. As a result much higher concentrations of women and
children could be found in the hill stations than existed in the expatriate
population as a whole.

This divergence from the predominantly adult masculine cast of the
British presence in India had important ramifications. It distinguished hill
stations as European enclaves where males and females, adults and children,
existed in much the same proportions as in British society. Almost alone
among the places where the colonizers tended to congregate in India, hill
stations managed to take on some of the social and biological characteristics

117

of self-sustaining communities. While the seasonality of hill-station life and the transience of residents might be thought to have undermined the social cohesion of these enclaves, such oscillations actually contributed in a curious way to their viability and their importance to the imperial endeavor. Because much of the subcontinent's scattered British population circulated through these remote resorts, with women and children constituting particularly sizable portions of the seasonal migration, the hill stations bound the colonizers together in ways that were essential to the perpetuation of their power.

In the hill stations the otherwise widely dispersed representatives of the raj could reproduce their numbers, restore their sense of themselves as bearers of a superior civilization, and transmit their norms and values to their children in a setting protected from the alien influences of India. For the Victorians and their heirs, these were the responsibilities of the family unit and the educational institution. Nowhere else in India did the sense of family become so pervasive and the choice of schools so extensive as in the hill stations. They were the preferred sites within the subcontinent for single young adults to conduct their courting rituals, for married and widowed matrons to exercise their skills as society hostesses, for pregnant women to spend their confinements and new mothers to care for their infants, for toddlers to take their first steps, and for boys and girls to enroll in boarding schools. The hill stations accommodated all the functions essential to the biological and ideological reproduction of the British population in India. They were the nurseries for the ruling race.

---

British women first began to enter India in significant numbers after the East India Company lost the power to restrict immigration in 1833. Most were the wives and daughters of senior company officials, merchants, planters, and of some missionaries. While figures for the first half of the century are hard to come by, females numbered no more than 19,306 out of a total British population of 125,945 in 1861, and they remained a distinct minority throughout the rest of the colonial era, with the 1901 census showing 384 women per thousand men.[1] They tended to concentrate in

---

1. PP, *Report of the Commissioners Appointed to Inquire into the Sanitary State of the Army in India,* XIX, 1863, 46; P. J. Marshall, "British Immigration into India in the Nineteenth Century," in *European Expansion and Migration: Essays on the International Migration from Africa, Asia, and Europe,* ed. P. C. Emmer and M. Morner (New York, 1992), 184.

Calcutta, Madras, and Bombay, although the expansion and stabilization of British imperial power across the subcontinent allowed increasing numbers of women to filter into the *mofussil*, or provinces.

Most of the women who spent time in hill stations in the early years were the wives of civil and military officers stationed in nearby districts. When some members of the family of John Briggs, resident at Satara, fell ill, he moved them to Mahabaleshwar. John Sullivan took his family to Ootacamund for the same reason: sadly, his wife and two children died there. Doctors ordered Henry Lawrence's wife to spend the 1839 hot season in Simla, and in the course of her stay she and her husband acquired an abiding affection for the place. Emily Eden observed that the ladies of Simla in the early 1840s were almost all the wives of high-ranking military officers; when these men departed for the disastrous Afghan campaign, British females outnumbered males in the station by forty-six to twelve.[2]

The number of women who went to the hills and the distances they traveled to do so increased dramatically in the second half of the nineteenth century. These increase occurred for two principal reasons. One was the conflagration that swept upper India in 1857. "The value of the hill towns, small as they then were, was shown during the mutiny," observed one advocate of the highlands. "They became places of refuge for many fleeing from the plains, and for the wives and children of those fighting in the field."[3] While the hill stations in the western Himalayas attracted refugees, even a station as far removed from the disturbances as Yercaud was fortified as a sanctuary for the women and children of Salem in case the rebellion spread to the Madras presidency.[4] The second reason was the construction of a railway network across India. The railway made it a great deal easier and more affordable for women to make the journey to a popular hill station at the onset of the hot weather without the assistance of a husband or other male chaperon.

One example of the opportunities for travel by British women in India in the latter part of the nineteenth century can be found in the diary of Mrs.

2. Perin Bharucha, *Mahabaleswar: The Club 1881–1981* (Bombay, c. 1981), app. B; Paul Hockings, "John Sullivan of Ootacamund," in *Journal of Indian History Golden Jubilee Volume*, ed. T. K. Ravindran (Trivandrum, 1973), 870; Sir Herbert Benjamin Edwardes and Herman Merivale, *Life of Sir Henry Lawrence*, 2d ed., vol. 1 (London, 1872), 210; Emily Eden, *Up the Country: Letters from India* (1930; reprint, London, 1984), 278.

3. Hyde Clarke, "The English Stations in the Hill Regions of India," *Journal of the Statistical Society* 44 (Sept. 1881): 559.

4. F. J. Richards, *Salem* (Madras, 1913), 254.

Robert Moss King, the wife of a colonial official stationed in Meerut. The nearest hill station was Mussoorie, and Mrs. King went there in the fall of 1878 in a journey that took a day and a half by train, coach, and pony. The following year she spent time in Naini Tal, with side trips to Ranikhet and Almora. In 1880 she returned to Mussoorie, or more precisely Landour, where she rented a house from March to November and took a trek into the Himalayan interior that included a stay at the hill cantonment of Chakrata. During the summer of 1881 she traveled via Murree to Kashmir, spending two months at Srinagar and its environs. Finally, before departing from India in 1882 she visited Matheran. Every year of her sojourn in the country included a lengthy stay in the highlands. Although her husband accompanied her on some of these journeys, just as often she led her children and an entourage of servants on her own.[5]

The peripatetic habits of women like Mrs. King arose not merely from an enthusiasm for the adventures they encountered in the hills but from an antipathy for the life they faced on the plains. This antipathy was usually traced to the tropical climate and its subversive effects on women's health. Maud Diver, the author of a number of successful novels about British India, insisted that memsahibs wilted under the heat much more rapidly than their menfolk. This invocation of the "weaker-sex" doctrine sparked some dissent. Another novelist, Flora Annie Steel, who had lived in India with her husband, a civil servant, between 1867 and 1889, claimed that women could cope with the climate just as well as men.[6] But her opinion was the exception, and it was certainly not shared by the medical fraternity. They believed that the physiology of females put them at a distinct disadvantage when the sweltering heat of summer set in, making their flight to the hills necessary. As one of the more popular nineteenth-century books of medical advice for women in India put it, "Women break down sooner than men."[7]

The problem with the weaker-sex argument, however, is that there was no epidemiological evidence to support it. The notion that British women in India suffered poorer health than their male counterparts is contradicted

5. Mrs. Robert Moss King, *The Diary of a Civilian's Wife in India 1877–1882*, 2 vols. (London, 1884), passim.

6. Maud Diver, *The Englishwoman in India* (Edinburgh and London, 1909), 8–9; F. A. Steel and G. Gardiner, *The Complete Indian Housekeeper and Cook*, rev. ed. (London, 1917), 204.

7. Edward John Tilt, *Health in India for British Women*, 4th ed. (London, 1875), 34.

by mortality data. A Parliamentary commission reported in 1863 that the death rate for women was just fourteen per thousand, compared with twenty per thousand for civil servants, thirty-eight per thousand for army officers, and sixty-nine per thousand for enlisted men.[8] Medical authorities could not, therefore, rest their case for sending women to the hills on the straightforward grounds of comparative life chances. Instead, they had to rely on exclusivist arguments about the physiology and sociology of the British female.

The physiological case centered on reproduction. The afflictions most often referred to in the health guides for memsahibs were miscarriages and menstrual irregularities.[9] Given what we know about the adverse effects of malaria, dysentery, and other diseases on female fertility, there can be little doubt that British women in India did suffer inordinately from miscarriages and other reproductive disorders. And given what we know about British colonial medicine's proclivity for tracing ill health in the tropics to climatic sources, it is hardly surprising that female patients were advised to go to the hills for convalescence. Hill stations thus came to be seen as places singularly suited to the reproductive needs of the British population in India. Women went there to relieve menstrual distress, to recuperate from miscarriages, and to ensure that pregnancies passed to term. Even hardy Flora Annie Steel went to a hill station—Dalhousie—for her two pregnancies.[10]

The other major argument for sending women to the hills was also couched in medical terms, but its real concern was the adverse effect of colonial social strictures on their lives. Many of the ailments that afflicted British women were attributed to their lack of purposeful activity. The stereotypical memsahib was a creature of leisure who spent her days in the darkened confines of her bungalow, surrounded by a compliant army of servants whose labor left her little to do besides nap, entertain, and gossip. This stereotype ignores the many British women who led active,

8. These figures are averages for the period 1800–56. *Report of the Commissioners Appointed to Inquire into the Sanitary State of the Army*, 18, 40, 47.

9. Francis R. Hogg, *Practical Remarks Chiefly concerning the Health and Ailments of European Families in India* (Benares, 1877), 2–4, 84; Major S. Leigh Hunt and Alexander S. Kenny, *Tropical Trials. A Handbook for Women in the Tropics* (London, 1883), 304–9; Tilt, *Health in India*, 34, 55–61. An excellent examination of these issues can be found in Nupur Chaudhuri, "Memsahibs and Motherhood in Nineteenth-Century Colonial India," *Victorian Studies* 31, no. 4 (summer 1988): 517–35.

10. Flora Annie Steel, *The Garden of Fidelity* (London, 1929), 46, 52.

productive lives in India.[11] At the same time, it obscures the degree to which the memsahibs' leisured existence helped to maintain the social boundaries of colonial privilege by marking their gendered role in racial terms.[12] But the fact remains that most British women in India were confined to a monotonous and trivial existence: they were "incorporated wives" whose roles and status derived solely from their husbands' occupations.[13] Diver observed that British ladies' "domestic duties are practically *nil.*" Steel was even blunter: "the majority of European women in India have nothing to do."[14] With no duties to keep them busy, the wives of the colonizers were believed to be particularly susceptible to nervous disorders.[15] "Half the cases of neuraesthenia and anaemia among English ladies," argued Steel, "and their general inability to stand the hot weather, arises from the fact that they live virtually in the dark, . . . [in a state of] forced inertia."[16] Medical authorities were equally convinced that the neurasthenic ills of the memsahibs could be traced to their inactivity. As one doctor put it, "Their lives, especially those in affluent or easy circumstances, are generally torpid, and too little relieved by occupa-

11. Much of the more recent literature on the memsahibs has endeavored to challenge or modify this stereotype. See Pat Barr, *The Memsahibs: The Women of Victorian India* (London, 1976); Pat Barr, *The Dust in the Balance: British Women in India 1905–1945* (London, 1989); Mary Ann Lind, *The Compassionate Memsahibs: Welfare Activities of British Women in India, 1900–1947* (New York, 1988); Margaret MacMillan, *Women of the Raj* (London, 1988); and Barbara N. Ramusack, "Cultural Missionaries, Maternal Imperialists, Feminist Allies: British Women Activists in India, 1865–1945," *Women's Studies International Forum* 13, no. 4 (1990): 309–21.

12. This point is made by Margaret Strobel, *European Women and the Second British Empire* (Bloomington, 1991), 15. Also see the essays by Mrinalini Sinha and Nancy L. Paxton in Nupur Chaudhuri and Margaret Strobel, eds., *Western Women and Imperialism: Complicity and Resistance* (Bloomington, 1992); and the provocative work of Vron Ware, *Beyond the Pale: White Women, Racism and History* (London, 1992), esp. pt. 3.

13. For an examination of this phenomenon and its application to the British colonial world, see the essays by Janice N. Brownfoot, Beverley Gartrell, and Deborah Kirkwood in Hilary Callan and Shirley Ardener, eds., *The Incorporated Wife* (London, 1984).

14. Diver, *Englishwoman in India*, 16; Steel, *Garden of Fidelity*, 122.

15. The same association between a dearth of meaningful tasks and nervous disorders has been suggested for upper-middle-class women in Victorian England. See the scathing critique of her own society by Florence Nightingale, *Cassandra* (reprint, New York, 1979); and see Elaine Showalter, *The Female Malady: Women, Madness, and English Culture, 1830–1980* (New York, 1985).

16. Steel and Gardiner, *The Complete Indian Housekeeper*, 178.

tion. . . . They become listless and apathetic, and they succumb to the climate sooner than men."[17]

Hill stations alleviated both the physical and the social ills that plagued colonial women. Insofar as the tropical heat confined women to their homes, the hill stations freed them, making it possible for them to enjoy fresh air and vigorous exercise. And insofar as their problems were precipitated by loneliness and monotony, the hill stations offered a refreshing change of pace, a new and enlarged network of companions with whom they could socialize and reinvigorate themselves. In either case, the hill stations held the promise of recovery for women whose lives had lost purpose.

For all these reasons, British women were drawn to hill stations in substantial numbers. A few statistics indicate the scale of the female presence. In Mussoorie, the imperial census of 1881 (conducted in February) counted nearly twice as many Christian men as women (289 males and 151 females), but a census carried out the previous September, near the end of the "season," found the Christian population to be almost evenly divided between men and women (960 males and 897 females). These figures suggest that females actually constituted a majority of the seasonal sojourners.[18] Moreover, their proportion increased over time. Summer European census figures for Simla show that the percentage of women grew from 44.6 percent in 1869 to 53.7 percent in 1904 to 57 percent in 1922.[19] Similarly, the imperial census for Ootacamund indicates that the female portion of the European population increased from 39 percent in 1871 to 41.5 percent in 1901 to 53 percent in 1921, and the percentages were almost certainly a good deal higher during the in-season months.[20]

17. R. S. Mair, "Medical Guide for Anglo-Indians," in Edmund C. P. Hull, *The European in India; or, Anglo-Indian's Vade-Mecum* (London, 1872), 216. Also see Hunt and Kenny, *Tropical Trials*, 178; and Tilt, *Health in India*, 64.

18. Edwin T. Atkinson, *The Himalayan Gazetteer*, vol. 3, pt. 2 (1882; reprint, Delhi, 1973), 597–98.

19. Annual Report of the Simla Municipality, 1904–5, 18, HPSA; "Simla Summer Census, 30 June 1921," Simla Municipal Corporation Records, 179/1933/123/1921/II, HPSA.

20. See Table 14.2 in Paul Hockings, "British Society in the Company, Crown and Congress Eras," in *Blue Mountains: The Ethnography and Biogeography of a South Indian Region*, ed. Paul Hockings (Delhi, 1989), 351. Although the proportion of women slips a bit in certain decades, the overall trend was one of growth.

"There are always plenty of females on the hills," observed the wife of a Madras Army officer, who proceeded to identify what seemed to her the principal categories:

> There are the wives who *can't* live with their husbands in the plains; the 'grass-widows.' . . . Then there are the young ladies whose parents are not able, or not willing, to send them to England just yet. . . . And, lastly, there are the mothers themselves, with their troops of little ones, for whose health, perhaps, they have consented to separate from their lords and masters; or wives who have accompanied their husbands thither.[21]

Most of these women were related to civil and military officers, and their status made lengthy stays to the hills both affordable and socially obligatory. Women with official affiliations were not the only ones to go to the hills however. Female missionaries were a major presence in certain hill stations.[22] Toward the end of the nineteenth century the railways and an increasing number of businesses established rest houses in the highlands for the use of their employees' families. The Indian Army provided accommodations in its hill cantonments for the wives and children of soldiers: in 1875 the Bengal command alone housed 712 women and 1,367 children in the hills, and others resided there without military assistance.[23] A number of widows and unmarried women also lived in hill stations. Some supported themselves by opening dame schools: Richard Burton reported the existence of two schools for young children at Ootacamund in 1847, one run by a Miss Hale and a Miss Millard, the other by a Mrs. James and a Miss Ottley.[24] Others found employment as estate agents for absentee landlords: the mother of Jim Corbett, the famed tiger hunter, established a successful estate agency in Naini Tal after the death of her husband.[25] Still others operated boarding houses and hotels or rented out houses they had acquired: a guidebook to Mahabaleshwar informed its readers of several cottages available for rent from the widow Mrs. Riley, a twenty-five-year

---

21. Florence Marryat, *"Gup." Sketches of Anglo-Indian Life and Character* (London, 1868), 101–2.

22. For example, Rachel Kerr Johnson was an American Presbyterian missionary who wrote about her visits to Landour. Barbara Mitchell Tull, ed., *Affectionately, Rachel: Letters from India 1860–1884* (Kent, Ohio, 1992), esp. 284–87.

23. Tilt, *Health in India*, 18.

24. Richard F. Burton, *Goa, and the Blue Mountains* (1851; reprint, Berkeley, 1991), 286n.

25. Martin Booth, *Carpet Sahib: A Life of Jim Corbett* (Delhi, 1990), 29.

resident of the station.[26] In Ootacamund, a sixth of the houses listed in an 1858 directory were held by women, and one had nine property titles to her name; by 1886, women owned a quarter of all European dwellings.[27] A government report on Dalhousie in 1902 revealed that women owned thirty-five of the eighty-two houses in the station, including nine in the possession of a Mrs. Higgins, and the station's three hotels were owned by women as well.[28]

An unusually rich source of evidence concerning the mix of single, married, and widowed women in the hill stations comes from a 1911 directory of Ootacamund's European residents. It lists 599 names, 352 of whom are female. Approximately three-fifths of these women are identified as wives and daughters in households with a husband or father or both (although many of the males were probably not in residence). The other two-fifths are equally divided between unmarried women, many of whom appear to have been teachers, governesses, and nurses, and women identified by the designation "Mrs." but unattached to any male name—most of the seventy women in this category can be assumed to have been widows.[29] While similar data from other hill stations are scarce, most likely the distribution of their female residents by marital status was similar.

With so many British women ensconced in the hills, it is easy to understand why these locales acquired reputations for romance and scandal.[30] By providing settings and occasions where men from widely dispersed and often isolated parts of the subcontinent could meet a substantial number of women of their own class and culture, the hill stations were conducive to intimate relationships. "Everybody there is prompted to be gay if only because they are on a holiday," explained one observer of British social life in the hill stations. "What wonder, then, that there should be much innocent gaiety, some frivolity, and here and there a man and a woman who have lost their heads."[31]

26. *Mahableshwur Guide* (Bombay, 1875), 12.

27. Sir Frederick Price, *Ootacamund: A History* (Madras, 1908), app. C; *A Guide to the Neilgherries* (Madras, 1886), 71–76.

28. *Report of the Commission Appointed to Deal with the Transfer of the Punjab Government to the Hill Station of Dalhousie* (Simla, 1902), app. E.

29. J.S.C. Eagan, *The Nilgiri Guide and Directory* (Mysore, 1911), iii–x.

30. This reputation survives in popular accounts of the British raj. See, for instance, Michael Edwardes, *Bound to Exile: The Victorians in India* (New York, 1970), ch. 17.

31. L. C. Ricketts, "English Society in India," *Contemporary Review* 101 (1912): 684.

In its most respectable guise, this aspect of hill-station social life can be seen as a mechanism for furthering the efforts of young people to meet, to court, and to marry. Many of the leading stations' social events—the dinners, the picnics, the balls—were staged at least in part as vehicles for the "coming out" of daughters, nieces, and other single women—an announcement of their interest in entertaining marriage proposals. Annual dinners and other events where young people could meet were hosted by bachelor societies such as Simla's Order of Knights of the Black Heart and Darjeeling's Knights-Errant.[32] Much like the spas and seaside resorts of England, the hill stations were locales for the circulation of marriageable women.

This amorous image also had a less reputable side. Colonel Robert Blackham, an Indian Army medical officer who visited Mussoorie around the turn of the century, recalls that the Charleville Hotel rang a bell every morning at six, "and it is hardly an exaggeration to say that it was a sorting-out signal for visitors to return to their own rooms." He also describes a parlor game in Simla. "The men went underneath and the ladies sat round the edge of a large table, dangling their legs. The men were allowed to inspect as far as the knee and to recognise the fair competitors by what we used to call . . . 'their lower extremities.'"[33] Such tales recur in the memoirs of the period. Licentious behavior was most often associated with the grass widows. Even with medical sanction, these women risked accusations of neglecting their marital obligations by leaving their husbands to labor on the plains while they played in the hills. The presence of so many young, uniformed, and fun-seeking officers in the hill stations was considered a serious temptation to unattached women. *Hobson-Jobson* suggests that the term *grass widow*, which it observes was "applied . . . with a shade of malignity" in India, may have derived from the Suffolk "grace-widow," an unmarried mother, or the low German *gras-wedewe*, "a dissolute low married woman living by herself."[34] It is clear from the discourse of the time that the adulterous grass widow was often seen as the sexual aggressor: one official's wife described her as "the most dangerous [woman] that the

32. Iris Butler, *The Viceroy's Wife: Letters of Alice, Countess of Reading, from India, 1921–25* (London, 1969), 113–14; E. C. Dozey, *A Concise History of the Darjeeling District since 1835* (Calcutta, 1922), 117–18.

33. Col. Robert J. Blackham, *Scalpel, Sword and Stretcher* (London, 1931), 87, 194.

34. Col. Henry Yule and A. C. Burnell, *Hobson-Jobson,* new ed. (1886; reprint, Delhi, 1989), 394.

idle young man could encounter."[35] Seldom did the male party suffer the same censure. A rare commentary on the double standard that operated here came from the anonymous (female?) author of an article about the hill stations of Kumaun:

> Let the breath of reproach justly sully any woman's name, and she is marked and avoided. Let it equally sully a man's, and he is not. He is not thought unfitted for taking his place in respectable society; and even when his character is known to be thoroughly bad, his acquaintance is sought, and his visits allowed, as though he were really an ornament to the society which lowers itself by admitting him. It is impossible to help feeling that this is not as it ought to be.[36]

Much of the gossip was, in fact, hyperbolic. Nothing is quite so certain to titillate an audience than suggestions of infidelities among the high and mighty, as Rudyard Kipling and other chroniclers of Simla knew full well when they regaled their readers with the intrigues of Mrs. Hauksbee and her kind. Such tales exploited social estrangements within the British Indian community. The nonofficial British inhabitants of Calcutta, Madras, and other commercial centers, who resented the power and snobbery of the "heaven-born," savored stories that portrayed Simla as a sink of iniquity. Perhaps this is why the summer capital acquired far more notoriety than Mussoorie, even though everyone who visited both resorts knew that Mussoorie was the place to go for a good time unrestrained by stuffy formalities and finger-wagging.[37] There was much truth in the assertion of a visitor to Simla in the early 1870s that "the balls and picnics, the croquet and badminton parties, the flirtations and rumoured engagements, are given an importance which they do not actually possess."[38] It must also be remembered that moral standards changed over time. Conduct that stalwarts of the age of muscular Christianity considered shocking seldom would have raised an eyebrow among their *fin-de-siècle* progeny.

Despite all these qualifications, evidence does suggest that the conduct of Europeans changed when they got to the hills. Scrutiny was directed toward sexual scandal in the hill stations at least in part because it was the

---

35. Marryat, "*Gup,*" 101.

36. "Kumaon and Its Hill-Stations," *Calcutta Review* 26 (Jan.-June 1856): 392.

37. See, for example, the remarks comparing Mussoorie and Simla by John Lang, *Wanderings in India: And Other Sketches of Life in Hindostan* (London, 1859), 402; as well as the comments on the respectable atmosphere at Simla during the Elgin years by Sir Claude H. Hill, *India—Stepmother* (Edinburgh, 1929), 50.

38. Andrew Wilson, *The Abode of Snow: Observations on a Journey from Chinese Tibet to the Indian Caucasus* (Edinburgh and London, 1875), 51.

most dramatic indicator of the transforming power of these places. Up among the clouds it seemed permissible to behave in ways that went beyond the limits of propriety elsewhere. Yet it was not merely nor mainly sexual license that characterized the sense of release that the journey to the hills provided. Consider, for example, the American missionary David Coit Scudder's account of the emotions that overcame him when he arrived in Kodaikanal in 1862: "I . . . seized our United States flag, shouted out 'Long may it wave!' . . . at the English collector . . . and did other uncouth things that I am capable of doing up here—not down there."[39] The key to this odd outburst is the final clause of Scudder's statement, the contrast he poses between "up here" and "down there." Arriving in the hills, many visitors experienced a similar heady rush of freedom, a sudden sense of escape from social constraints, and its varied expressions encompassed not only the sexual irregularities that gave the leading stations their colorful reputations but such minor misdemeanors as the waving of an American flag in the face of a local British collector.

To understand this seeming intoxication, it is necessary to appreciate the degree to which it was a reaction to the confining commands of imperial power. Respectable British opinion accepted that certain things simply could not be done in the colonial context because they eroded the facade that the colonizers considered essential to the maintenance of their authority. In the parlance of the times, "prestige" was at stake. This preoccupation with prestige led to strict regulation of the actions of the expatriate population—rules that attempted to stifle those coarse and contrary aspects of human nature that could demean British rulers in the eyes of Indian subjects. But those restrictions did not apply—or at least did not apply with the same force—in the hill stations. The *Times* correspondent William Howard Russell, recently seared by what he had seen of the mutiny and its suppression, took the residents of Simla to task for their apparent neglect of so vital a matter as prestige. He described bacchanals of drinking, gambling, and other excesses, and warned that "not a season passes without damage to reputations, loss of fortune, and disgrace to some of the visitors; which are serious social evils affecting the British community directly, but which also bear a very grave aspect in relation to the influence we exercise over the natives."[40] While this argument had enor-

---

39. Horace E. Scudder, *Life and Letters of David Coit Scudder, Missionary in Southern India* (New York, 1864), 304.

40. William Howard Russell, *My Diary in India*, vol. 2 (London, 1860), 145. He goes on to remark: "Nothing is more remarkable during one of these little

mous resonance on the plains, where it represented the norm, what Russell either did not understand or could not concede was that the hill stations were special realms where the rules of the colonial world did not apply. Thus, his rebuke did not stand out for its message, which was commonplace, but for its intended targets, who must have found it a surprising and singular outburst. For most Europeans in India, hill stations were places where they could find relief from the constraints that were elsewhere imposed on their behavior.

The implication to be drawn from this analysis is not that the British regarded their visits to hill stations as licenses to do anything they pleased—moral sanctions remained firmly in place—but rather that they regarded them as opportunities to free themselves at least temporarily from the colonial strictures that prevented them from doing what they would have done in the metropolitan milieu. If hill stations acquired reputations for scandalous conduct, it must be understood that this was in comparison to the straitened context of colonial society. From the perspective of metropolitan culture, such behavior represented little more than the normal workings of a regular community, albeit compressed and quickened somewhat by its seasonality. Members of the opposite sex met, socialized, courted, married, and occasionally engaged in adultery. They conceived children and perpetuated their breed. They did those things that were essential to the reproduction of the ruling race.

Thus we return to the prominent place of women in the hill stations. Their seasonal concentration in these enclaves can be seen as an ingenious response to two of the demographic problems that plagued the British in India: the huge disparity between the male and female portions of the white population and the wide dispersal of that population across a vast subcontinent. By establishing centers where relatively equal numbers of men and women could interact in ways that were culturally comfortable to them, where they could meet an array of possible marriage partners in a social milieu carefully conceived for that purpose, where they could engage in dalliances that caused less opprobrium than such behavior provoked on the plains (and certainly less than the alternative of interracial liaisons), and, finally, where they could raise families with less fear of the physical and social perils of an alien land, the British established environments that

---

effervescences than the behaviour of the native servants. They stand in perfect apathy and quiescence, with folded arms, and eyes gazing on vacancy as if in deep abstraction, and at all events feigning complete ignorance of what is going on around them" (148).

affected the entire imperial endeavor. By concentrating their women in the hill stations, the British sought to strengthen their demographically precarious position in their Indian realm.

———

Those mothers who spent their summers in hill stations invariably brought their offspring with them. Many other parents sent their children to boarding schools in the hills while they remained on the plains. Even orphans and the children of poor whites were frequently placed in institutions located in the vicinity of major hill stations. The British had always regarded their young as the most problematic element of their strategy to establish a permanent presence in India, and the uses they made of hill stations for raising children tell us a great about the centrality of these mountain resorts to the British raj.

Like women, children were considered fragile creatures, especially susceptible to the diseases of the tropics; and indeed the mortality rate for European children in India was more than twice that of their cohort at home. The most dangerous period was the first five years of life: a report issued in 1870 calculated 148.10 deaths per thousand in the Bengal presidency compared with 68.58 per thousand in England. The death rate dropped after the age of five, but it was still double the domestic figure. This terrible toll gave some biological basis to the widespread conviction that Europeans could not sustain a permanent population in India past the third generation.[41]

From the start, hill stations were seen as promising retreats for ailing youngsters. Darjeeling, the station closest to Bengal with its large European population, was singled out for effusive praise. In an oft-quoted passage, Joseph Hooker exclaimed, "It is incredible what a few weeks of that mountain air does for the India-born children of European parents: they are taken there sickly, pallid or yellow, soft and flabby, to become transformed into models of rude health and activity."[42] This assessment was affirmed repeatedly, and Simla, Ootacumund, Mahabaleshwar, and other hill stations received similar endorsements.

41. The child-mortality figures, and an interesting commentary on them, can be found in Sir Joseph Fayrer, *Tropical Dysentery and Chronic Diarrhoea* (London, 1881), 341ff.
42. Joseph Dalton Hooker, *Himalayan Journals*, vol. 1 (London, 1854), 120. Also see *The Dorjeeling Guide* (Calcutta, 1845), 28, 37–38; *Darjeeling*, pamphlet reprinted from the *Calcutta Review*, no. 55 (1857): 25; and Capt. J. G. Hathorn, *A Hand-Book of Darjeeling* (Calcutta, 1863), 66.

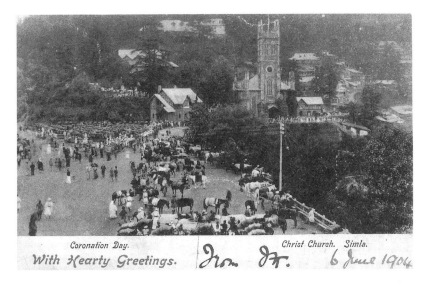

*Coronation Day.*

*With Hearty Greetings.*

*Christ Church. Simla.*

Figure 8. Children riding ponies on the Mall at Simla. From a postcard in the possession of the author.

Consequently, children were a significant presence in the hill stations. They made an important contribution to the social character of these mountain enclaves—a contribution that is too often overlooked. They helped to give their summer homes the sights, the sounds, and the feel of a cohesive and permanent community. In contrast to the widespread practice on the plains of sequestering children indoors to protect them from a climate and a culture that seemed poised to snatch them away, in the hills these same children were generally set free to experience and explore their surroundings: the younger ones could be seen on the Mall in carriages pushed by ayahs and on ponies led by syces (Figure 8); the older ones could be met walking across the station to and from school and wandering in groups through the lanes of the ward and the alleys of the bazaar on adventures of their own. They were everywhere. Those who resided with their parents in the larger stations attended birthday parties and costume parties, picnics and fetes; they participated in theatricals and *tableaux vivants*; they mirrored their parents' social lives with startling exactitude.[43] So incessant were such activities that the author of one handbook for

43. The memoirs of M. M. Kaye, who spent her youth in Simla, are particularly enlightening in this regard: *The Sun in the Morning: My Early Years in India and England* (New York, 1990), passim.

women in India warned, "The innumerable parties, dances, and elaborate entertainments for children, which are a striking feature of fashionable hill stations, make the children blasé and dissatisfied with simple pleasures; and they become over-tired and over-excited."[44]

Parents in the upper echelons of British Indian society seemed especially eager to provide their children with lavish entertainments; it is possible to view these actions as compensation for the wrenching separations that loomed ahead, for it was widely accepted that British children should be shipped back to Britain before they reached adolescence. Their removal from India was one of the most rigidly enforced customs of the British in India. Most medical men and other self-styled authorities agreed that it was essential for boys in particular to be gone by the age of six or seven; for girls an early departure was considered less imperative.[45] The children's health was offered as the rationale for their removal, with warnings that prolonged presence in the tropics would make them feeble and "weedy." But their physical well-being was not as central a consideration as colonial rhetoric suggested. After all, the most precarious years in the lives of children occurred well before the age recommended for departure, and the natural dangers they faced were not peculiar to boys. The main motivation to ship children back to the motherland was concern about their social and cultural development and the role of this development in the perpetuation of the British imperial presence.

The child-rearing practices of the British in India—or more precisely of the great majority of parents who saw themselves as respectable—resembled the practices of the upper middle class at home: both used servants as surrogates for all but the least onerous of their parental responsibilities.[46] In India, these surrogates were with few exceptions Indians, and their most prominent and pervasive representative was the ayah, or nursemaid. She became a colonial institution, an essential element of the British Indian nursery. She was responsible for dressing her charges, feeding them, bathing them, entertaining them, and settling them into bed. Indian women were often employed as wet nurses for European infants, although

---

44. Kate Platt, *Home and Health in India and the Tropical Colonies* (London, 1923), 143.

45. See, for example, Joseph Ewart, *Goodeve's Hints for the General Management of Children in India in the Absence of Professional Advice*, 6th ed. (Calcutta, 1872), 28; Fayrer, *Tropical Dysentery*, 344; and Hull, *The European in India*, 133.

46. See Chaudhuri, "Memsahibs and Motherhood."

this practice declined toward the end of the nineteenth century.[47] Some of the wealthier British families sought white or mixed-race women as nurses or governesses for their children, particularly in the latter period of colonial rule, but even in these households an ayah carried out the menial tasks of the nursery. In addition to the ubiquitous ayah, cooks, gardeners, syces, and many other Indian domestics in colonial households influenced the daily lives of young residents. The results were predictable: British children grew emotionally attached to their ayahs and other Indian attendants, and they frequently acquired more familiarity with and fondness for the language and culture of these people than they did for the European heritage of their parents.[48]

The colonial literature was replete with laments about how children were being corrupted morally by their intimate association with servants. The acquisition of an Indian dialect roused particular concern since it gave children immediate access to a world apart from parental supervision or even comprehension. For example:

> [I]f left to the society of native servants, not only will [children] most assuredly contact native habits in the way of eating, gesticulating with the hands when talking, etc., . . . but, rapidly picking up the language, their little minds will soon become contaminated with ideas and expressions that would utterly horrify a mother did she herself understand the language of the country.[49]

Whatever the parents' response may have been to their children's drift into an alien embrace—and the persistent use of ayahs suggests that it caused them less anguish than we might suppose—its implications for imperial policy were profoundly disturbing. How could the British assert the superiority of their culture if their own children forsook it for indigenous alternatives? How could they maintain imperial authority in the face of this dissolution of difference? The inescapable answer is that they could not. This stark realization provided a powerful rationale for the British to

47. See, for example, the contrasting advice offered by "A Lady Resident," *The Englishwoman in India* (London, 1865), 96–97; and by Steel and Gardiner, *The Complete Indian Housekeeper*, 163–66.

48. See Rudyard Kipling, *Something of Myself and Other Autobiographical Writings*, ed. Thomas Pinney (Cambridge, 1990), 4; and Kaye, *The Sun in the Morning*, 91–94, 151.

49. Hunt and Kenny, *Tropical Trials*, 403. Similar statements appear in "A Lady Resident," *Englishwoman*, 106; Diver, *Englishwoman in India*, 42–43; Steel and Gardiner, *The Complete Indian Housekeeper*, 166; and Platt, *Home and Health in India*, 138–39.

send their children away, to remove them from the seductive influence of India before it could make a permanent mark on their psyches, to place them in the sober environment of British homes and British boarding schools, where their socialization in British values could be assured.

The problem was that many parents either could not afford to send their children back to Britain or were unwilling to do so. The financial costs—the fare for the passage, the expense of maintenance with strangers or even relatives, the fees for schooling—were simply prohibitive for many families in India, especially those employed in the uncovenanted services (telegraph, mail, police, forestry, customs, opium), the railways, the army, and various commercial enterprises. Moreover, the emotional costs of shipping off one's children at the age of five or so, with little expectation of seeing them again (apart from the brief opportunities presented by periodic leaves) until they had become adults themselves, were understandably more than some parents could bear. Even those willing to make this sacrifice for what they regarded as their children's sake were often eager to postpone the fateful day as long as possible.[50]

The English saw hill stations, from their inception, as attractive sites for the education of children who were not sent to British boarding schools. A description of Darjeeling in its infancy praised it for possessing "one advantage . . . inestimable beyond all others"—an environment suitable for the schooling of younger children, whose parents could "so escape the pain and anxiety of a separation little less than those [sic] of death." The Nilgiris were described by an early promoter as a place where "those parents who cannot afford to send their children home" could meet their educational needs in a salutary setting.[51] At Ootacamund, the Church Missionary Society established a school for European children in the early 1830s, and although it soon vanished, the Fern Hill School, "a boarding-school for young gentlemen," appeared in 1847 and lasted for eight years. More durable was the school founded at Mussoorie in 1835 for "parents who are too poor to send children home." These were the words of Eden, who encountered a party of several children traveling to this institution

---

50. The emotional estrangement this practice creates for a mother and daughter is the theme of "A Mother in India," an insightful short story by Sara Jeannette Duncan in her book *The Pool in the Desert* (1903; reprint, Harmondsworth, 1984).

51. J. T. Pearson, "A Note on Darjeeling," 1839, reprinted in Fred Pinn, *The Road to Destiny: Darjeeling Letters 1839* (Calcutta, 1986), 92–108; James Hough, *Letter on the Climate, Inhabitants, Productions, etc. of the Neilgherries, or Blue Mountains of Coimbatoor* (London, 1829), 137.

across the north Indian plains under the care of Indian bearers.[52] Mussoorie soon acquired a reputation as a center for European education. Several institutions in addition to the original Mussoorie school, which became a Diocesan school for boys in 1867, were successfully established in Mussoorie in the years before the 1857 rebellion—the Convent of Jesus and Mary (a girls' school founded in 1845), St. George's College for boys (1853), and the Woodstock School for girls (1856).

An important advance in the development of European schooling in the hill stations took place in the midcentury decades. This increased educational activity was propelled both by the needs of European residents and by the concerns of colonial authorities. New employment opportunities in commerce, planting, and other nonofficial enterprises, as well as in the railroads and the uncovenanted services, accounted for a rapid increase in the number of Britons entering India during this period. The nonofficial population exploded from little more than two thousand prior to the removal of restrictions on their entry in the early 1830s to nearly fifty thousand by 1861 and seventy thousand by 1871. As we have already seen, an increasing portion of the European population consisted of women, and their appearance also suggested the development of a larger and more significant domiciled community. While most railway engineers, telegraph operators, postal clerks, policemen, planters, boxwallahs, and others of similar socioeconomic standing could not afford to send their children back to England for schooling, they realized that an English-style education was important to their children's career chances. This was the principal social stratum that the hill schools tapped for fee-paying pupils.

At the same time, the colonial state and its ruling elite were growing concerned about the increasing numbers of poor whites in India. They were the inevitable residuum of the enlarged uncovenanted and nonofficial population, the underclass of unemployed workers, discharged sailors, abandoned and widowed women, orphaned children, alcoholics, lunatics, and others who lived on the margins of European society, often resorting to beggary, burglary, and prostitution to survive. Their presence was a reproach to British assertions of superiority, a menace to the social, moral, and above all racial underpinnings of the colonial order. Imperial authorities responded to this threat in two distinct ways: adults they sought to deport or incarcerate in workhouses, prisons, hospitals, asylums, and other holding facilities, claiming them to be incorrigible, but orphans and other

52. Price, *Ootacamund*, 96; Burton, *Goa*, 285; Eden, *Up the Country*, 102.

children they considered redeemable when placed in suitable environments, such as orphanages and similarly regimented educational institutions, particularly when those institutions were removed from the subversive influences of the plains.[53]

The Lawrence Military Asylum was the earliest and most influential institution established to redeem orphans and other poor white children by transferring them to the hills. Its founder was the famed imperial consul Henry Lawrence, whose Evangelical solicitude for barrack children's moral and social fate inspired him in 1845 to propose the establishment of a military-style boarding school in the Indian highlands for the sons and daughters of British soldiers. His aim, as he described it, was to create "an Asylum from the debilitating effects of the tropical climate, and the demoralizing influence of Barrack-life; wherein they may obtain the benefits of a bracing climate, a healthy moral atmosphere, and a plain, useful, and above all religious education, adapted to fit them for employment suited to their position in life." Although Anglo-Indian children could and did gain admittance, Lawrence insisted that preference be given to children of "pure European parentage" since they were "more likely to suffer from the climate of the plains."[54] The first of these military asylums was opened at Sanawar near Simla in 1847, its construction financed by donations from fellow officers and a large grant from the maharaja of Kashmir. Subsequent branches appeared at Mount Abu in 1854, Ootacamund (later moved over a ridge to Lovedale) in 1858, and Murree in 1860, by which point the government had assumed responsibility for their finances. The success of the Lawrence Asylums was confirmed by the decision to close the government orphanages in Calcutta and Madras and to send their inmates to these highland institutions in 1872.[55]

The Lawrence Asylums offered an education that stressed discipline, obedience, piety, respectability, and acquiescence to a future of limited opportunity. Boys wore artillery uniforms, girls drab jackets and white bonnets, and both were divided into military-style companies that marched

53. See David Arnold, "European Orphans and Vagrants in India in the Nineteenth Century," *Journal of Imperial and Commonwealth History* 7, no. 2 (Jan. 1979), 104–27; and Kenneth Ballhatchet, *Race, Sex and Class under the Raj: Imperial Attitudes and Policies and Their Critics, 1793–1905* (New York, 1980), ch. 5.

54. Quoted in *The Lawrence Military Asylum* (Sanawur, 1858), 3 and Appendix, i. Edwardes and Merivale, *Life of Sir Henry Lawrence*, vol. 2, gives an account of the origin of the Lawrence Asylum.

55. Arnold, "European Orphans," 108.

on parade grounds. They did not depend on Indian servants; they did most tasks themselves so that they would become "trained in industrial habits."[56] Lawrence envisioned his wards taking up manual trades like carpentry and smithing, creating the nucleus for a British artisanal class in India. The schools' directors, however, soon realized this goal was not feasible in the face of indigenous competition.[57] Instead, the most talented boys were trained in telegraphy, civil engineering, and other skills that prepared them for employment in the technical branches of government service, while the rest enlisted in the army or obtained work with the railroads. The girls received training for domestic service, but for most the future lay with the noncommissioned officers who "came up to select them as fast as they could be married."[58] David Arnold observes rather pointedly that, "for all the concern to rescue them from the barracks and the backstreets, the orphans were trained and fed back into society at almost precisely the same level at which they had been extracted from it."[59] Although Arnold is right, Lawrence and his followers never intended the asylums to become vehicles for social mobility, ladders on which young unfortunates could climb their way into the ranks of the covenanted class. Rather, the founders wanted these institutions to instill the moral discipline and occupational skills that their pupils would need to live as respectable members of the British working class in India, content with their social lot yet aware of their racial responsibilities.

Lawrence's conviction that the redemption of poor white youths lay in their removal to the hills was shared by other authorities, who sought to extend the opportunity for a highland education beyond those born in the barracks. In 1860, Bishop Cotton of Calcutta called upon the government to take the initiative on behalf of European and Anglo-Indian children who were in "great moral and spiritual danger" because their parents could not afford to provide them with a proper education. A Cambridge-educated cleric who had been a master at Thomas Arnold's Rugby and the first headmaster of Marlborough prior to his Indian appointment, Bishop Cotton envisioned a string of boarding schools arising in the hill stations, each of them modeled after the newly reformed, Christian-infused public schools of England. His entreaty helped to persuade the governor-general,

56. *A Guide to the Neilgherries*, 29.
57. Lawrence's views appear in Edwardes and Merivale, *Life of Sir Henry Lawrence*, vol. 2, 34.
58. Russell, *My Diary in India*, vol. 2, 140.
59. Arnold, "European Orphans," 111.

Lord Canning, to issued an important minute on education in late 1860. In this minute, Canning emphatically endorsed the Bishop's plan. He addressed the dangers that the lack of schooling among poor European and Anglo-Indian children posed not only for their souls but for the colonial order as well: "if measures for educating these children are not promptly and vigorously encouraged and aided by the Government, we shall soon find ourselves embarrassed in all large towns and stations with a floating population of Indianized English, loosely brought up, and exhibiting most of the worst qualities of both races; whilst the Eurasian population . . . will increase more rapidly than ever." Unless immediate measures were taken to forestall these developments, the children would present "a glaring reproach to the Government" and give rise to "a class dangerous to the State." Canning announced his intention to act with what many of his contemporaries must have seen as great audacity given the religious rivalries and suspicions that plagued British educational policy at home and abroad: he promised government grants for all Christian denominations—Nonconformist and Catholic as well as Anglican—that established schools for European children in the hills. The matter was regarded as too important to be held hostage to denominational differences. However, Canning drew a rigid line between the education of Europeans and that of Anglo-Indians. Anglo-Indians, he felt, would be best served by day schools on the plains, especially since "the climate of the hills . . . is held to be injurious to them, if at all weakly."[60]

Canning's minute was, in the words of an official writing a dozen years later, "the Magna Carta of European education in India."[61] It provided the financial security that made possible the proliferation of boarding schools in the Indian highlands. Many of the newly founded hill schools were all-male institutions. St. Paul's, an Anglican school originally located in Calcutta, was moved to Darjeeling in 1864. The Church of England also established a school in Simla named in memory of Bishop Cotton (1866), and diocesan schools in Mussoorie (1867), Naini Tal (1869), and Panchgani (1876). The Catholics opened St. Thomas College of Murree (1882) and St. Joseph's of Darjeeling (1888) (Figure 9), of Naini Tal (1889), and of Coonoor (1889), in addition to expanding the pre–Canning-era schools, St. George's of Mussoorie (1853) and St. Joseph's of Ootacamund (1854). The

60. Bishop Cotton's remarks and Lord Canning's minute appear in A. J. Lawrence, *Report on the Existing Schools for Europeans and Eurasians throughout India* (Calcutta, 1873), 1–4.
61. Ibid., 5.

Figure 9.   St. Joseph's College, Darjeeling. Photograph by the author.

American Protestant missions sponsored Oak Openings at Naini Tal (1880) and the Philander Smith Institute in Mussoorie (1885). Several nondenominational institutions also arose, notably Stanes' School in Coonoor (1861), Breeks' Memorial School in Ootacamund (1873), and the Modern School of Mussoorie (1896).

Educational opportunities in the hills were no less abundant for girls. Roman Catholics dominated the field, with the Loreto Convents particularly active. In addition to the branches it founded in Darjeeling and Ootacamund in the premutiny era, this Irish order opened schools in Murree (1876), Naini Tal (1878), Kurseong (1890), Simla (1895), and Shillong (date unknown). Other Catholic institutions for girls were the Convent of Jesus and Mary in Simla (1866), the Nazareth Convent School in Ootacamund (1875), and St. Joseph's Convent in Coonoor (1900). The Anglicans countered with Cainville House, Mussoorie (1864), Auckland House, Simla (1866), diocesan schools at Naini Tal (1869) and Darjeeling (1875), and St. Denys' School, Murree (1882). The American Presbyterian Mission took over the preexisting Woodstock House of Mussoorie (1872); the American Methodist Episcopal Church opened Wellesley School in Naini Tal (1880); and the Calcutta Christian Schools Society founded Queen's Hill School of Darjeeling (1895). Nondenominational schools included Wynberg, Mussoorie (1894), Hampton Court, Mussoorie (1895),

Petersfield, Naini Tal (1899), and Arycliff, Simla (1888), which subsequently affiliating with the Church of Scotland.

In addition to these institutions, a myriad of other schools arose in the hill stations. Most were private coeducational enterprises operated by widows and unmarried women in private homes. Some, such as Miss Twentyman's Darjeeling Home School for "young ladies" and boys under the age of ten, established themselves as successful, even venerable, institutions. The life of a great many others, however, was fleeting. Only one of the four schools for younger children referred to in an 1857 guidebook to Ootacamund was noted by Burton during his stay at the station in 1851, and none received mention in subsequent guidebooks.[62] A succession of these dame schools no doubt opened their doors and closed them a few years later.

Despite the intentions of Bishop Cotton and Lord Canning, the large denominational hill schools drew most of their students from the middle levels of British society in India, while doing their best to keep the lower orders out. Several government reports provide detailed information on the occupations of pupils' fathers. They included planters, merchants, missionaries, engineers, railway officials, clerks, and others employed in the uncovenanted services, but not the elite members of the Indian Civil Service or the Indian Army. As a general rule, "every European in India who can afford to send his children to Europe to be educated, does so. Similarly, it may be said in almost equally general terms that every parent, who can afford it, sends his children to the hills in preference to a school in the plains."[63]

The hill schools modeled their appearance and approach after English public schools, pitching themselves both to those parents who wanted their child to obtain the schooling needed to prepare them for "finishing" at an English institution and to those who wanted their child to receive the benefits of an English-style education without incurring the financial cost or facing the emotional loss entailed in sending them to England. For example, St. Paul's of Darjeeling was said to provide an education "after the model of the best English public schools," St. George's College of Mussoorie was "conducted after the best models of the English public school system," and St. Joseph's of Coonoor operated "on the lines of that given

---

62. Robert Baikie, *The Neilgherries,* 2d ed. (Calcutta, 1857), Appendix, iv.
63. Committee upon the Financial Condition of Hill Schools for Europeans in Northern India, Vol. 1: *Report* (Simla, 1904), 11. This report and Lawrence, *Report on the Existing Schools,* are filled with information about the occupations of parents.

in an English public school."[64] Students wore school jackets, played cricket on the pitch, and shared in their governance through the prefect system.[65] Some schools specialized in preparing students for transfer to particular home institutions, and the majority designed their curricula with the Cambridge Local exams in mind. At the turn of the century, a third of the boys who enrolled in the Himalayan hill schools went to England for further education (the figure for girls was one-sixth).[66] However, it was the other two-thirds (or five-sixths) who received the bulk of attention. Hill schools promised an education specially suited to those who did not leave India, an education that usually led to careers in the provincial or uncovenanted service for boys and to marriage for girls. They prepared male students for entry into administrative departments such as public works, surveys, police, opium, salt, telegraph, mail, forestry, subordinate medical service, and customs. Some institutions provided industrial training courses, including technical classes in civil and mechanical engineering.[67] St. Joseph's of Darjeeling specialized in preparing students for Rurki College, an engineering school, and most other schools established close ties with particular branches of the provincial service. After all, their reputations depended ultimately upon their success in garnering respectable jobs for their graduates, and those jobs were generally to be found in government.

Equally important to the reputations of hill schools was the racial composition of their student body. Although the state defined European schools as those that catered to pure *and* mixed-race Europeans who retained "European habits or modes of life,"[68] Anglo-Indians were not welcome at most of the better schools, and Indians were almost entirely prohibited from enrolling in them until the interwar years. British parents often objected to their children rubbing shoulders with mixed-race students. M. M. Kaye and her sister were pulled out of Simla's Auckland House by their horrified

64. L. S. S. O'Malley, *Darjeeling* (Calcutta, 1907), 178; T. Kinney, *The Echo Guide to Mussoorie* (Mussoorie, 1908), 78; *Madras District Gazetteers, Statistical Appendix for the Nilgiri District* (Madras, 1928), 66.

65. See the observations about St. Paul's of Darjeeling by Oscar Browning, *Impressions of Indian Travel* (London, 1903), 38.

66. Committee upon the Financial Condition of Hill Schools for Europeans in Northern India, *Report*, 12.

67. Dick B. Dewan, *Education in the Darjeeling Hills: An Historical Survey, 1835–1985* (New Delhi, 1991), 196.

68. Austin A. D'Souza, *Anglo-Indian Education: A Study of Its Origins and Growth in Bengal up to 1960* (Delhi, 1976), 6. The problems posed by this definition of "European" are alluded to by Alfred Mercer, *Report on the Progress of Education of European Children during the Quinquennium 1912–13—1916–17* (Calcutta, 1917), 1.

mother when they began to acquire the so-called "chi-chi" accent of Anglo-Indian classmates.[69] Breeks' School in Ootacamund led a highly checkered existence, with several financial crises and restructurings, because it failed to overcome its origins as a day school for poor Europeans, Anglo-Indians, and Indians.[70] It lacked the simple expedient most hill schools had to restrict the entry of undesirables—boarding fees. Bishop Cotton School was taken to task by the government of India for prohibiting the sons of Simla's "subordinate officials," mostly Anglo-Indians, from attending the institution as day students. But school authorities objected that day students "are not as amenable to discipline as boarders are; they are less regular in their attendance; they carry home school tales; and in many ways are a thorn in the flesh to masters." They went on to insist that the cultural shortcomings of Anglo-Indian households made students from such environments unsuitable for Bishop Cotton School.[71] This episode was characteristic of efforts by hill schools in the late nineteenth and early twentieth centuries to improve their reputations by imposing racial and social barriers to admission. Among the more dramatic examples was the transformation of Stanes' School in Coonoor from a day school for poor Europeans and Anglo-Indians to a high school divided into two sections, with the first serving the "sons of officials and missionaries."[72] Adding to the forces that ratcheted the social composition of the hill schools as high as it would go was the increasing expense of education in England. More and more parents were persuaded in the late nineteenth century to delay or even abandon the overseas education of their children.

As the elite schools sought to solidify their social standing through restrictive practices, the educational needs of poorer children attracted renewed attention. An inquiry by the Bengal department of education in 1875 aroused calls for the establishment of hill schools for children who occupied those subordinate tiers of society where Europeans and Anglo-Indians most often merged.[73] The railway companies began to establish

69. Kaye, *The Sun in the Morning,* 194–95.

70. See the references to Breeks' School in the Ootacamund Municipal Reports, 1888–89, 1892–93, 1894–95, 1897–98, 1899–1900, 1900–1, TNSA; and Price, *Ootacamund,* 96.

71. This correspondence appears in Lawrence, *Report on the Existing Schools,* 121–23.

72. *The Visitors' Handbook of the Nilgiris* (Madras, 1897), 58–59; Eagan, *The Nilgiri Guide,* 152–53.

73. See the correspondence in Education Department, June 1875, File 70, Proceedings of the Lieutenant Governor of Bengal, WBSA.

schools for the children of their British and Anglo-Indian employees, and although these schools sprang up across the subcontinent, some of the most notable ones were placed in the hills. The Victoria School of Kurseong began as a coeducational institution for the children of Bengal railway workers in 1879, although it subsequently became an all-male boarding school open to others. A separate facility for girls, the Dow Hill School, was established in 1897. The Bombay Baroda and Central India Railway founded a school in Mount Abu in 1887; later, it was christened St. Mary's High School and began to admit nonrailway pupils. The East India Railway School of Mussoorie appeared around 1888, and the Great Indian Peninsular Railway sponsored a school at Lonavala. Various other institutions in the hills served orphans and other children on the margins of European society. Three orphanages were established in Mussoorie—one Anglican, one Catholic, and one Nonconformist—as was the Summer Home for Soldiers' Children (its purpose evident in its name), which strictly prohibited the admission of Anglo-Indian pupils.[74] Simla was the site of the Himalayan Christian Orphanage and Industrial School, later renamed the Mayo Industrial School. Other institutions for poor European and Anglo-Indian children included St. Andrew's Colonial Homes of Kalimpong (1900), Goethal's Memorial School of Kurseong (1907), and St. George's Homes of Kodaikanal (1914), which later moved to Keti, in the Nilgiris. Note should be taken of the sites selected for these institutions. They, like the Lawrence Asylums, were located more often in the secondary and satellite stations than in the central ones—Kurseong and Kalimpong rather than Darjeeling, Lovedale and Keti rather than Ootacamund, Sanawar rather than Simla—suggesting that their pupils' social standing made it desirable to keep them at a distance from the major hill stations.

Most of these institutions shared the same goal as the Lawrence Asylums—to imbue their wards with the Christian rectitude and work ethos that would prepare them for their place in society. "No attempt has been made here . . . to raise the children out of their natural position in life," declared one visitor to the Mayo Industrial School. The pupils of this all-female institution were taught needlework and other "industrial occupations." Some Indian children were admitted to the school in its early years but only as servants, and the experiment ended in 1872, most likely because of fears that the European and Anglo-Indian children would ac-

74. John Northam, *Guide to Masuri, Landaur, Dehra Dun, and the Hills North of Dehra* (Calcutta, 1884), 57.

quire inflated opinions about their own station in life.[75] Indian servants
were strictly prohibited from St. Andrew's Colonial Homes as a way of
"removing the distaste for manual labour which is characteristic of the
Anglo-Indian and poor European . . . [and thereby] instilling principles of
self-respect, self-reliance and self-help." The same was true of St. George's
Homes: "no servants are employed so that from infancy the children learn
to do everything for themselves; . . . the Homes try and equip them to play
their part as good citizens of the country of their birth—India."[76] And what
part was this? Most of the male graduates of St. George's Homes and its
counterparts found work on the railways and in other industries where
Europeans were in demand to supervise Indian laborers, while the girls got
jobs as hospital and children's nurses or, more often, found husbands and
nursed their own children. One notable exception was St. Andrew's Colonial Homes, where boys worked at the school's farms in preparation for
their emigration from India to Australia or New Zealand: the governors of
the school believed there was no place for their wards in India.[77]

By the turn of the century, hill stations had become the primary locus
of European education in India. To be sure, a number of children continued
to attend schools in the plains, and many others did not go to school at all.
A study conducted in 1879 found that nearly half of the European and
Anglo-Indian children of Bengal were receiving no formal education, but
these were mainly Anglo-Indians living in the slums of Calcutta.[78] The
children who counted most in the imperial scheme of things—those of
"pure" European descent—were likely to attend a hill school at some point
in their youth. The Himalayan region alone harbored some sixty educational institutions with enrollments totaling around fifty-four hundred in
1905.[79] The only school on the plains to rival the reputations of the better
hill schools was the Lucknow Martinière. Otherwise, parents who sought
a respectable education for their children in India or an adequate preparation for their entry into a British public school sent them to the hills,

75. W. H. Carey, comp., *A Guide to Simla with a Descriptive Account of the
Neighbouring Sanitaria* (Calcutta, 1870), 55–56; Punjab Government, *Gazetteer of
the Simla District, 1888–89* (Calcutta, n.d.), 89.
76. *Newman's Guide to Darjeeling and Neighbourhood*, 6th ed. (Calcutta,
1919), 47–48; *Madras District Gazetteers, Statistical Appendix for the Nilgiri
District, 1928*, 70.
77. Dewan, *Education in the Darjeeling Hills*, 187–88, 197.
78. D'Souza, *Anglo-Indian Education*, 115.
79. Arnold, "European Orphans," 109.

while even those who occupied the lower levels of the colonial order found it increasingly feasible for their children to enroll in highland institutions.

The European hill schools had enormous significance for the raj. They made it possible to remove the younger generation from the dangers that lay lurking in the plains without removing them from India altogether. The sons and daughters of poor whites, as well as other British children, were inculcated in the hill schools with the social and cultural values that set them apart from Indians. These schools allowed the British to envision the prospect of their permanent domicile in the subcontinent without fear that physical and moral degeneration would inevitably ensue. A passage from the prospectus of St. Andrew's Colonial Homes explained its intent: "it is a well known fact that the domiciled community deteriorates in the environments of a tropical country and oriental standards; and the object of the Homes is to break down the influence of heredity and of such environments, by removing the children at an early age to surroundings which are healthier, both physically and morally, than the towns in the plains."[80] This statement might be translated as follows: it is clear that the British cannot retain the racial solidarity upon which their imperial position depends if their children grow up in an environment that dissolves the cultural identity meant to distinguish them as representatives of a ruling elite; to maintain and strengthen this identity necessitates their physical removal from the forces that subvert it and their immersion in a total institution that inculcates the values appropriate to the place they have been deemed by authorities to occupy within the imperial system. Simply put, the hill schools held the promise of the social and ideological reproduction of Britain's imperial emissaries.

---

Ann Stoler has sought in several important articles to rehistoricize our understanding of the social world of European colonizers. She argues that the social identity of the colonizers was never unproblematic, that it was in fact repeatedly beset by pressures that required a refashioning of what it meant to be part of the privileged order. Central to the endeavor to define affinities and align boundaries was the regulation of reproduction, and hence of women. "What is striking," Stoler observes, "when we look to identify the contours and composition of any particular colonial community is the extent to which control over sexuality and reproduction [was]

80. Quoted in *Newman's Guide to Darjeeling,* 47.

at the core of defining colonial privilege and its boundaries."[81] Stoler's insights help us to discern the significance of the hill stations' peculiar demographic attributes. They alert us to the fact that the unusual concentration of women and children in these enclaves constituted a message about the construction of a British colonial identity. And that message was the determination of colonizers to isolate the agents of their reproduction from the alien influences of the realm they ruled and thereby to retain and renew the cultural and ethnic markers that set them apart.

This endeavor was played out in terms of a public/private dichotomy that stood at the center of the bourgeois liberal ethos. From the British perspective, the public sphere was the world of business, politics, and the state; the private sphere was the world of women, children, and the family: the distinction lay between production and reproduction. Situated as they were in the profoundly public role of rulers over a foreign land, the British found it difficult to carve out a space for their private lives. Hill stations arose in part to supply that space. The physical remoteness of these enclaves was a measure of their distance from the public obligations of imperial authority, and their attraction for large numbers of women and children was a testimony to their success in constituting a private domestic domain. Here was a realm insulated from the repercussions of power where those who oversaw the raj could renew themselves, produce their scions, and reaffirm the creed that sustained their imperial endeavors.

81. Ann Laura Stoler, "Rethinking Colonial Categories: European Communities and the Boundaries of Rule," *Comparative Studies in Society and History* 13, no. 1 (1989): 154. Also see Ann Laura Stoler, "Making Empire Respectable: The Politics of Race and Sexual Morality in 20th-Century Colonial Cultures," *American Ethnologist* 16, no. 4 (Nov. 1989): 634–59.

# 7 The Pinnacles of Power

There is nothing that is not political. Everything is politics.
—Thomas Mann, *The Magic Mountain*

Delhi, most certainly, is not the symbol of India's slavery. The place which is the real headquarters of the rulers is Simla.
—Mahatma Gandhi, "Five Hundredth Storey"

The British presence in India was mainly political in nature. The imperial state's civil and military servants made up the overwhelming majority of the subcontinent's European population, and their role was a clear one—to rule. Whether this rule found expression in the brute force of military campaigns and police actions, the stately ceremonials of parades and durbars, the daily decisions of political agents and district commissioners, or the numerous other forms through which the colonial state exercised power, it occurred within what was seen as the public sphere.

Although the British found the hill stations enticing places to which to escape from their imperial obligations, these havens of private pleasure assumed public roles as well. This claim may seem odd, but its incongruity recedes when we recall that the private and public were bound together in a dialectical web. The outlines of this web could be discerned even in the hill stations' high concentrations of women and children, those parties thought to be least implicated in the public sphere. As Linda Colley has observed with regard to British society, the existence of separate spheres affirmed that the woman was "indispensable to the well-being of the state through her private influence on her citizen husband and education of her children."[1] If women played this role in the homeland, they did so even more emphatically in the colonial realm. The British recognized that one of the greatest threats to their rule in India was the erosion of cohesion within their ranks, the loss of a sense of common identity and purpose under the onslaught of alien influences; and it was precisely for this reason that they gathered their women and children together in highland cottages and schools where the values essential for the continuation of their power

1. Linda Colley, *Britons: Forging the Nation 1707–1837* (New Haven, 1992), 273.

could be cultivated. What occurred within those domestic and institutional walls was never as fully detached from the public realm of the raj as it seemed.

Nor were the reputations of hill stations as purely private sites inconsistent with the increasing importance they acquired as seasonal headquarters for various official agencies. In the second half of the nineteenth century, the public sphere began to intrude directly on Simla and many of its sister stations through the formal transfer of government offices to these summer resorts. The main impetus for this move was the great mutiny and rebellion. What had previously been individual officials' personal preferences for holidays in the hills was transformed in the aftermath of the events of 1857–58 into a formal policy of shifting various government headquarters into the higher elevations during the hot months. At least in part, this annual migration occurred because the hill stations appeared aloof and secure; they seemed immune from the paroxysms that had shaken imperial authority in the plains. The intent behind the retreat of the government to the hills, then, was to make it difficult for Indians to breach the walls of power. Yet this security could be achieved only by turning the hill stations themselves into public places. They became increasingly drawn into the political processes of the colonial realm, with the result being their inexorable erosion as places apart from the rest of India.

———

How could the British maintain their control over India's multitudes? This question lay at the heart of every decision made by the representatives of the raj but especially the one that determined the size and the role of the British population on the subcontinent. The planting of settlers in foreign soils had been an integral feature of British colonialism in its early Irish and North American manifestations, but in South Asia it showed little promise. For over a century and a half, the British had clung to the margins of this densely populated land, surviving because of the sufferance of Indian rulers. The prospects for colonists remained slight even after the East India Company wrested control from the Mughal empire and its successor states in the late eighteenth and early nineteenth centuries. The company extracted its profits from the indigenous inhabitants. Its European agents consisted of a small administrative elite—whose collective goal was to acquire a fortune and retire to an English landed estate—and a much larger body of mostly lower-class Irish and Scottish troops, whose death rate was so high that the fate of those few who managed to make it through their lengthy terms of service was a matter of little concern. Not until the company lost its monopoly in 1833 did a significant number of planters, merchants, and other independent entrepreneurs enter the country to seek their fortunes, but few of them showed much inclination to raise their children and live out their lives in this distant land. India remained a realm distinct and separate from the settler colonies of the empire.[2]

Most authorities strongly objected to white colonists, and for good reasons.[3] As the American experience had shown, colonists tended to be politically contentious, often raising their voices against imperial rule and stirring up strife with native peoples. They also presented social problems by engendering a large poor-white and mixed-race population that blurred the boundaries between ruler and ruled and thereby weakened British claims of superiority. Nor did they offer significant economic advantages in India since most could find no viable niche in a society that already possessed a large and productive indigenous population of farmers, artisans, merchants, and others.[4] Lord William Bentinck did suggest in an abortive 1829 minute that the East India Company support European settlement as a means of diffusing Western skills and values among Indians, but the London court of directors dismissed the proposal as "absurd," and Bentinck himself conceded that the country offered little or no opportunity for the average emigrant from Britain.[5]

Yet the vision of an India colonized by white settlers never fully faded from view: it shimmered like a mirage over the highland regions of the

2. European settlement in India has been examined by David Arnold, "White Colonization and Labour in Nineteenth-Century India," *Journal of Imperial and Commonwealth History* 9, no. 2 (Jan. 1983): 133–58; P. J. Marshall, "The Whites of British India, 1780–1830: A Failed Colonial Society?" *International History Review* 12, no. 1 (Feb. 1990): 26–44; Raymond K. Renford, *The Non-official British in India to 1920* (Delhi, 1987), ch. 1; and John Riddy, "Some Official British Attitudes towards European Settlement and Colonization in India up to 1865," in *Essays in Indian History*, ed. Donovan Williams and E. Daniel Potts (London, 1973), 17–41.

3. See C. A. Bayly, *Imperial Meridian: The British Empire and the World, 1780–1830* (London, 1989), ch. 3.

4. Ironically, this view was often shared by members of the nonofficial commercial community in India. In an 1833 pamphlet demanding greater rights for Europeans under East India Company rule, the author sought to deflect criticisms that colonists were not "sufficiently respectable" by arguing that it was only "the highest class" that could establish itself on the subcontinent. "The poorer classes of society could not find their way to India; or, when there, could not find employment." John Crawford, *Notes on the Settlement or Colonization of British Subjects in India* (London, 1833), 23.

5. C. H. Philips, ed., *The Correspondence of Lord William Cavendish Bentinck*, vol. 1 (Oxford, 1977), 201–13, 225.

subcontinent. Some of the earliest advocates of hill stations were enthusiastic about their potential as sites for permanent colonies of Europeans. They argued that the elevation and isolation of the highlands would allow settlers to thrive there. Particular interest was paid to the Nilgiris. The commander of the Pioneer Corps, which constructed the first road into the Nilgiris, argued in a series of letters to the *Madras Gazette* that the region was an ideal location in which officials could retire, soldiers could recuperate, and merchants and farmers could prosper. He urged authorities to grant tracts of land to planters, suggesting in a prescient aside that coffee and tea held promise as commercial crops.[6] Others advocated the Nilgiris as a site for colonization, notably the medical officer and publicist for Ootacamund in its early years, Robert Baikie.[7]

Far to the north, an officer in the Bengal cavalry spoke of the Himalayas as "a great natural fortification, a stronghold for Europeans."[8] This was a tempting vision, and among those taken by it was Major-General Sir S. F. Whittingham, the commander of the Meerut and Cawnpore divisions of the army. In 1830 he urged Lord Bentinck to offer soldiers grants of land in the area around Mussoorie in lieu of pensions. In a flight of fancy, he envisioned a feudal-like colony of veterans ensconced in the Dehra Dun valley below Mussoorie, where they would raise pigs, chickens, and other products for the local market, while on the heights above "well behaved Europeans might hope to be taken into the service of gentlemen having estates on the hills, as overseers."[9]

This desire to re-create the lineaments of English agrarian society in the Indian highlands inspired several settlement schemes in the 1820s and 1830s. The Madras council approved a modest plan in 1825 to send five British military pensioners to the Nilgiris, where they were to be given land, tools, livestock, and other supplies necessary to establish themselves as small farmers. What became of this endeavor is unclear, but again in 1830 the government of Madras issued orders to provide plots of land and

6. Major William Murray, *An Account of the Neilgherries, or, Blue Mountains of Coimbatore, in Southern India* (London, 1834), 27, 32, 37, 43.

7. Robert Baikie, *Observations on the Neilgherries*, ed. W. H. Smoult (Calcutta, 1834), 39. Another early commentator recommended the colonization of the Nilgiris by "Eurasians or Indo-Britons," but this proposal cut against the grain of the efforts to establish ethnic enclaves in the highlands, and it received little attention or support. See James Hough, *Letters on the Climate, Inhabitants, Productions, etc. of the Neilgherries, or Blue Mountains of Coimbatoor* (London, 1829), 137–38.

8. Capt. H. Drummond, *Notes on the Colonization of the Himalayas* (Edinburgh, 1845), 3.

9. Philips, *Correspondence*, 456.

tools to fifty-six invalid soldiers, whom it hoped would become the nucleus for a community of "small farmers of hardy, active, persevering and industrious habits" in the Nilgiris.[10] At about the same time, a number of East India Company pensioners began to congregate in Dehra Dun, and many of them acquired summer cottages in Mussoorie. Few, however, took up farming, so in 1838 the government sought to encourage the development of European commercial agriculture in the area by alienating large tracts of land. The scheme came to an ignominious end when it became clear that most of the property had gone to officials whose intentions were almost entirely speculative.[11] Nor did the Nilgiri effort to place pensioners on small holdings leave any perceptible trace. The popular explanation for the failure was that the "class of men" who remained in India on pensions "but rarely offer an example of industry or sobriety, while the effects of their long residence in the low country, added to their (generally) advanced age, render them . . . insensible to the advantages of the change" to the hills.[12]

Many members of the colonial administration doubted whether even the most industrious and sober British pensioners could succeed as small farmers. When in 1856 the Indian government inquired into the prospects for settling retired army officers and soldiers on the land, officials all across India responded in the same vein: alienable land was too scarce, hired help too dear, Indian farmers too fierce as competitors, and British pensioners too poorly prepared for the physical demands of agricultural labor.[13] Although the report that summarized these reactions did refer to Darjeeling and the Nilgiris as possible sites for colonization, it concluded that India otherwise offered little or no hope for white settlers.

Brian Hodgson, the British envoy to Nepal, was the only official among the respondents to express enthusiastic support for European colonization. He devised a scheme that went well beyond the bounds of the government's inquiry about army pensioners, suggesting that large numbers of impecunious Scottish and Irish peasants be planted in the Himalayas. As he saw

10. See report dated 10 Nov. 1830, E/4/939, Madras Dispatches, IOL; and PP, *Papers Relative to the Formation of a Sanitarium on the Neilgherries for European Troops,* Session 729, XLI, 1850, 29, 34–35, 50.

11. G.R.C. Williams, *Historical and Statistical Memoir of Dehra Doon* (Roorkee, 1874), 314–32; Capt. O.E.S. Powers, *Dehra Dun Past and Present: Guide and Directory to Dehra and the Doon District* (Dehra Dun, 1929), 4–5.

12. Baikie, *Observations,* 39.

13. See the correspondence reprinted in "Report on the Transactions of the Government of India in the Military Department in 1856–57," in *General Report on the Administration of the Several Presidencies and Provinces of British India, 1856–57,* pt. 1 (Calcutta, 1858), 1–25.

it, they could supply wholesome foodstuffs for themselves and other Britons in India, as well as provide "some fifty to one hundred thousand loyal hearts and stalwart bodies of Saxon mould" (an honorary upgrade for peoples usually sniffed at as Celts) to serve as a reserve force against internal threats to imperial rule.[14] While Hodgson's voice may have been a lonely one within the government in 1856, various individuals and groups outside its ranks were calling for the creation of European colonies in the highlands.[15] Perhaps the most prominent of these advocates was Hyde Clarke, an agent for Indian railway and planter interests. In 1857 he published *Colonization, Defence and Railways in Our Indian Empire,* a book that provided detailed accounts of the development of Darjeeling, Simla, and some twenty other hill stations around the subcontinent. Its main purpose was to persuade readers (especially the governors of the East India Company, to whom it was dedicated) that the construction of the railway and telegraph made possible the colonization of the highlands with European planters, soldiers, invalids, pensioners, and others. Clarke, like Hodgson, believed these colonists would supply a "copious reserve" prepared to sweep down from their highland abodes at the earliest signs of trouble on the plains: "the colonization of the hill regions of India with English will give us a hold which can never be shaken off."[16]

Composed immediately prior to the outbreak of revolt in 1857, the strategic arguments of Clarke and Hodgson acquired a prophetic quality as disorder swept northern India. The realization that a large body of colonists might provide a useful line of defense against rebellion convinced Parliament in 1857 to appoint a select committee to investigate the prospects for European colonization in India. After collecting five fat volumes of testimony, however, the committee concluded that the subcontinent was best suited for "a class of superior settlers" who could serve as overseers of Indian laborers. It believed that the colony offered scant "inducements to

14. Hodgson's report reappears under the title "On the Colonization of the Himalaya by Europeans" in B. H. Hodgson, *Essays on the Languages, Literature and Religion of Nepal and Tibet,* pt. 2 (1874; reprint, Varanasi, 1971), 83–89.

15. See, for example, the claims for Darjeeling as a suitable site for European settlers in *Friend of India,* 20 Nov. 1856, cited in Capt. J. G. Hathorn, *A Hand-Book of Darjeeling* (Calcutta, 1863), 110, and in the pamphlet *Darjeeling,* reprinted from the *Calcutta Review,* no. 55 (1857): 29. Robert Baikie, *The Neilgherries,* 2d ed. (Calcutta, 1857), makes much the same claim for the Nilgiris.

16. Hyde Clarke, *Colonization, Defence and Railways in Our Indian Empire* (London, 1857), 126. Also see his postmutiny assessment, "On the Organization of the Army of India, with Especial Reference to the Hill Regions," *Journal of the Royal United Service Institution* 3 (1860): 18–27.

the settlement of the working classes of the British Isles" because of the harshness of the tropical climate, the scarcity of alienable land, and the abundance of indigenous labor.[17] These conclusions seemed so sweeping in their rejection of white colonization that most historians have lost sight of a subtext that made an exception of the highland regions. The committee expressed its confidence that the hills could serve as sites for permanent colonies of Europeans. Its views were shaped by the testimony of those who claimed some knowledge of the Indian highlands.

Major-General George Tremenheer, the first person to testify to the committee, set the tone for the inquiry by insisting that India's general unsuitability for colonization did not apply to the hill stations. The precipitous terrain of the Himalayas prevented colonization on "a large scale," he conceded, but the example of the Lawrence Asylum convinced him that many poor Europeans who currently languished in the plains could become productive if transferred to the hills. Send the children of British soldiers and similarly marginal Europeans to the Himalayas, he urged, where they might be protected from the degenerative influences on the plains and trained in the mechanical and other skills appropriate for the supervision of Indian laborers.[18] The benefits of the highlands for domiciled European children and their parents were stressed by other witnesses as well. A veteran of twenty-five years of service in the Bombay presidency recommended Mahabaleshwar as a convalescent station for British soldiers and as an asylum for their children.[19] Dr. James Ranald Martin, a leading authority on the diseases of India, advocated the removal of all British troops to highland cantonments.[20] Captain John Ouchterlony, an army engineer who had spent several years in the Nilgiris, testified at great length about their potential for colonization, insisting that European planters, soldiers, pensioners, women, and children could reside there in health and security.[21] Numerous people who had worked in India in nonofficial capacities also voiced enthusiasm for hill colonies. Thus, it is hardly sur-

17. PP, *Report from the Select Committee on Colonization and Settlement (India)* (1859), Session 2, V, iii.

18. PP, *First Report from the Select Committee* (1858), Session 1857–58, VII, pt. 1, 1–13. Tremenheere also urged that access to the hill stations be improved by constructing rail lines to the foot of the ranges where they were located.

19. Major George Wingate, in PP, *Fourth Report from the Select Committee* (1858). Session 1857–58, VII, pt. 2, 56.

20. PP, *First Report from the Select Committee* (1858), Session 1857–58, VII, pt. 1, 18.

21. PP, *Third Report from the Select Committee* (1858), Session 1857–58, VII, pt. 1, 1–41.

prising that the committee itself reached the conclusion that the highland regions of India held genuine potential as sites for colonization by Europeans: it referred specifically to Darjeeling, Ootacamund, and other hill stations.[22]

The post-1857 period did see a dramatic expansion of European agricultural settlement in the highlands. The extension of the railway system into the vicinity of these hitherto remote regions and the state-assisted development of commercial crops that thrived at higher altitudes—notably tea, coffee, and cinchona—made it economically feasible for settlers to come to the hills, and Lord Canning assisted the process by liberalizing the rules for alienating land to Europeans.[23] British planters began to congregate in substantial numbers on the slopes around Almora, Darjeeling, Kalimpong, Shillong, Ootacamund, Coonoor, Kodaikanal, Yercaud, and various other hill stations in the second half of the nineteenth century. They brought an added dimension to the social and economic life of the hill stations they encircled, a dimension that derived from the primal appeal of an agrarian existence—its stability, rootedness, permanence—and that was especially apparent when the men who owned or operated estates were accompanied by their wives and children. Many of the planters, however, were bachelors who were employed by large companies and who had no lasting attachment to the land. In addition, nearly all the planters were members of that "class of superior settlers" who oversaw the work of indigenous laborers rather than farmers who worked the fields themselves. In the subtle but useful semantic distinction drawn by David Arnold, they were settlers rather than colonists.[24]

Thus, the tantalizing social vision of scattered highland sites densely populated by white colonists who lived like simple yeomen on the fruits of their own labors and loomed like avenging angels over the troubled plains never materialized. The Nilgiris was virtually the only location that

---

22. PP, *Report from the Select Committee* (1859), Session 2, V, iv. Testimony by nonofficials in support of European settlement in the hills includes that by John Freeman, in PP, *First Report from the Select Committee* (1858), Session 1857–58, VII, pt. 1, 113; Joseph Gabriel Waller, in PP, *Second Report from the Select Committee* (1858), Session 1857–58, VII, pt. 1, 201; Alpin Grant Fowler, in PP, *Third Report from the Select Committee* (1858), Session 1857–58, VII, pt. 1, 49; Joseph Hooker and George Howard Fenwick, in PP, *Report from the Select Committee* (1859), Session 1, IV, 6, 39.

23. Riddy, "Some Official British Attitudes towards European Settlement," 39.

24. Arnold, "White Colonization," 134. Settlers, Arnold suggests, were planters and others who had the capital to hire laborers, while colonists were expatriate agriculturalists who had to rely on their own labor.

continued to attract serious attention as a site for colonization. In the early 1870s the Madras government, responding to pressure from the British Indian press, directed the superintendent of government farms to investigate the prospects for European agricultural settlement. His report proved to be an exercise in ambivalence. He asserted that the natural conditions were suited to the establishment of colonists on the land but that small farmers would require extensive training and assistance from the state in order to succeed. He doubted whether military pensioners or rural laborers from England and Scotland were up to the task, and so he focused his attention instead on locally born children trained from an early age in technical hill schools like the Lawrence Asylum.[25] Even this modest recommendation was dismissed by the state, which was content with the status quo. In the Himalayas, a rare effort to start a European agricultural colony was the sadly misnamed Hope Town, a place some ten miles from Darjeeling where missionaries attempted to establish a few dozen poor whites as petty farmers. Within a short time, Hope Town had become a ghost town.[26] Some years later, an Anglican clergyman proposed that a colony of destitute Europeans be established at the foot of the Darjeeling hills, but authorities concluded that the money would be better spent by sending them to Australia.[27]

The government's brushing aside of the occasional proposal to transplant poor whites to the hills was thus the sorry denouement of the debate about the colonization of the Indian highlands. While a few officials were doubtless still drawn to the notion that those on the margins of British Indian society might redeem themselves and buttress the raj as successful, small, highland farmers, most held that poor whites (though perhaps not their children) were beyond personal redemption or political benefit. And if they were unsalvageable, what purpose would be served by encouraging new colonists of the same class from Britain? India's imperial rulers could not bring themselves to add to the very element that seemed in their eyes to demean the social standards of the white community and to drain the resources of the state. Thus, the lengthy flirtation with highland colonies

25. W. R. Robertson, *Report on the Agricultural Conditions, Capabilities, and Prospects of the Neilgherry District* (Madras, 1875). A summary of the report appears in *Report on the Administration of the Madras Presidency, 1874–75* (Madras, 1876), 121–23.

26. See Hathorn, *Hand-Book*, 110–18.

27. Correspondence in General Department, Miscellaneous, June 1876, Proceedings of the Lieutenant Governor of Bengal, WBSA.

of white farmers amounted to little in the end. The British raj sought other means to sustain its power. Yet these too would involve the hill stations.

————————

While the Indian government believed that it had little to gain from concentrating colonists in the highlands, it did grant the hill stations a place in its strategic and political designs. Their enlarged significance in the operations of the raj gave them an unmistakably public importance in the latter half of the nineteenth century.

The army saw the hill stations with new eyes in the aftermath of the 1857 revolt. It had long recognized the health benefits of these places, but it now began to appreciate their strategic value. When violence erupted on the plains below, the hill stations of the western Himalayas remained tranquil, providing sanctuary for many British women and children. With the subsequent boost in the number of British troops committed to Indian service and the improvements in transportation brought about by the railway, it seemed both sensible and feasible to station a larger portion of the army in hill cantonments. In 1859–60 the military department of the government of India launched an extensive survey of highland locations suitable for quartering British soldiers. Its aim was both to determine the prospects for expanding existing sanitaria and cantonments and to identify new sites for development.[28] The results were striking. In India's strategically vital northwestern quadrant, a number of highland cantonments were established in the decade after the revolt. These included Balun, Chakrata, Ranikhet, and Solon. Dalhousie, although surveyed for use as a cantonment in 1853, was not occupied until 1860. In central India, a military station was established at Pachmarhi. Far to the east, Shillong's origins could be traced to the military department's efforts in the early 1860s to find a site in the region to settle soldiers on the land.[29] In the Nilgiris, a small military sanitarium known as Jackatalla was renamed Wellington and transformed into a major cantonment for the Madras Army. Other sleepy stations experienced similar surges of expansion. In addition, military au-

————————

28. *Selections from the Records of the Government of India (Military Department)*, nos. 1–3: *Report on the Extent and Nature of the Sanitary Establishments for European Troops in India* (Calcutta, 1861, 1862).

29. See the memoranda in nos. 7–10, 7 Jan. 1863, Home Dept. Proceedings, Public Branch (A), INA.

thorities investigated a number of highland locations across India that proved unsuited for development because of the lack of water, the prevalence of malaria, or other limiting factors.[30] A Parliamentary commission reporting on the sanitary state of the Indian Army in 1863 added to the reputations of highland cantonments by recommending that a third of British forces be placed in hill quarters on a rotating basis.[31]

For many critics, this shift of British forces to the hills did not go far enough. The Liberal politician Charles Dilke insisted that there was "no reason except a slight and temporary increase in cost to prevent the whole of the European troops in India being concentrated in a few cool and healthy [hill] stations."[32] An 1869 *Lancet* editorial, reprinted in the *Times*, argued that health considerations made it essential for authorities to place still more soldiers in hill stations.[33] The medical case for sending most if not all British troops to highland cantonments reappeared in various other forums.[34] A great deal of attention was also given to the unrealized strategic potential of the highlands. Some enthusiasts were convinced that the advent of the railway and the telegraph made it possible to harbor all British forces in the hills, where they would be secure from surprise attack but positioned to respond quickly to troubles anywhere in the subcontinent. Advocates of white colonization were enamored with the idea that soldiers stationed in the hills could be convinced to settle there when their terms of service came to an end and thereby could become the nucleus of permanent settlements that would serve as reliable reserves of military man-

30. *Selections from the Records of the Government of Bengal,* no. 36, pt. 2: *The Maghassani Hills as a Sanatarium* (Calcutta, 1861); *Selections from the Records of the Government of Bengal,* no. 38: *Papers Relating to a Sanatarium upon Mount Parisnath* (Calcutta, 1861); and the reports by Lt.-Col. (later Gen.) Douglas Hamilton, *Report on the Shevaroy Hills* (Madras, 1862), *Report on the Pulni Mountains* (Madras, 1864), and *Report on the High Ranges of the Annamullay Mountains* (Madras, 1866).

31. PP, *Report of the Commissioners Appointed to Inquire into the Sanitary State of the Army in India,* XIX, 1863, 143–52. The commissioners would have recommended that a greater proportion of British troops be quartered in hill stations except for concerns about the effects on military security.

32. Charles Wentworth Dilke, *Greater Britain: A Record of Travel in English-Speaking Countries,* vol. 2 (London, 1869), 244–45.

33. *Times* (London), 16 Jan. 1869, p. 5, col. 6.

34. See "Hill Stations of India as Sanitaria for the British Soldier," *Calcutta Journal of Medicine* 1, no. 8 (Aug. 1868); William Curran, "The Himalayas as a Health Resort," *Practitioner* (Jan. 1871); and William Curran, "Further Evidence in Favour of a Hill Residence for European Soldiers in India," *Irish Journal of Medical Science* 52, no. 104 (1871).

power. Ootacamund's local newspaper argued in favor of settling soldiers and their families in the Nilgiris, asserting, "When it comes to the question of defencibility, Ootacamund, and for that matter almost every spot on these hills, is unapproached by any in India as a place of security."[35] Kashmir excited the imagination of Rudyard Kipling, who had the narrator of his short story, "His Private Honour" (1891), fantasize about planting army pensioners in that lovely vale, where they would "breed us white soldiers."[36] Perhaps the most important proponent of the strategic value of the hills was Major-General D.J.F. Newall. In the two-volume *The Highlands of India Strategically Considered* (1882), he sought to show that the colonization of the highlands by European troops was both feasible and essential to the "future for British India." The book provided a detailed region-by-region survey of the many stations and cantonments scattered across the Indian highlands. Little more was required, it suggested, than the authorities' open-mindedness in order to transform these stations into military colonies that would ensure the security of British rule.[37]

The arguments of Newall and his confreres were not enough, however, to initiate a full-scale withdrawal of European troops from the plains to the hills. Senior army planners could not be convinced of the strategic merits of removing the bulk of their forces from active duty on the plains, and they had little incentive to invest their resources in efforts to settle ex-soldiers in the hills. Nor did the prospect of occupying the pristine highlands with drunk and debauched "Tommies," as the army's rank-and-file were often perceived, do much to relieve official anxieties about white colonization in general. Despite all of these concerns, it remains incontestable that hill stations acquired an importance to the military in the late nineteenth century that they had never before possessed. By the 1870s, a sixth of the British forces in India were located in hill cantonments, and two decades later the proportion was nearer a quarter.[38]

Not only did the hill stations provide billets for British troops; they also provided headquarters for their officers. The consolidation of the commander-in-chief's staff and offices in Simla and the transfer of other army

---

35. *South of India Observer,* 27 January 1877.
36. Rudyard Kipling, "His Private Honour," in *Many Inventions* (New York, 1925), 134.
37. Major-Gen. D.J.F. Newall, *The Highlands of India Strategically Considered* (London, 1882).
38. David Arnold, *Colonizing the Body: State Medicine and Epidemic Disease in Nineteenth-Century India* (Berkeley, 1993), 79.

command centers to Murree, Ootacamund, and elsewhere in the hills were among the signs that a profound shift was taking place in the geographical concentration of imperial power.

————

But the hill stations acquired their most significant public role in the raj as political capitals. When Gandhi wrote in 1921 that Simla was the true headquarters of the rulers of India, he was stating what everyone knew to be the case. Simla had become the principal residence of the viceroy of India, the commander-in-chief of the Indian Army, the lieutenant-governor of Punjab, and a host of other government dignitaries; it had become a vibrant political capital with an imposing array of public buildings from whence the affairs of state were conducted; it had become the nerve center of the raj. The changes at Simla, moreover, had been replicated on a provincial scale in Ootacamund, Darjeeling, Mahabaleshwar, and elsewhere: hill stations throughout India had become hubs of imperial power.

In the first half of the nineteenth century, however, hill stations did not operate as official centers of power, even though their inhabitants and visitors were intrinsically political beings. Governors-general and governors went to highland sanitaria for much the same reasons as other visitors—the appeal of the climate, the search for health, the desire for relaxation. While they were there, they continued to conduct the affairs of state, to be sure, but most of the panoply of power and the bureaucracy that carried out its pedestrian transactions were left behind. No fixed pattern of "seasons" governed the peregrinations of the heads of state. Some governors-general, such as Lord Auckland, enjoyed extended stays in Simla; others, notably Lord Canning, disliked the place and avoided it after one brief sojourn. The duration and frequency of visits to hill stations varied among governors and other regional authorities as well. Occasionally the length of a governor-general's holiday in the hills gave rise to concern that he was neglecting his official duties. Lord Dalhousie in particular was subjected to repeated attacks by the Calcutta press and critics in England for spending so much time in Simla; even the court of directors of the East India Company took him to task for his fondness for the place in 1853.[39]

39. Minute by Dalhousie, 17 May 1853, enclosure to Dispatch #16 (1887), L/PJ/6/199/643, IOL. Also see Marquess of Dalhousie, *Private Letters of the Marquess of Dalhousie*, ed. J.G.A. Baird (Edinburgh and London, 1910), 168, 186; and Sir William Lee-Warner, *The Life of the Marquis of Dalhousie,* vol. 1 (London, 1904), 301, 370.

Usually, however, imperial heads of state managed to escape the realm of politics when they went to the hills.

The politicization of the hill stations occurred in the second half of the nineteenth century. In this matter as in so many others, 1857 marked an important turning point. After the revolt the authorities' sojourns to the hills acquire a powerful, if often tacit, new motive—the desire to carry out official duties in an environment secure from the perils that had arisen with such dramatic force on the plains. Even though Lord Canning had himself spent little more than three weeks in the hills over a span of six years, in 1861 he granted governors and lieutenant-governors permission to reside for four months of every year "at the most convenient hill station." He allowed the Madras and Bombay governments to augment their official presences in Ootacamund and Mahabaleshwar, approving a request by Bombay for funds to assist its annual migration and a proposal by Madras to sell one of the governor's two residences in Madras so as to purchase one in the hill station. He also approved a medical request by the lieutenant governor of the North-West Provinces to spend his summers in Naini Tal. Although he avoided addressing the broader implications of these separate decisions and expressed reservations about the wisdom of the governor-general's making it a practice to leave Calcutta for the summers, Canning in effect took the first step toward an official endorsement of governments' seasonal flights to the hills.[40]

A rationale for this nascent policy came from Sir Bartle Frere, one of the most respected members of the governor-general's council. Railing against "the absurdity of forcing our Governors to live all the year round in the worst climate in their charge," he grounded his case in part on claims for the health benefits of the highlands. However, he also proffered an argument based on historical precedent. Citing examples from China, Persia, and, of course, Mughal India, he declared: "Every great oriental ruler, with any pretensions to civilization has his summer and winter residence." In effect, Frere sought to legitimize the seasonal migration of government to the hills by associating it with what was seen as an indigenous, "oriental" model of governance. This, in turn, was simply one aspect of a sweeping endeavor by the British in the post-1857 era to restructure their rule along

40. Minute by Canning in no. 34, 13 May 1861, Home Dept. Proceedings, Public Branch, INA. Also see correspondence on Bombay hill stations in nos. 117–21, 28 Aug. 1861, Home Dept. Proceedings, Public Branch (A), and correspondence of the lieutenant governor of the North-West Provinces about Naini Tal in nos. 52–54, 28 Feb. 1861, and nos. 64–66, 30 April 1862, Home Dept. Proceedings, Public Branch, INA.

increasingly aloof and autocratic lines and to imbue it with symbols that evoked past patterns of authority.[41]

The decisive moment in the establishment of a highland headquarters for this self-styled oriental regime occurred in 1864. The new viceroy, Sir John Lawrence, brought his executive council and some five hundred government staff members with him on his summer sojourn to Simla in that year. The transfer of the council, which served as the viceroy's cabinet, represented a formal shift of decision-making power away from Calcutta, the official capital. The secretary of state for India, Sir Charles Wood, realized the move would set an important precedent and was reluctant to approve it for that reason. But Lawrence refused to accept the viceroyship unless he could conduct the affairs of state from Simla. Every year thereafter at the onset of hot weather the British rulers of India removed themselves and an ever-expanding contingent of bureaucrats to their Himalayan hideaway, where they remained for the subsequent six months or more.[42]

As Simla began to overshadow Calcutta in political importance, the position of Calcutta as the official seat of government became a topic of debate (and it continued to be one until the transfer of the capital to Delhi was announced at the imperial durbar of 1911). In 1867, Sir Stafford Northcote, Wood's successor at the India Office, appointed a special committee to consider whether the lieutenant-governorship of Bengal should be raised to a governorship and, if so, whether the capital of India should be moved to a different location. To Northcote's apparent surprise and dismay, this committee exercised its mandate to beat back what it saw as Simla's threat to Calcutta. Not only did it conclude that Calcutta should remain the capital, but it urged that the viceroy and his entourage be "prohibited" from undertaking their annual migration to Simla.[43] The

41. Minute by Frere in no. 35, 14 May 1861, Home Dept. Proceedings, Public Branch, INA. For the shift in the British strategy of governance, see Thomas R. Metcalf, *The Aftermath of Revolt: India 1857–1870* (Princeton, 1964); Bernard S. Cohn, "Representing Authority in Victorian India," *The Invention of Tradition,* ed. Eric Hobsbawm and Terence Ranger (Cambridge, 1982); and Francis G. Hutchins, *The Illusion of Permanence: British Imperialism in India* (Princeton, 1967), ch. 8.

42. Pamela Kanwar, *Imperial Simla* (Delhi, 1990), 34–39.

43. Report of the Special Committee, 14 Nov. 1867, in L/PJ/6/190/2034, Public and Judicial Dept., IOL. Simla's role in the considerations of the committee and in the subsequent half-century of debate about the transfer of the capital from Calcutta is entirely ignored in Robert Grant Irving, *Indian Summer: Lutyens, Baker, and Imperial Delhi* (New Haven, 1981).

committee and its sympathizers argued that the move to and from Simla cost the government too much time and money, that it alienated the Indian clerks who were forced to abandon their homes and families in Calcutta, and that it isolated authorities from the salutary sway of public opinion. These would remain the principal charges against Simla for decades to come. The most forceful response to the committee's complaints came from Henry Maine, the distinguished legal member of the viceroy's council. Maine mocked Simla's critics by insisting that it was the capital already in all but name: "the theory that Calcutta was the capital was preserved only by a fiction, and a fiction so transparent that, did I not know something of the power of fictions, I should wonder at men being blinded by it." Maine argued that the cost of the annual migration and the time spent in transit had been substantially reduced by recent improvements in transportation and communication, and that the cool highland climate made officials more productive in the summer months. Moreover, "almost all governments originating in the conquest of hot countries by persons born in a cooler climate have been, as a matter of history, more or less peripatetic," an assertion that echoed Frere. A more conciliatory stance was taken by Lord Lawrence, who assured Calcutta's defenders that he had no desire to abandon it as the official capital of India. Nevertheless, he forcefully defended the seasonal shift of government to Simla: it was salubrious, unlike Calcutta with its summer saunas; it was secure, as had been proven by the loyalty of the local chiefs and their subjects during the recent uprising; and it was located near the strategic heart of India, which consisted of the Punjab and the North-West Frontier.[44] Lawrence's defense proved decisive: an uneasy truce ensued that left Calcutta with the outward guise of power but Simla with most of its substance.

Simla's position as the principal headquarters of the imperial government soon became all but unassailable. The viceroy and his council began to spend so much time in the hill station that the secretary of state felt obliged in 1877 to insist that they remain in Calcutta from November 1 through April 15 each year. The order was simply ignored.[45] A growing army of clerks and other state functionaries accompanied the viceroy to Simla to conduct the everyday business of the raj. Not only did major

44. Minutes by Lawrence, 19 Feb. and 23 March 1868, and Maine, 2 Dec. 1867 and 16 March 1868, L/PJ/6/190/2034, Public and Judicial Dept., IOL. Others active in this exchange of minutes were Henry Durand and James Strachey.

45. Salisbury to Lytton, 20 Dec. 1877, L/PJ/6/190/2034, Public and Judicial Dept., IOL.

departments such as the foreign office, finance, and public works transfer their operations to Simla for the bulk of each year, but so did a great many lesser agencies, among them the offices of the surgeon general and sanitary commissioner, the director general of the post office, the commissioner of salt revenue for northern India, the inspector general of forests, the surveyor general, the meteorological reporter, the director general of telegraphs, the director general of railways, the commissary general-in-chief and the commissary general for transport, the director general of ordinance, and the director of army remounts.[46] The annual cost of moving the government from Calcutta to Simla and back averaged around Rs. 800,000 through most of the 1880s.[47]

The physical appearance of the station underwent a transformation as it sought to accommodate this enlarged bureaucratic presence. What had been an overgrown village consisting of fewer than three hundred privately owned European cottages in the mid-1860s soon became a small metropolis, its center bounded by a chain of multistoried government buildings and its boundaries pushed in all directions by the rapid increase in population. The greatest spate of public construction occurred in the 1880s (Figure 10). Arising in this decade were the secretariat and the army headquarters, two great iron and concrete structures said to have been modeled after the Peabody building in London; the Tudor-style post office; the fortresslike telegraph office; the rambling Swiss Gothic Ripon Hospital; the large stone courthouse and cutcherry of the deputy commissioner; the public-works building; the town hall, an ambitious Victorian Gothic complex that housed municipal offices, the police station, an assembly hall, a Masonic hall, and the Gaiety Theater; and the Swiss chalet–influenced foreign office, which was pronounced "the most picturesque of all the Government buildings."[48] The greatest of these public projects, however, was the Viceregal Lodge, a castlelike edifice of gray limestone that served as the official residence of the viceroy. Prior to its completion in 1888, governors-general and viceroys had leased a series of private homes for their stays in Simla, most recently a half-timbered Tudor villa known as Peterhof. The decision to built the

46. Dispatch #25, Lansdowne to Cross, 2 April 1889, L/PJ/6/250/687, Public and Judicial Dept., IOL.

47. Dispatch #16, Dufferin to Cross, 15 March 1887, 22, L/PJ/6/199/643, Public and Judicial Dept., IOL.

48. See Public Works Department, *Completion Reports of Public Office Buildings and Clerks' Cottages at Simla,* serial no. 21 (Calcutta, 1889). The comment on the foreign-office building comes from Edward J. Buck, *Simla Past and Present,* 2d ed. (1925; reprint, Simla, 1989), 106.

General View of Government Offices.                              Simla.

7147.

Figure 10.   Government office buildings perched along the ridge in Simla. From a postcard in the possession of the author.

Viceregal Lodge was a statement in stone of the government's intention to establish a permanent presence in Simla. Designed by the public-works department's principal architect, Henry Irwin, in a dark and heavy Elizabethan Renaissance style and located atop Observatory Hill at the western end of Simla, it was built to impress, with the entry hall paneled in teak, the ballroom hung with tapestries of silk, and the dining room embellished with heraldic shields. It cost Rs. 970,093 to construct.[49]

Although new construction slackened after the 1880s, the stones of state continued to cast a heavy shadow over Simla. In 1897 the army took over the secretariat building, and its previous tenants acquired a new building; the Punjab government rebuilt and expanded an existing structure to serve as its impressive new headquarters in 1902; the Walker Hospital for Europeans arose in the same year. The government of India purchased a series of houses in the late nineteenth and early twentieth centuries for use as residences by council members and other high-ranking officials. It also constructed a number of cottages, hostels, and barracks for its European, Anglo-Indian, and Indian clerks, who found it increasingly difficult to

49. Public Works Department, *Completion Report of the New Viceregal Lodge at Simla,* serial no. 22 (Calcutta, 1890).

afford the high rents on the open market. Small wonder so many visitors felt that the weight of officialdom was intolerable in Simla.[50]

Similar public-building projects were undertaken at other hill stations as they acquired recognition as political headquarters. London had rejected several requests by the government of Madras in the 1860s to transfer its council to Ootacamund for the summer months, but Madras continued to press for the move. A pamphlet published in 1869 argued that Ootacamund's "commanding position," its ease of defense, its space for troops, its salubrious climate, and its economic potential made it the logical site for the Madras government.[51] When another plea from Madras was made in 1870, the secretary of state relented, approving a three-month stay by the governor and his council in Ootacamund.[52] The India Office was persuaded to reverse itself because of the precedent established by the viceroy's inhabitancy of Simla. Still, London officials remained wary: Sir Erskine Perry warned that "the evil of a small official clique living exclusively with one another without any of the advantages to be derived from contact with an independent intelligent non official community cannot well be exaggerated." For this reason, the secretary of state insisted that the Ootacamund residency be limited to three months annually. But this restriction was soon ignored, as Perry had suspected it would be when he asked, "What is there to prevent the three months being changed eventually into the whole year."[53] What indeed? By the 1880s the governor and his council were spending as many as eight months annually in Ootacamund.

Once the barrier posed by London's opposition had been breached, nothing apart from the natural constraints of geography could prevent bureaucrats from marching across the length and breadth of India into the hills. Mahabaleshwar soon established itself as the so-called summer headquarters of the government of Bombay, although authorities actually occupied the station from early April to mid-June (when they fled the monsoons to Poona) and again from mid-October till the end of November. The official season soon extended from April to October or even November in many of the Himalayan stations. The lieutenant-governor of Bengal

50. For fuller treatment of the subjects discussed in this paragraph and the preceding one, see Buck, *Simla Past and Present,* chs. 2, 6; and Kanwar, *Imperial Simla,* ch. 4

51. *Ootacamund as the Seat of the Madras Government,* pamphlet reprinted from the *Madras Mail,* 1869, 3, passim.

52. Minutes on the removal of the government of Madras to the Nilgiris, nos. 151–52, 15 Jan. 1870, Home Dept. Proceedings, Public Branch, INA.

53. Note by Sir Erskine Perry, 4 Feb. 1870, L/PJ/6/35/448, Public and Judicial Dept., IOL.

began to take his government to Darjeeling, while the government of the United Provinces followed its lieutenant-governor to Naini Tal. The lieutenant-governor of the Punjab established his first summer residence at Simla in 1871, moved it to Murree for the 1873–75 seasons, then returned to Simla again. Pachmarhi became the summer headquarters for the chief commissioner of the Central Provinces in 1873. Shillong was sanctioned to serve as the year-round capital for the government of Assam in 1874, although by the early twentieth century its governors began to imitate the migration of their counterparts elsewhere in India by repairing to a chateau on a hill above Shillong during the summer months.

This formal transfer of provincial authority to the hill stations led to the proliferation of government buildings, especially stately homes for heads of state. The Punjab government in 1878 purchased Barnes Court, a large Tudor-style manor house, as the official Simla residence for its lieutenant-governor. In Darjeeling, a mansion previously owned by the maharaja of Cooch Behar was acquired and remodeled in 1879 to serve as an official residence for the lieutenant-governor of Bengal. In Mahabaleshwar, a government house was built in 1886 for the governor of Bombay. A lavish residence for the lieutenant-governor of the United Provinces was completed at the turn of the century on a site overlooking Naini Tal. The most significant spate of public-works projects occurred, however, in Ootacamund. In 1877 the Duke of Buckingham and Chandos, then governor of Madras, began construction of a governor's mansion on the slopes of Dodabetta peak, above the rest of the station. Modeled after his own country home, Stowe House, the lavish Italianate structure proved so expensive to build—Rs. 783,000 including furnishings, with an additional Rs. 60,000 for a ballroom in 1900—that it became known as "Buckingham's Folly" (Figure 11).[54] Cutcherry Hill was the name attached to a cluster of administrative buildings that arose near the symbolic center of Ootacamund, St. Stephen's church. John Sullivan's original home, Stonehouse, was turned into government offices in 1870 and rebuilt in 1875–77, when a new council chamber, offices, and a clock tower were added for Rs. 31,400. Further additions and improvements cost Rs. 44,962 in 1883–84, Rs. 17,660 in 1899, and Rs. 68,000 in 1906–07. In 1884 the Madras Army spent Rs.

54. Sir Frederick Price, *Ootacamund: A History* (Madras, 1908), 56–57. Also see Judith Theresa Kenny, "Constructing an Imperial Hill Station: The Representation of British Authority in Ootacamund" (Ph.D. diss., Syracuse University, 1990), 185–92, who reproduces on p. 158 a shrewd and scathing ditty, "This Is the House the Duke Built," which first appeared in the *Madras Mail*, 24 July 1880.

Figure 11. The Madras governor's mansion, Ootacamund. From Sir Frederick Price, *Ootacamund: A History* (Madras, 1908).

70,000 to move its headquarters into a nearby building. Married clerks' quarters were built in 1884–85 at a cost of Rs. 22,676, a postal and telegraph office in 1884 for Rs. 56,960, and a printing-press building in 1904 for Rs. 84,495. Lesser sums were spent on items like a saluting battery to acknowledge the arrival and departure of the governor and other dignitaries.[55] Furthermore, the cost of moving the government from Madras to Ootacamund increased from some Rs. 25,000 per annum in the 1870s to Rs. 43,341 in 1884–85.[56] These expenditures were one measure of the metamorphosis of Ootacamund into a permanent headquarters for the Madras government.

The spate of public building was also, however, a provocation to the nonofficial public in Madras and other towns in the presidency. In 1881 the secretary of state for India received a memorial from the citizens of Madras, protesting the annual migration of the presidency government to

55. Price, *Ootacamund*, 20–21, 100; W. Francis, *The Nilgiris* (Madras, 1908), 358–59. Also see Kenny, "Constructing an Imperial Hill Station," chs. 5, 6.

56. Minute by Henry Waterfield, 6 April 1881, L/PJ/6/35/448, and minute on the annual cost of the move to Simla and Ootacamund, 1886, L/PJ/6/190/2034, Public and Judicial Dept., IOL.

Ootacamund. The memorial complained that the move was an unnecessary expense, that it led to the construction of a lavish mansion for the governor at a time of famine, that it caused suffering for Indian clerks and servants who found the highland climate uncongenial, that it inconvenienced those obliged to conduct regular business with the government, and that it removed officials from public scrutiny for as much as nine months every year. The document concluded by addressing the broader implications of the government migration to the hills:

> Your Memorialists are convinced that the growing tendency of Governments throughout India to desert their respective capitals for the greater portion of the year, and to retire to places at great distances therefrom whence they cannot exercise the control and do the duty required of them, has much to do with bringing about the present financial embarrassment of the Empire, and the consequent heavy taxation now prevailing throughout India.

Appended to the memorial were some 220 pages filled with approximately thirteen thousand signatures in English, Tamil, and Telegu.[57]

Madras was the scene of an even more impressive protest against the government's migration to the hills in 1884. The apparent spark was the transfer of the Madras Army headquarters to Ootacamund, but the causes of discontent clearly went much deeper. A public meeting drew "the largest assemblage within the recollection of the oldest inhabitants" of the city, attracting some nine to fifteen thousand people to the Esplanade, according to the London *Times*.[58] The crowd divided into English-, Tamil-, and Telegu-speaking groups to listen to speeches by various local notables, including Bishop Coglan of the Roman Catholic Church; Sir Alexander MacKenzie, a prominent businessman and member of the governor's council; Raja Sir Madhava Rao, who had served as dewan for the princely states of Travancore, Mysore, and Baroda; Ananda Charlu, who helped to found the nationalist Madras Mahajan Sabha in 1884 and later became president of the Indian National Congress; and a number of British and Indian lawyers. Here, then, was an issue on which a heterogeneous array of parties, otherwise polarized by race, class, and other distinctions, could find common ground. The assemblage approved a memorial that resembled the one drafted in 1881, again objecting to the expense of the transfer of government to the hills and warning that the authorities' isolation there

57. Memorial to the Marquis of Hartington, 4 March 1881, L/PJ/6/35/448, Public and Judicial Dept., IOL.
58. *Times* (London), 7 July 1884, p. 5, cols. 1–2.

"deprives them of feeling the pulse of the country, . . . estranges them from their native fellow subjects, and . . . exposes them to the risk of forming erroneous opinions of the requirements of the times."[59] The leaders of the 1884 protests, however, exhibited a good deal more political savvy and determination than had been shown three years earlier. Public meetings were held throughout the presidency to coincide with the Madras event; telegrams of "sympathy" were sent by groups in Bellary, Salem, Coimbatore, and elsewhere. The petition drive garnered over twice as many signatures as the earlier initiative, and the petition itself was sent not to the India Office, where its predecessor had sunk with scarcely a ripple, but to Parliament, where its complaints received a public airing.[60] Members of both houses spoke to the protesters' concerns, with several lords especially critical of the transfer of the government to the hills. Lord Napier, whose long and distinguished military career in India had culminated in his appointment as commander-in-chief of the Indian army (1870–76), insisted on the floor of the Lords that "the Government and Council should have their abode in the places where the citizens spend their days." Lord Stanley, who had been secretary of state for India (1859–60), warned that the "chief evil [of the use of Ootacamund as government headquarters] was that the officials became more and more separated from the inhabitants of the country, and more ignorant of their wants and feelings."[61] The London *Times* gave these remarks and other ramifications of the Madrasi events extensive attention in its pages.

While it was the protests over the annual migration of the Madras government to the Nilgiris that had attracted the attention of members of Parliament, the *Times*, and others, critics both in India and in Britain meant their objections to apply more broadly to include other provincial governments as well as the imperial government. In effect, the entire raj was on trial. The practice of transferring the agencies of authority to the hill stations had become so widespread among so many tiers of the imperial government that the resentments against it boiled up not only in Madras

59. The full text of the memorial appears as app. A of Kenny, "Constructing an Imperial Hill Station."

60. A petition containing 26,717 signatures was presented to the House of Lords; another 7,299 appeared on a petition to the House of Commons. *Times* (London), 21 July 1884, p. 5, col. 2. Telegrams of "sympathy" from twenty-five civic and other groups are reproduced in Kenny, "Constructing an Imperial Hill Station," app. B. Chapter 5 of Kenny's dissertation provides a good account of the 1884 protest meeting and its political ramifications.

61. PP, *Hansard Parliamentary Debates*, 3d ser., vol. 293 (1884), cols. 1346, 1349.

but all across India. In Calcutta and elsewhere, public meetings were held to protest the annual migration.[62] Evidence of the widespread resentment can be found in the private papers of Sir George Russell Clerk. A distinguished veteran of the Indian political service, Clerk had been twice governor of Bombay (1847–48, 1860–62), permanent undersecretary of state for India (1858–60), and, finally, a member of the viceroy's council (1863–67). He grew increasingly disturbed after his retirement by the tendency of the Indian government to spend most of its time in the hills. He collected clippings from English-language and vernacular newspapers that complained about the practice, and he interspersed these items with his own scathing comments. One clipping spoke derisively of "government by *picnic,*" another of "the frivolous and fatal atmosphere of Simla." Clerk himself warned, "It is a fatal mistake to disregard the mortification and the contempt with which the people view their highly paid functionaries secluding themselves thus for ten months yearly, and so shirking their duties." In the view of this grizzled veteran, the actions of the current coterie of officials stamped them as "Sybarites," whose "frivolities and effeminacy" jeopardized the foundations of British rule.[63]

The migration of the government to the hills did, to be sure, have its supporters as well. Kipling weighed in on the issue with his poem "A Tale of Two Cities," which cast Calcutta residents' complaints about Simla as simple envy: "'Because, for certain months, we boil and stew, so should you.'" Its final lines asserted that "for rule, administration, and the rest, Simla's best."[64] Similarly, an article in the *Calcutta Review* dismissed the objections to Simla and Darjeeling as self-interested, coming as they did from Calcutta merchants and lawyers, especially the lawyers, who saw their income and influence diminish because of the seasonal flight to the hills.[65] Yet the voices of Kipling and the author of the *Calcutta Review* piece were scarcely audible above the loud chorus of complaints.

Despite the remonstrances from press and public in Madras, Calcutta, and elsewhere in India, the critics could do little to prevent the annual migration by the government to the hills. Neither, it seems, could Parliament. Although the India Office, responding to the petitions and pro-

62. See, for example, H. M. Kisch, *A Young Victorian in India: Letters,* ed. Ethel A. Waley Cohen (London, 1957), 213.

63. Sir George Russell Clerk Collection, MSS. Eur.D. 538/6, IOL.

64. Rudyard Kipling, "A Tale of Two Cities," in *Verse: Definitive Edition* (Garden City, N.Y., 1952), 75–77.

65. C. J. O'Donnell, "Simla, Calcutta and Darjeeling as Centres of Government," *Calcutta Review* 83 (Oct. 1886): 398–419.

tests, demanded a closer accounting of the costs entailed in the annual migrations and sought to impose limits on the number of officials who took part, it conceded that the use of hill stations for political headquarters was a *fait accompli*. This conclusion came after an 1887 investigation revealed just how thoroughly the hill stations had become woven into the fabric of British rule in India.[66] "It does not seem possible," sighed one India Office bureaucrat, "for the Secretary of State to forbid the practice [of migration of the hills] or to lay down a limit of 3, 4, or 6 months, as the maximum period of hill-residence in any year." Another observed that "the time has come for recognizing the fact that Simla is the place where the Government of India is, as a rule, carried on."[67] Lord Cross, the secretary of state for India, officially conceded the point in a dispatch to the viceroy, Lord Lansdowne:

> The annual transfer of the Government to Simla has now been a recognized practice for twenty-four years; it has been acquiesced in by successive Secretaries of State in Council; the head-quarters of the Army have long been established there; large expenditures have been incurred in the provision of public buildings; and I am not in the circumstances prepared to disturb existing arrangements.[68]

The secretary of state's surrender did nothing to silence the public outcries against the official migration to the hills. Increasingly, however, those objections came from one quarter in particular—Indian nationalists. Time and again, Indian members of the Legislative Assembly complained about the public costs of the annual governmental migration to the hills.[69]

66. See Dispatch #16, Dufferin to Cross, 15 March 1887, L/PJ/6/199/643, and the memoranda by regional governments responding to the request for information on their use of hill stations in L/PJ/6/226/732, Public and Judicial Dept., IOL.

67. Memorandum by Henry Waterfield, 8 June 1888, and letter by J.A.G., 14 June 1888, L/PJ/6/226/732, Public and Judicial Dept., IOL.

68. Dispatch #116, Cross to Lansdowne, 25 Oct. 1888, L/PJ/6/226/732, Public and Judicial Dept., IOL. Cross did demand that the government remain in Calcutta from November 1 through April 15, reiterating a requirement ineffectually imposed by Lord Salisbury in 1877, and Cross insisted that the same limitations apply to provincial governments. But he backed down from these demands when the viceroy objected. See Dispatch #9, Lansdowne to Cross, 29 Jan. 1889, and Dispatch #37, Cross to Lansdowne, 18 April 1889, L/PJ/6/224/252, Public and Judicial Dept., IOL.

69. See the memoranda generated by these challenges in nos. 223–36, Oct. 1911, Home Dept. Proceedings, Public Branch (A); no. 75, March 1917, Home Dept. Proceedings, Public Branch (B); no. 136, April 1917, Home Dept. Proceedings, Public Branch (B); no. 1/54/1927, 1927, Home Dept. Proceedings, Public Branch; and no. 1/12/1930, 1930, Home Dept. Proceedings, Public Branch; all in IOL. The

Gandhi's objections to the practice were enunciated in his essay on Simla, "Five Hundredth Storey." He compared the government to a shopkeeper who placed his shop in the topmost floor of a building, inconveniencing his customers. "The thirty crore customers of this Government, the country's shopkeeper, have to climb not 60 feet but 7,500 feet! . . . Is it any wonder that the country starves?" Carrying his metaphor to its logical conclusion, he declared, "To win swaraj means to oblige the Government . . . to descend from the five hundredth floor to the ground floor and introduce naturalness in its relations with us."[70] Despite its distinctive rhetorical cast, the essential thrust of Gandhi's criticisms was largely the same as those that had been voiced in the late nineteenth century: a government that isolated itself in the hills lost touch with the needs of its subjects. Yet the many British Indian merchants, lawyers, and other nonofficials who had played prominent roles in the earlier protests no longer did so. Whatever measure of collaboration they had forged with Indians against a regime that both parties regarded as aloof and arrogant was fleeting, and it dissolved in the racial polarization that accompanied the rise of militant nationalism in the twentieth century.

────────

Power and privilege were at the heart of the debate about the annual migrations of the supreme and provincial governments to hill stations, just as they were at the heart of the debate about the European colonization of the highlands. The key questions concerning colonization were these: What role existed for white settlers in this densely populated land? Would their exclusion leave imperial authority exposed and unprotected? Would their inclusion subvert the boundaries between colonizer and colonized? Questions of a similar gravity arose over the choice of political headquarters: What locations were best suited to be centers of imperial authority? Should the rulers' proximity to their subjects be the primary criterion in determining the sites of power, or should the security and comfort of the rulers take precedence? All these questions were answered in different ways by different parties, demonstrating that a multiplicity of interests operated within this colonial polity.

────────

1927 memorandum cites similar questions by Indian members of the Legislative Assembly in 1920, 1921, 1925–26, and 1926–27.

70. Gandhi, "Five Hundredth Storey," in *Collected Works*, vol. 20 (Delhi, 1966), 117.

Yet the interests that counted most were those of the mandarins, the high officials who oversaw the operations of imperial rule, and the answers they gave to the preceding questions were the ones that took precedence in determining the character of the raj. Despite the lobbying efforts of advocates of white settlement, the recommendations to make the highlands sites for colonies of European agriculturists, or even military and political centers, attracted little support from the government in the first half of the nineteenth century. Around midcentury, several developments, above all the 1857 revolt, reoriented official opinion. Authorities acquired a new appreciation for the highlands, and they sought various ways to put them to imperial use. They may have remained unconvinced that the settlement of poorly capitalized men on small plots of land could succeed, but the remarkable proliferation in the second half of the nineteenth century of tea, coffee, and cinchona estates was a significant step toward the establishment of a permanent European presence in the highlands, and it was made possible through the state's alienation of land, construction of a railway system, experimentation with plants, and other active subventions. The most significant indication of the increased appreciation of the highlands, however, was the effort to turn hill stations into centers of government. For the viceroys who found Simla a more congenial place from which to conduct the affairs of state than Calcutta, for the governors, the lieutenant-governors, the chief commissioners, and even district officials who sought out highland headquarters of their own, and, indeed, for the thousands of clerks and servants who followed their superiors on these annual migrations and the tens of thousands of lawyers and merchants and others who resented the practice, it became apparent that a massive shift in the geography of power occurred in the latter part of the nineteenth century, a shift from the plains to the hills.

Sandria Freitag has argued that an indigenous Indian public sphere in the colonial era took shape in "a world from which the British had excluded themselves; and it was this overt act of exclusion by the state itself which marks the greatest difference between the colonial public arena and the public sphere of western Europe."[71] While Freitag herself makes no reference to hill stations, it has been suggested here that they were in fact the

71. Sandria B. Freitag, "Enactments of Ram's Story and the Changing Nature of 'The Public' in British India," *South Asia* 14, no. 1 (June 1991): 89. Also see the other essays in this issue of *South Asia*, which is devoted to an examination of a colonial public sphere.

logical outcome of this exclusionary process. The British determination to impose an aloof and vigilant system of authority over the Indian population in the aftermath of 1857 was realized through the progressive concentration of political and military might in the hill stations. The consequences of this action would be not only the rise of a distinctively Indian public arena but also the struggle to sustain an exclusively British one.

# 8　The Intrusion of the Other

You are dividing the world up into two hostile camps, which I may
tell you, is a grievous error, most reprehensible!
　　　　　　　　　　—Thomas Mann, *The Magic Mountain*

He led the horses below the main road into the lower Simla
bazar—the crowded rabbit-warren that climbs up from the valley to
the Town Hall at an angle of forty-five. A man who knows his way
there can defy all the police of India's summer capital; so cunningly
does verandah communicate with verandah, alley-way with
alley-way, and bolt-hole with bolt-hole. Here live all those who
minister to the wants of the glad city—jhampanis who pull the
pretty ladies' rickshaws by night and gamble till the dawn; grocers,
oil-sellers, curio-vendors, firewood-dealers, priests, pickpockets, and
native employees of the Government.
　　　　　　　　　　　　—Rudyard Kipling, *Kim*

**W**hat sustained the hill stations was their image of aloofness. It was no
less essential to their public than to their private purposes that they present
themselves as exclusively European enclaves, isolated from the pressures
and perils of India and its inhabitants. Yet the British were not alone: they
were surrounded by Indians. One of the paradoxes of the hill stations is
that their success as places where the British imagined it possible to get
away from Indians depended on the contributions of Indians.

From the start, the development of highland sanitaria generated enormous demands for native labor. Roads and bridges had to be constructed,
land cleared and dwellings erected, provisions produced and marketed,
visitors and their baggage brought up, fodder and fuel and water provided,
and a myriad of domestic drudgeries carried out. These tasks the British
relied upon Indians to do, and in large numbers: hill station censuses
suggest that at least ten Indians were necessary to support each European.
Much of the initial labor force came from the surrounding hills, coerced
in many cases to work without pay. The demand gradually spread to more
distant parts of the country, necessitating an elaborate network that carried
a stream of male migrant workers to and from the hill stations. A wide array
of people amassed each season within the confines of the station bazaars
(Figure 12).

Figure 12.   View of the main bazaar at Darjeeling. From Eastern Bengal State Railway, *From the Hooghly to the Himalayas* (Bombay, 1913).

The British found the intrusion of these people highly problematic. They came in such large numbers from such varied origins that it was almost impossible to "know" and manage them. They clustered in crude, crowded quarters along narrow, labyrinthian lanes that were all but impenetrable to municipal authorities. These densely packed tenements came to be seen as reservoirs of disease, cradles of crime, wellsprings of subversion. Kipling's description of the Simla bazaar as a "rabbit-warren" where a man could easily "defy" the police suggests the sense of disorder and danger they evoked. The British were presented with an ongoing dilemma: how to maintain the labor that made their lives in the hill stations so pleasant without eroding the psychic and social walls that set them apart from the rest of India and that helped them sustain a common identity and purpose.

———

The British had sought to incorporate the indigenous inhabitants of the hills within their pristine vision of these areas by imagining them as noble savages, whose supposed innocence and intimacy with nature made them emblematic of the Edenic qualities of their highland surroundings. To preserve this image, the Todas of the Nilgiris were exempted from employment in the colonial economy. Most other hill peoples, however, soon found themselves enmeshed in the multifarious demands for labor that arose when the British arrived—and often quite literally *as* they arrived. Lord Amherst required the services of a thousand hill men to carry his entourage and their effects to Simla in 1827. Lord Auckland needed more than fifteen hundred to take him up to the hill station in 1838 and double that number to return him to the plains at the end of the season. A decade later, at least nine thousand local men were conscripted to transport Lord Dalhousie and his party, and later still the figure had risen to fifteen thousand and more.[1] Nearly every European who went to a hill station in the early years relied on local peoples for porterage services. It was not uncommon for a visitor to employ fifty or more men to carry the clothing, crockery, and other effects needed for a season's stay in the hills. A traveler en route to Mussoorie recalled encountering a party of twenty-four coolies

---

1. H. Montgomery Hyde, *Simla and the Simla Hill States under British Protection 1815–1835* (Lahore, 1961), 39; Emily Eden, *Up the Country: Letters from India* (1930; reprint, London, 1984), 105, 176; Sir William Lee-Warner, *The Life of the Marquis of Dalhousie*, vol. 1 (London, 1904), 270; Sir George Russell Clerk Collection, 60–68ff., MSS. Eur.D. 538/6, IOL.

struggling to haul a piano up the road to the station.[2] While these numbers were small in comparison with the armies of porters involved in the seasonal migrations of governors-general, the total volume of labor required for the movement of visitors and their goods to and from the hills must have been huge.

Porterage may have constituted the largest sector of employment for the peoples who inhabited the environs of the hill stations, but it was hardly the only one. The opening of the stations to regular traffic depended on the construction of roads through rugged mountain terrain, and most of the muscle for this enormously labor-intensive enterprise came from neighboring villages. Major John Briggs, resident of Satara, used eight hundred local men in 1825 to build a road to Mahabaleshwar. Simla's first road was constructed by laborers conscripted from the surrounding hill states. In Darjeeling, some twelve hundred local men were set to work on the roads by Captain G. S. Lloyd in 1839.[3] Public-works projects of various sorts required large quantities of labor in and around hill stations.

So too did the service economy. The seasonal influx of visitors created a heavy demand for domestic servants, including khitmatgars (butlers or head waiters), khansamahs (cooks), malis (gardeners), dhobis (washermen), bheestis (water carriers), jhampanis (coolies who carried sedan chairs and later pulled rickshaws), mehtars (sweepers), and others. While many visitors brought personal servants with them from the plains, all but a few depended on local peoples for menial tasks. According to Charles Dilke, a "small family" in Simla required the services of "three body servants, two cooks, one butler, two grooms, two gardeners, two messengers, two nurses, two washermen, two water-carriers, thirteen jampan-men, one sweeper, one lamp-cleaner, and one boy . . . or thirty-five in all." When the *Times* war correspondent William Howard Russell and a friend rented a house in Simla, they felt obliged to employ thirty servants, including ten woodcutters. Even transport within the station had surprisingly large labor ramifications. Mrs. Robert Moss King marveled at the sight of two hundred

2. "Mountaineer," *A Summer Ramble in the Himalayas* (London, 1860), 8. Mrs. Robert Moss King was one of those who required the labor of fifty coolies to move her baggage to and from Landour, and this figure does not include those who carried her piano. *The Diary of a Civilian's Wife in India 1877–1882*, vol. 2 (London, 1884), 45, 94.

3. Perin Bharucha, *Mahabaleswar: The Club 1881–1981* (Bombay, c. 1981), 23; Marquess of Dalhousie, *Private Letters of the Marquess of Dalhousie*, ed. J.G.A. Baird (Edinburgh and London, 1910), 181; H. Hosten, "The Centenary of Darjeeling," *Bengal: Past and Present* 39, pt. 2, no. 78 (April-June 1930): 118.

dandies (hammocklike vehicles), six hundred coolies (to carry the dandies), one hundred ponies, and one hundred syces (grooms) crammed together outside the Anglican church in Mussoorie on Sunday.[4]

How was this labor obtained? In the early years, much of it was coerced, especially for hard and heavy work like road building and porterage. The most notorious instances occurred in the western Himalayas, where the British got manpower through the system of begar, or forced labor.[5] While local chiefs had long imposed a corvée on their Pahari subjects, the British pushed this practice far past its traditional limits. They impressed thousands of peasants at a time, often expecting them to feed and shelter themselves for the weeks or even months that their services were required: the result was that "many perish on the road; but that is considered as a matter of very little consequence."[6] As the political agent for the Simla hill states, Captain Charles Kennedy was responsible for collecting the labor needed to take governors-general and other dignitaries to and from Simla. He claimed that begar, in accord with custom, was used simply for purposes of state, ignoring the fact that the scale of the British requirements exceeded anything demanded by indigenous rulers.[7] His assurances were in any case untrue. Victor Jacquemont reported that Kennedy had constructed his own home with forced labor: "some hundreds of mountaineers were summoned, who felled the trees around, squared them rudely, and, assisted by workmen from the plains, in one month constructed a spacious house."[8] And he did little to prevent visitors to the area from impressing local inhabitants as porters, wood cutters, water gatherers, and the like. Further east, the assistant commissioner at Dehra Dun was besieged by complaints from early visitors to Mussoorie because "I would not force the inhabitants of the Doon to carry loads up the hill," which he feared would lead to "the desertion of the province by those forced." Such fears were well-founded. When subsequent officials sanctioned the seizure of local inhabitants for porterage, they responded in the time-worn fashion of peasants—they

4. Charles Wentworth Dilke, *Greater Britain*, vol. 2 (London, 1869), 242; William Howard Russell, *My Diary in India*, vol. 2 (London, 1860), 96, 101; King, *Diary of a Civilian's Wife*, vol. 1, 144.

5. For a discussion of begar, see Ramachandra Guha, *The Unquiet Woods: Ecological Change and Peasant Resistance in the Himalaya* (Berkeley, 1989), 25–26.

6. Russell, *My Diary in India*, vol. 2, 161–62.

7. Kennedy to W. H. Macnaghten, 12 Sept. 1832, no. 25, Political Proceedings, Foreign Dept., INA.

8. Victor Jacquemont, *Letters from India*, vol. 1 (London, 1834), 226.

simply abandoned their villages.[9] Reactions such as these helped to persuade authorities of the need to place restrictions on the use of begar, which one memorandum bluntly described as "a species of extortion, almost amounting to plunder."[10] By midcentury, porterage services to and from the major hill stations had become commercialized, and private parties could no longer impress local people as they liked. They continued to do so, however, in outlying areas. A few years after Dalhousie was occupied in 1860, a local official reported that the routes leading to the station were "being steadily depopulated and impoverished through the people losing heart at the frequent and heavy exactions upon their time and labour which the yearly recurring 'season' entails." The problem continued through the end of the century at this remote hill station, and a guidebook published in 1898 felt obliged to warn its readers that "travellers requiring coolies should never impress them themselves."[11] Furthermore, the use of begar for official purposes did not come to an end until 1921.[12]

While begar was limited to the western Himalayas, other forms of forced labor were employed elsewhere in the highlands, especially during the early years of colonial rule. Sometimes, for example, convicts were put to work on roads and other public-works projects. More often neighboring zamindars and rajas were prevailed upon to provide unpaid manpower. The British resorted to these practices for reasons that went beyond the crudely extortionistic desire to obtain the cheapest labor available. They were convinced that mountain peoples, most of whom operated within the tight orbit of subsistence economies, were not susceptible to the attractions of work for wages. Captain Lloyd complained that the Lepchas of Darjeeling knew nothing of money and were "unaccustomed to the idea of working

9. E. J. Shore to Adjutant General of the Army, 4 Aug. 1828, in Municipal Department, Jan. 1905-A, Proceedings of the Government of the United Provinces, IOL; G.R.C. Williams, *Historical and Statistical Memoir of Dehra Doon* (Roorkee, 1874), 196. For an insightful examination of peasant strategies of resistance, see Michael Adas, "From Avoidance to Confrontation: Peasant Protest in Precolonial and Colonial Southeast Asia," in *Colonialism and Culture*, ed. Nicholas B. Dirks (Ann Arbor, 1992), 89–126.

10. Memorandum dated 25 Aug. 1841, E/4/767, India and Bengal Dispatches, IOL. Also see Macnaughten to Committee for Improvement of Simla, 17 Sept. 1832, no. 26, Political Proceedings, Foreign Dept., INA.

11. Extract from Chumba diary of superintendent of Chumba, May 1865, no. 273, Foreign Dept. Proceedings, Political Branch (A), INA; Capt. J. B. Hutchinson, *Guide to Dalhousie and the Neighbouring Hills*, 2d ed., rev. H. A. Rose (Lahore, 1898), 9.

12. Vipin Pubby, *Simla Then and Now: Summer Capital of the Raj* (New Delhi, 1988), 88.

for hire."[13] Few of the hill peoples, however, were as fully detached from market forces as the British imagined them to be, and they became less so as the British established summer retreats in their midst. The problem for the British was that there were other, more attractive avenues of entry into the colonial economy than wage labor. Hill stations created a voracious demand for foodstuffs, fodder, and fuel. The peasants who inhabited the surrounding hills were often perfectly placed to meet this demand. Many of them turned to market gardening as station bazaars sprang up. Others collected firewood and grasses from surrounding woodlands for sale in the stations. Agricultural production increased as farmers worked their fields more intensively, expanded the acreage they put under cultivation, and adopted higher-yielding, more marketable crops such as the potato.[14]

Some of the more enterprising local inhabitants became petty traders. The author of the Naini Tal district gazetteer observed:

> The increasing importance of the hill stations in Kumaun has affected the pattis [villages] which lie near the rail and along the chief routes in a very perceptible manner. The number of roadside shops and small bazars which have sprung up in recent years . . . is ample evidence of this. The people themselves are losing the characteristics of the hillman. . . . They are adverse to, and above, carrying loads.[15]

Similar developments in the vicinity of other hill stations led observers to note the increased prosperity of the local peasant population.[16] Thus, the market forces in the hill stations created countervailing trends, one pressing toward proletarianization, the other providing an alternative to it.

If the British wished to close this avenue of escape, they had to restrict the peasants' access to land. One place where authorities did precisely that was Mahabaleshwar. In 1853 a five-mile-wide forest reserve was

---

13. Quoted in H. V. Bayley, *Dorje-ling* (Calcutta, 1838), 52. Also see Lloyd's correspondence in nos. 129–133, 3 April 1839, Foreign Dept. Proceedings, INA.

14. According to the provincial gazetteer, the cultivated areas of the districts of Naini Tal and Garhwal increased 50 percent from 1872 to 1902 and from 1864 to 1896 respectively, and the cultivated area in the district of Almora increased 22 percent from 1872 to 1902. *Imperial Gazetteer of India, Provincial Series: United Provinces of Agra and Oudh,* vol. 2 (reprint, New Delhi, 1984), 252, 268, 282.

15. H. R. Neville, *Naini Tal: A Gazetteer, Being Volume XXXIV of the District Gazetteers of the United Provinces of Agra and Oudh* (Allahabad, 1904), 117.

16. Mrs. A. K. Oliver, *The Hill Station of Matheran* (Bombay, 1905), 125; H. G. Walton, *Dehra Dun: A Gazetteer, District Gazetteers of the United Provinces of Agra and Oudh,* vol. 1 (Allahabad, 1911), 68.

established around the station, eliminating cultivation on some two-thirds of the plateau's land surface. Local inhabitants who had hitherto grown crops for their own subsistence and the local market suddenly found themselves alienated from the land and forced to find wage employment. The district gazetteer frankly admitted that the upheaval "caused considerable hardship to a population then purely agricultural," observing that "manual labour while more precarious demanded more continuous and severe exertion than agriculture." It added that the changes experienced by the local population "involved a loss of social position carrying with it feelings of degradation only to be removed in process of time."[17] This honest appraisal of the impact of land alienation in Mahabaleshwar made it quite clear why the peasants surrounding other hill stations clung so ardently to their agrarian existence.

The switch to wage employment occurred elsewhere, though rarely in such an abrupt fashion. Revenue settlements put pressure on poorer peasants to find outside sources of income. The introduction of government cinchona plantations and the spread of commercial tea and coffee estates on the slopes surrounding hill stations pushed people off their land, often leaving them with little alternative but to seek employment with the very enterprises that were responsible for their loss. The creation of forest reserves and tree plantations closed large blocks of highland territory to the native inhabitants who had traditionally depended on them for grazing, fuel, fodder, game, and other resources. Lepchas, Paharis, and various others were victimized by these measures.[18]

Over time, then, a significant number of hill peoples did filter into local labor markets. The young, who had few opportunities or obligations within their villages, and the poor, who had little or no property to sustain their needs, probably made up the majority of these workers. Droughts and other natural disasters periodically pushed others onto the scene. Most likely viewed their entry into the labor market as a temporary expedient. "Occasionally," observed the author of the Dehra Dun district gazetteer, "one or more superfluous members of a large family takes service either in a hill

17. *Gazetteer of the Bombay Presidency*, vol. 19: *Satara* (Bombay, 1885), 497.
18. One result was incendiarism and other forms of resistance, as Ramachandra Guha and Madhav Gadgil show in "State Forestry and Social Conflict in British India," *Past and Present* 123 (May 1989): 141–77. Also see Guha's *Unquiet Woods* and "Saboteurs in the Forest: Colonialism and Peasant Resistance in the Indian Himalaya," in *Everyday Forms of Peasant Resistance*, ed. Forrest D. Colburn (New York and London, 1989), 64–92.

station or in the forest department, but the motive is simply to earn enough money to pay the revenue or the rent as the case may be."[19]

This pattern of seeking wage employment to supplement an agrarian existence made hill peoples troublesome for the British. They were seen as undisciplined and unreliable workers. They did not exert themselves as hard as their employers believed they should, and they could not be counted on to stick to their jobs through the season. Those engaged in domestic service were thought to be especially troublesome. A typical outburst condemned them as "a very bad class; dirty in person and habits, addicted to excessive drinking, thievish, and insolent."[20] The steady stream of complaints about their work habits, their wage demands, and their readiness to return to their villages indicates that they retained some degree of control over their own labor. They also retained a large reservoir of suspicion concerning British intentions, particularly in the regions where begar had been imposed on the population. They often fled their jobs when census takers, vaccination teams, and other representatives of imperial authority arrived on the scene, and they were susceptible to the chilling, recurrent rumor that the British abducted Indians to extract oil from their brains or bodies for use as medicine for ailing viceroys and other dignitaries. This rumor emptied the western Himalayan hill stations of their local labor forces on numerous occasions.[21]

The economic relationship between the hill stations and the inhabitants of the surrounding slopes was a complicated one, and this summary account cannot do justice to the wide variations in practices from place to place. But two generalizations seem warranted. First, most of the peasants who lived in the shadows of hill stations managed to escape the harness of

---

19. Walton, *Dehra Dun*, 68.

20. E. F. Burton, *An Indian Olio* (London, 1888), 138. See also E. B. Peacock, *A Guide to Murree and Its Neighbourhood* (Lahore, 1883), 9; W. H. Carey, comp., *A Guide to Simla with a Descriptive Account of the Neighbouring Sanitaria* (Calcutta, 1870), 18; *The Visitors' Handbook of the Nilgiris* (Madras, 1897), 61; and *Newman's Guide to Darjeeling and Neighbourhood* (Calcutta, 1900), 29. Richard F. Burton was one of those whose confrontations with Ootacamund's servants brought him before the local magistrate, an experience he angrily recounts in *Goa, and the Blue Mountains* (1851; reprint, Berkeley, 1991), 306–8.

21. Constance F. Gordon Cumming, *In the Himalayas and on the Indian Plains* (London, 1884), 484–85; Hyde, *Simla and the Simla Hill States*, 19; "Mountaineer," *A Summer Ramble*, 8–9. British efforts to send plague victims to hospitals stirred similar rumors in Bombay and Poona (now Pune) at the end of the century, reports David Arnold, *Colonizing the Body: State Medicine and Epidemic Disease in Nineteenth-Century India* (Berkeley, 1993), 220–21.

proletarianization as a primary or permanent mode of production. Second, their escape increased the local demand for labor from other sources.

---

A panoply of Indians followed the British up to the hill stations. Khitmatgars, khansamahs, ayahs, syces, and other servants accompanied their masters on their seasonal sojourns. Stonemasons, carpenters, and artisans of other sorts journeyed from the plains to offer their skills to Europeans. Merchants and shopkeepers made the most of the economic opportunities that arose where the British congregated by importing goods and opening shops.

A dearth of census data makes it difficult to determine the rate of Indian migration to the hill stations in the first half of the nineteenth century, though anecdotal evidence indicates that the influx began early and involved significant numbers. The Indian population of Panchgani, for example, nearly doubled in size within seven years of the arrival of the first European settler.[22] A reliable run of population statistics does exist for the larger hill stations by the latter part of the century, and these figures demonstrate the scale of the influx by Indians from other regions. In the Punjab, for example, the census of 1881 found that the hill stations there had grown far more quickly since the previous census (1868) than any other towns in the province, with Simla expanding by 74 percent and Murree by a whopping 84 percent over the intervening thirteen years. The population of the Nilgiris more than doubled between 1871 and 1901, and in the course of the 1890s alone, Ootacamund and Coonoor grew by 22 percent and 20 percent, respectively, compared with an average of 7 percent in the rest of the presidency. Darjeeling's population mushroomed from around 3,000 in 1871 to nearly 17,000 in 1901, and the entire district (including Kalimpong and Kurseong) experienced the most rapid rate of growth on record for nineteenth-century Bengal, expanding from 10,000 in 1850 to nearly 250,000 in 1901. By 1900, roughly half or more of the inhabitants of the Simla, Nilgiri, and Darjeeling districts had been born elsewhere.[23]

The overwhelming majority of the Indians in the hill stations were adult males engaged in seasonal migrant labor. That few brought wives or

22. John Chesson, "Hill Sanitaria of Western India: Panchgunny," *Bombay Miscellany* 4 (1862): 337.
23. Denzil Ibbetson, *Report on the Census of the Panjab, Taken on February 1881*, vol. 1 (Calcutta, 1883), Tables A, C, F; W. Francis, *The Nilgiris* (Madras, 1908), 123–24; L. S. S. O'Malley, *Darjeeling* (Calcutta, 1907), 35–36.

children with them was one of the most striking features of the hill stations' demography. In Simla, the ratio of Indian men to women was about five to one for the summer months (slightly less in the winter) and the ratio of adults to children was much the same.[24] Emily Eden observed that there were "very few children ever to be seen in [the bazaar]. Natives who come to open shops, etc., never bring their families, from the impossibility of moving women in a sufficiently private manner."[25] While Eden may have been right in pointing to purdah as a factor in accounting for the absence of women, economic constraints almost certainly predominated in the considerations of most migrants.[26] They simply could not afford to move their families to Simla or to house them once they arrived. The absence of women was noted in other hill stations as well. "The traders and domestic servants are unable to afford the expense of the journey for their families, who have consequently to remain down in the plains," the report of the 1911 summer census for Dalhousie stated. The male/female ratio for that station's Indian population was 100/30. In Murree, the same conditions applied, and there the male/female ratio was 100/28. The disparity was a bit less stark in Darjeeling, where there were roughly twice as many men as women. In Ootacamund and Coonoor, "native traders, servants, coolies, and other temporary residents . . . are not, to any great extent, accompanied by their women." The Nilgiris as a whole had a "smaller proportion of females to males than any other [district] in the Presidency."[27] It is highly unlikely that there was a single hill station where Indian males did not outnumber females by a wide margin.

24. Summer-census data showed the female portion of the Indian population to be 19.2 percent for 1869, 19.3 percent for 1889, 22.0 percent for 1898, and 20.6 percent for 1904. The winter census of 1868 found that females constituted 27.1 percent of the population; the 1891 winter census showed them to constitute 23.4 percent. Only 17 percent of the Indian population in the 1898 census were children. See Annual Report of the Simla Municipality, 1904–5, 18, HPSA; and *Report of the Simla Extension Committee, 1898* (Simla, 1898), annexture A(2).

25. Eden, *Up the Country*, 301.

26. The Indians who could most easily afford to bring their families to Simla were the Bengali government clerks, who received a rent subsidy and a family maintenance allowance in the late nineteenth century. Yet 82 of the 158 Indian clerks who accompanied the government to Simla in 1889–90 left their families behind in Calcutta. Appendix to Simla Allowance Committee Report, 17, in Dispatch #19, 1890, L/PJ/6/276/723, Public and Judicial Dept., IOL.

27. *Report on the Summer Census of Dalhousie, 1911* (Lahore, 1912), 6–7; *Report on the Summer Census of Murree, 1911* (Lahore, 1912), 5; *Darjeeling District Gazetteer, Statistics, 1901–02* (Calcutta, 1905), 2–3; H. B. Grigg, *A Manual of the Nilagiri District* (Madras, 1880), 29; Francis, *Nilgiris*, 124.

The British could find some comfort in this demographic disequilibrium. A population that consisted predominantly of adult males lacked the biological means to perpetuate itself, to beget the progeny that would secure it an enduring place in the stations where it labored. This was a problem the British understood quite well, of course, since it plagued their own presence in India. Only in the hill stations had they managed to establish the demographic balance between men and women—and adults and children—that resembled that of normal reproductive communities. The absence of a similar balance among the Indians acquired all the more significance from this contrast. In effect, the colonial demographics of gender and age had been turned on their heads in the hill stations. This made it easier for the British to convince themselves that the Indian inhabitants of the hill stations were mere transients, alien and evanescent parties who had no claim to these places. "This station is not a native town," insisted a public health official who sought the removal of most menial laborers from Simla. Similarly, the Ootacamund Municipal Council declared in 1877 that the station "should be regarded as an English and not a native town . . . [since] the whole native population is directly or indirectly dependent on the presence of the European community."[28]

Where did these laborers come from? Each hill station drew its migrant population from many sources, and the larger the station, the larger the hinterland that supplied its needs. Different sectors of employment tended to attract different clusters of people from different regions and different castes, classes, and religions. The forces that drove these people to seek employment in the hill stations were equally varied. While a full appreciation of the complex contours of these movements of migrant labor must await further research at the local and regional level, their general patterns can be discerned. The influence of those patterns on British uses of the hill stations is what concerns us here.

The Indian population of Simla was composed overwhelmingly of outsiders to the district during the summer season, and a substantial minority were outsiders to the province of Punjab as a whole.[29] Pamela Kanwar's study provides a richly detailed analysis of this remarkably varied, highly

28. W. A. C. Roe, "Report on the Sanitary Inspection of the Municipal Town of Simla," 10 May 1894, 5, Simla Municipal Proceedings, vol. 6, 1893–94, HPSA. Ootacamund Municipal Council quoted in Judith Theresa Kenny, "Constructing an Imperial Hill Station: The Representation of British Authority in Ootacamund" (Ph.D. diss., Syracuse University, 1990), 173.
29. The summer census of 1921 showed that only 20 percent of the station's Indian population had been born within Simla district, and nearly 30 percent had

balkanized population.[30] Among the lowliest inhabitants were the sweepers, who consisted largely of untouchables from the Jullundur and Hoshiarpur districts to the west of the Simla hill states. Poverty-stricken peasants from these districts as well as the Kangra hills north of Simla filled the ranks of the rickshaw-coolie force. Most of the porters who carried heavy loads through the station, as well as many construction workers, came from Kashmir and Ladakh. Taken together, the porters, rickshaw coolies, sweepers, and other low-skilled laborers made up about 20 percent of the employed Indian population, according to the summer census of 1904.[31] Another 25 percent or so of the population consisted of shopkeepers and other merchants, petty artisans, and a small contingent of professionals. Soods from Kangra and, to a lesser extent, the Punjab plains dominated this sector of employment. They counted among their numbers lawyers and doctors, moneylenders, timber contractors, forest lessees, and traders in various goods. They owned the greater part of the lower bazaar, as well as properties elsewhere in the station. Other groups found niches in commerce as well, including Jain shopkeepers, Sikh building contractors and tailors, Kashmiri shawl and dried-fruit merchants, and Punjabi Muslim butchers. Another 12 percent of the Indian working population consisted of government clerks, most of whom were Bengalis until the government began to recruit Punjabis in significant numbers in the early twentieth century. Finally, servants were the largest single occupational category among the Indian population of Simla, constituting 37 percent. This category probably included the chaprassis (office messengers) who carried out menial tasks for government agencies. They came for the most part from the neighboring hill states. Unfortunately, we know a good deal less about the large number of domestic servants in private homes. Anecdotal sources suggest that they were an extremely mixed group, with local peoples dominating the lower ranks, especially as bheestis and mehtars, while the more skilled employees, such as khansamahs and khitmatgars, often came with their employers from sundry parts of northern India.

"The people of the Nilgiris consist . . . very largely of immigrants," observed the author of the 1908 district gazetteer.[32] Ootacamund's pop-

been born outside of Punjab province. See Summer Census of Simla, 1921, Table IIA, in Simla Municipal Corporation Records, 179/1933/123/1921/II, HPSA.

30. Pamela Kanwar, *Imperial Simla* (Delhi, 1990), esp. chs. 9–12.

31. The 1904 census data on occupations come from the Annual Report of the Simla Municipality, 1904–5, 19, HPSA.

32. Francis, *Nilgiris*, 124.

ulation grew from 12,335 to 18,596 and Coonoor's from 4,778 to 8,525 between 1881 and 1901. The district's tea, coffee, and cinchona estates attracted thousands more. The great majority of these immigrants came from the immediately surrounding regions—Coimbatore, Malabar, Canara, and Mysore—but there were people "from every part almost of India," according to one knowledgeable source.[33] As a result, the Nilgiris was the "most polyglot area in the Presidency," with some 30–40 percent of the population who spoke either Tamil or Badaga, and smaller portions for whom Telegu, Canarese, Malayalam, Hindustani, and, of course, the local Kurumba, Kota, and Toda were the native tongues.[34] Different groups occupied different niches in the local economy. Most of the government employees and professionals of various sorts were said to be Vellalas, a rather amorphous caste that dominated government service throughout Tamil India. Vellalas also constituted a significant portion of the shopkeeper population, which also included Muslims from Malabar and a caste of traders and artisans known as Chettis. The most prominent businessmen, however, were Parsis from Bombay, who first appeared in the Nilgiris in the mid-1820s. Although their numbers were small, they had their own burial ground, and they owned a great deal of property in Ootacamund and Coonoor. As was the case in Simla, the servant sector seemed to encompass a variety of peoples, both indigenous and immigrant. Many servants, as well as laborers on the coffee and tea estates, were identified as Paraiyans, an agricultural laborer caste from Coimbatore and other Tamil districts.[35]

Although Darjeeling has been described as a "Babel of tribes and nations,"[36] suggesting the sort of ethnic diversity that characterized the other large hill stations, this phrase is rather misleading. Darjeeling was, in fact, dominated by immigrants from Nepal. Dr. Arthur Campbell estimated that the district had no more than one thousand inhabitants when he became superintendent in 1839, and he encouraged Nepali settlers to take up so-called waste land since the station's growing demand for foodstuffs was not being met by the Lepchas, with their predilection for *jhum* (shifting cultivation). Nepalis also came to Darjeeling to enlist at its army recruiting station.[37] It was the founding of the tea industry in the mid-1850s, how-

33. Capt. J. Ouchterlony, *Geographical and Statistical Memoir of a Survey of the Neilgherry Mountains* (Madras, 1868), 69.

34. Francis, *Nilgiris*, 124.

35. Grigg, *Manual*, 33–34.

36. O'Malley, *Darjeeling*, 41.

37. See Joseph Dalton Hooker, *Himalayan Journals*, vol. 1 (London, 1854), 118–19.

Figure 13.   Coolie carrying a chest of Darjeeling tea. From *Darjeeling and Its Mountain Railway* (Calcutta, 1921).

ever, that brought the inflow of Nepalis to full flood. By 1874, there were 113 tea gardens in the area, employing 19,424 workers, and at the end of the century the labor force had risen to 64,000, a third of the district's entire population (Figure 13). Nearly all of these tea workers—96 percent, according to the 1941 census—were Nepalis. In the district's hill subdivisions as a whole the Nepalis constituted over 86 percent of the population. This "pushing, thriving race," as the British were fond of calling them, had come to dominate the district.[38] In the township of Darjeeling itself, however, the population was rather more heterogeneous, as it was in Kalimpong and Kurseong as well. The rickshaw and dandy coolies were said to be mostly Bhutia and Lepcha men, and their women were prized as ayahs. One guidebook told its readers, in a telling turn of phrase, that the Bhutias and Lepchas, *"when caught young,* make excellent cooks and khitmutgars, and they have the advantage of having no caste prejudices, and of being able to turn their hands to any kind of work."[39] Tibetans dominated the trans-Himalayan trade. Most of the merchants, professionals, and other middle-class Indians were Marwaris, Biharis, and Bengalis. The occupations of bheesti, dhobi, and tailor were also dominated by people from the plains, and the butchers were generally Muslim immigrants. Still, some two-thirds of the station's population were Nepalis, who found employment as servants, bearers, syces, carpenters, blacksmiths, and small traders.[40]

Nepalis also moved in significant numbers further east to Shillong. A Gurkha garrison was stationed there in the mid-nineteenth century and the first Assamese tea estates recruited Nepali laborers. Shillong, however, attracted a much wider range of peoples than Darjeeling did. The indigenous Khasis, who worked as porters, carpenters, masons, domestic servants, graziers, and market gardeners, made up about half the population of the station. The other half consisted primarily of Bengali government clerks and professionals, Bihari dhobis and small traders, Marwari merchants, Assamese servants, and Nepali porters and graziers. The tea industry, meanwhile, increasingly turned to Chotanagpur and other parts of central India to supply its labor needs, and some of these peoples filtered into the bazaar wards of Shillong as well. The population of the hill station quadrupled between 1878 and 1901, increasing from 2,149 to 8,384. What

38. W. W. Hunter, *A Statistical Account of Bengal,* vol. 10: *Districts of Darjiling and Jalpaiguri, and State of Kuch Behar* (London, 1876), 53, 165; O'Malley, *Darjeeling,* 74–75; Arthur Jules Dash, *Bengal District Gazetteers: Darjeeling* (Alipore, 1947), 63–64. For a general examination of the Nepalis in Darjeeling, see Tanka B. Subba, *Dynamics of a Hill Society* (Delhi, 1989).

39. R. D. O'Brien, *Darjeeling, the Sanitarium of Bengal; and Its Surroundings* (Calcutta, 1883), 27 (my emphasis). This statement recurred in later guidebooks.

40. In addition to ibid., see *Newman's Guide to Darjeeling,* 30; G. Hutton Taylor, *Thacker's Guide Book to Darjeeling and Its Neighbourhood* (Calcutta, 1899), 28; and G. S. Bomwetsch, *Before the Glory of the Snows: A Hand Book to Darjeeling* (Calcutta, 1899), 25–27. A detailed breakdown of the population of Darjeeling in 1941 is supplied in Dash, *Bengal District Gazetteers,* 84.

had been the home of a few dozen Khasi tribesmen at midcentury had become a crowded and remarkably cosmopolitan town by the century's end.[41]

———

The preceding examples demonstrate that at least the major hill stations acquired a very different demographic and ethnic shape than the British had intended for them. Far from remaining small and intimate enclaves isolated from the influences of India and Indians, the hill stations became bustling centers of commerce, service, and administration, bursting at the seams with Indians from far and wide. How could the essential Englishness of these places persist in the midst of such multitudes? How could the presumption that they stood apart from India and its peoples survive the presence of so many and such varied Indians? The British sought to sustain the enclavist flavor of their hill stations through the manipulation of space, sanitation, and social behavior.

Although the massive influx of seasonal laborers to the hill stations produced dreadfully overcrowded and unsanitary conditions, the British were initially reluctant to acknowledge, much less confront, this problem, clinging instead to the illusion that their highland retreats were pristine and unpolluted. It was especially easy for the British to ignore the conditions in the bazaars since so few of them ever entered those areas, but the neglect of sanitation requirements extended quite literally into their own backyards. "Very few private houses in Simla," reported municipal officials in 1877–78, "were provided with latrines for the use of servants and natives living in the compounds, many had only mere mat or wooden enclosures, and all were of such faulty construction as to be most offensive."[42] Individual employers simply assumed that their servants would fend for themselves, as they generally did on the plains. The Ootacamund municipality's request for homeowners to erect latrines for their servants was a "dead letter" when the Madras sanitary commissioner conducted an investigation in 1868, and as a result "there is a general foecal taint to the atmosphere" due to defecation in the surrounding undergrowth. Conditions were hardly better in the station's main bazaar, where not a single latrine existed for

41. See H. C. Sarkar, *Guide to Shillong* (Calcutta, n.d.); K. D. Saha, "The Study of Community-wide Distribution and the Growth of Population in Shillong," in *Cultural Profile of Shillong*, ed. B. B. Goswami (Calcutta, 1979), 4–31; and M. L. Bose, *Social History of Assam* (New Delhi, 1989).

42. Annual Report of the Simla Municipality, 1877–78, 27, HPSA.

an estimated three to four thousand inhabitants. Open sewers flowed into the lake, which supplied drinking water for much of the population.[43] Other large hill stations faced similar sanitation problems.

It is hardly surprising, then, that typhoid fever, cholera, and other diseases of human contamination broke out with increasing frequency in the hill stations in the latter part of the nineteenth century. Once it became obvious that the lack of sanitation facilities for Indians posed a health threat to Europeans, authorities began to act. As a result of the Bengal Presidency Act X of 1842 and the India-wide Act XXVI of 1850, hill stations were able to establish municipal governments with powers to impose conservancy regulations.[44] The new municipalities built public latrines, regulated private privies, dug sewer systems, and established safe water supplies. By the late nineteenth century, Kanwar notes that Simla had the same number of municipal health inspectors and sweepers as did Allahabad, which was twice its size.[45] Yet the expanding populations of the hill stations continued to overwhelm efforts to keep them clean. One irritated health official in Simla described the situation:

> [A] very large number of the lower classes of Natives yearly flock
> into this station and with them may come epidemic disease of all kinds;
> in fact . . . all details sink into insignificance compared with the ever-
> increasing coolie population. . . . [E]very idler, every cooly out of work
> at his home, every servant who cannot obtain employment swarm into
> Simla every season hoping for a job.[46]

A 1905 study found that Simla's most crowded bazaar averaged 17.4 residents per house, the highest population density in the Punjab. Sanitary-inspection reports from Naini Tal and Mussoorie at the turn of the century declared that dreadful overcrowding had made these stations "hotbed[s] of disease." Shillong's health officer warned that "congested localities are becoming a growing menace to the public health of this hill-station."[47]

43. J. L. Ranking, *Report upon the Sanitary Condition of Ootacamund* (Madras, 1868), 6, 18.

44. Hugh Tinker, *The Foundations of Local Self-Government in India, Pakistan and Burma* (New York, 1968), 28–29.

45. Pamela Kanwar, "The Changing Image of Simla," Urban History Association Occasional Papers Series 10, 1989, 5.

46. Roe, "Report on the Sanitary Inspection," 5.

47. *Report of the Simla Sanitary Investigation Committee* (Simla, 1905), 11. For Naini Tal, see correspondence in Municipal Department, March 1904-A and Sept. 1908-A, Proceedings of the Government of the United Provinces, IOL. For Mussoorie, see reports on sanitary conditions in Municipal Department, Dec.

Scholars have shown that British municipal policies regarding sanitation and disease often served as a rationale for colonial urban segregation.[48] John Cell argues that this was not the case in India, as opposed to Africa, but his definition of segregation—"the conscious manipulation of physical space on the part of the dominant group in order to achieve or maintain a psychological gap between itself and a group it intends to keep in an inferior place"—does in fact correspond to the aims of public health authorities and other officials in the hill stations.[49] Repeated efforts were made to regulate the boundaries between European and Indian zones and to remove bazaars from sites that impinged too directly upon neighboring European areas. When a fire destroyed Matheran's market in 1865, authorities used the opportunity to remove it from the center of the station, arguing that it threatened to contaminate the lake, the station's source of drinking water. In 1893–94, the market was moved once again, this time to the very edge of the plateau, where its "rubbish can without difficulty be thrown into the Ravine away from human habitation."[50] In Simla, a similar initiative occurred when the outbreak of cholera in 1875 provided officials with the pretext to prohibit Indians from rebuilding shops and homes lost to fire on the Upper Mall, which became as a consequence reserved for European-owned stores. The Simla Improvement Committee of 1877 sought an even more radical excision of the Indian community. Disturbed by the way "the native town has sprung up and extended to the very heart of the station," it advocated the demolition of the entire lower bazaar, which was "saturating the site with filth and polluting its limited water-supply."[51] This plan proved impossible to carry out, and in 1907 the bazaar's "insanitary excrescences upon the European quarter" again

---

1905-A, Feb. 1906-A, and June 1906-A, Proceedings of the Government of the United Provinces, IOL. For Shillong, see Sarkar, *Guide to Shillong,* 47.

48. See Maynard W. Swanson, "The Sanitation Syndrome: Bubonic Plague and Urban Native Policy in the Cape Colony, 1900–1909," *Journal of African History* 18, no. 3 (1977): 387–410; Philip D. Curtin, "Medical Knowledge and Urban Planning in Tropical Africa," *American Historical Review* 90, no. 3 (June 1985): 594–613; and John W. Cell, "Anglo-Indian Medical Theory and the Origins of Segregation in West Africa," *American Historical Review* 91, no. 2 (April 1986): 307–35.

49. Cell, "Anglo-Indian Medical Theory," 307.

50. Oliver, *The Hill Station of Matheran,* 28–29.

51. Simla Improvement Scheme Report of 1877, in Simla Municipal Corporation Records, 103/1150/1/1877/I, and Annual Report of the Simla Municipality, 1877–78, 29, HPSA.

occupied the attention of a municipal improvement committee.[52] While authorities could not make the lower bazaar disappear, they could at least ensure that it did not encroach on European areas by delineating the precise boundaries beyond which it could not grow—a policy that had the natural effect of increasing the population density of the bazaar and thus its health problems.[53] Much the same sequence of events occurred in Mussoorie. There the anxieties over pollution and disease reached such a fever pitch in 1905 that the army prohibited a regimental band from returning to the station for the summer season until conditions had improved. The solution proposed by a medical inspector and a committee of investigation was the removal of the main bazaar, although again it proved easier to cordon it off than raze it.[54]

In Ootacamund, however, authorities did manage to move a substantial portion of the bazaar population to peripheral sites. Distress about sanitation in the station had inspired calls to "re-build the native town in a less central" location as early as the 1860s.[55] The appearance of plague in 1903 provided the pretext for undertaking the drastic measures that health officials had long been urging.[56] Armed with broad powers under newly instituted plague regulations, authorities began to demolish portions of the main bazaar and the adjacent Mettucherry and Agaraharam quarters, as well as to prohibit further construction in these areas. By 1911, 158 Indian houses had been cleared away as a plague-prevention measure, and another 298 were razed to make way for the railway. Thousands of people were displaced from their homes, and while some were relocated in the Kandal bazaar at the western outskirts of the station, the net effect of this so-called slum clearance was increased overcrowding. Municipal authorities knew that the "clearing of congested areas does not in itself reduce but increases overcrowding if no provision is made for the occupants of the condemned houses," and they conceded that "no remedy has been discovered for this

52. *Report of the Simla Improvement Committee* (Simla, 1907), 17.

53. See Kanwar, *Imperial Simla*, 58–60, 137–38.

54. See Inspection Report on Sanitary Conditions in Mussoorie by Major J. Chaytor-White, 30 Aug. 1905, Municipal Department, Dec. 1905-A, and Report of Committee on Sanitation of Mussoorie, 28 Dec. 1905, Municipal Department, June 1906-A, Proceedings of the Government of the United Provinces, IOL.

55. Report of A. Wedderburn, president of the Municipal Committee of Ootacamund, in Ranking, *Report,* app. A.

56. For a fascinating study of the varied social and political ramifications of the plague in imperial India, see David Arnold, "Touching the Body: Perspectives on the Indian Plague," in *Selected Subaltern Studies,* ed. Ranajit Guha and Gayatri Chakravorty Spivak (New York, 1988), 391–426, which appears in revised form as ch. 5 of Arnold's *Colonizing the Body.*

[overcrowding]."[57] From their perspective, however, the operation had succeeded in its main task of driving large numbers of Indians out of the central part of the station and establishing a cordon sanitaire around those who remained.[58]

The outbreak of plague at the end of the nineteenth century was used to sanction another policy for controlling the influx of Indians to the hill stations.[59] In Simla the British opened medical-inspection posts on the main routes into the station in 1899. The most important of these posts was at Tara Devi, one of the final stops on the train journey to Simla. All third-class passengers were required to disembark for a physical examination that seemed designed to humiliate them. Those suspected of carrying contagions were turned away; the rest were fumigated and their belongings disinfected. The post continued to operate long after the epidemic had subsided. In 1926, vehement protests from Indians persuaded the Punjab's director of public health to close the inspection post, which he condemned as "that medieval anachronism," but others missed its powers, and it reopened in 1930. It was widely thought to have been used to prevent nationalist agitators from entering Simla.[60]

Sanitation policies and other public health measures were not the only means by which the British sought to regulate the Indians in their midst. In 1883, the Darjeeling Municipal Porter's Act was enacted in response to what local authorities described as "insolent, clamorous and turbulent" behavior and "extortionate" fee demands by the stations' porters. The act regulated porters' rates, required them to obtain licenses and wear brass identity badges, and imposed penalties on those who deserted or otherwise failed to fulfill their terms of service. Similar legislation was introduced in Simla, Mussoorie, and other Himalayan hill stations.[61] The conduct and

57. Ootacamund Municipal Report for 1911–12, 7–8, Municipal G.O. #1676, TNSA.

58. Ootacamund Municipal Reports for 1903–4, 1906–7, 1908–9, and 1911–12, Municipal G.O. #1847, #1686, #1076, #1676, TNSA. Also see Kenny, "Constructing an Imperial Hill Station," 222–29.

59. Arnold, *Colonizing the Body*, 208.

60. Inspection Report of Simla, 1926, and Simla Inspection Note, 1930, in Simla Municipal Corporation Records, 1/2/4/1925–28/IV and 1/2/4/1929–35/V, HPSA; Raja Bhasin, *Simla: The Summer Capital of British India* (New Delhi, 1992), 87–88; Pubby, *Simla Then and Now*, 92.

61. "Report on Working of Act V (Darjeeling Porter's Act)," 16 March 1885, Municipal Branch, Municipal Dept., Proceedings of the Lieutenant Governor of Bengal, WBSA. Also see Municipal Branch Proceedings for June 1883, Aug. 1884, and Oct. 1899, WBSA; and O'Brien, *Darjeeling*, 8–9, 27–28. For Simla's adoption of the Darjeeling Act, see President, Municipal Council, to Deputy Commissioner,

composition of Indian migrants were influenced in other ways as well. Most hill stations expelled beggars and other vagrants as a matter of course. The Simla municipality introduced a bylaw in 1891 that prohibited all porters, except those carrying the baggage of European visitors, from appearing on the Mall from 4 to 8 P.M. between the months of April and October—when, in other words, the Mall was most heavily frequented by Europeans. Similar rules were adopted in Naini Tal. Public-works projects also reduced contact between Indians and Europeans. In Darjeeling, for example, a new road was constructed in 1886 so that Europeans could visit the Lloyd Botanic Gardens without having to pass through the bazaar. Simla went even further, cutting a tunnel under the Mall in 1905 to divert coolie traffic from the notice of Europeans.[62] Whatever other purposes these road projects and labor regulations and sanitation measures were intended to serve, each had the effect of making the Indians' presence less visible and vexatious to the British.

Above all, however, the use of topography made the Indian inhabitants of the hill stations "invisible." The British understood the symbolic significance of altitude. As one of them put it, "Nothing is more likely to maintain British prestige than the occupation of commanding ground by the British race."[63] Invariably, the British took the high ground for themselves, consigning the Indians to the lower elevations, where they were usually out of sight and out of mind. This practice was especially apparent in the Himalayas, where the precipitous terrain favored the strict segregation of Briton and Indian across a vertical plane. But it could be seen in other hill stations as well. In Shillong, "the hills in the neighbourhood of the Government offices . . . have been reserved for the European population."[64] Even the highland plateaus of peninsular India often had sufficient variations in elevation for racial boundaries to follow their contours. The

---

Simla, March 1892, Simla Municipal Proceedings, vol. 5, HPSA. For Mussoorie, see Rules for Regulation of Porters and Jhampanis, Aug. 1912, Municipal Department, Proceedings of the Government of the United Provinces, IOL.

62. Simla Municipal By-law, Section 144, Act XX of 1891, Simla Municipal Proceedings, vol. 6, 1893–94; C. W. Murphy, *A Guide to Naini Tal and Kumaun* (Allahabad, 1906), Appendix; "Annual Report of Royal Botanic Gardens for Year 1885–86," 3, July 1886, Medical Branch, Municipal Dept., Proceedings of the Lieutenant-Governor of Bengal, WBSA; Kanwar, *Imperial Simla*, 63–64.

63. *Selections from the Records of the Government of India (Military Department)*, no. 2: *Report on the Extent and Nature of the Sanitary Establishments for European Troops in India* (Calcutta, 1861–62), 153.

64. Sarkar, *Guide to Shillong*, 47.

British justified this use of topography, as they did so many other measures to separate themselves from Indians, on sanitary grounds:

> The natural separateness of the European from the Native part of the town . . . is of supreme importance from a sanitary point of view. Above, the air is fresh and pure, and cannot be contaminated by that below. The undulating surface and slopes of the hills carry away in their surface drainage all decaying matter and there is no chance for stagnation. So distinct are the two localities, that they bear but slight relationship [to one another].[65]

To reduce the relationship between the European and Indian sectors of the hill stations to its sparest utilitarian essentials was precisely the point behind the use of altitude in site selection. The entire social structure of a hill station was often embedded in its topography like successive layers of geological strata, as Nora Mitchell and others have noted.[66] In Simla, the government deliberately reinforced this association by providing senior officials with fine houses upon the ridge, English and Anglo-Indian clerks with cottages along the slopes, and Indian clerks with rooms in dormitories further below.[67] The process occurred with less deliberation in other hill stations, but the results were much the same. As one medical official put it with reference to Ootacamund, the British lived "away from, and out of sight of, the native town."[68]

———

As long as the Indians remained sequestered in the bazaar wards at the lower reaches of the hill stations, the British could to some degree retain their illusion of seclusion. As one visitor remarked about the Simla bazaar, "This is a place where no Europeans ever dream of going."[69] They had no reason to do so, given the physical and social structure of the hill stations. But when Indians began to infiltrate the station wards that the British themselves inhabited, this illusion experienced intolerable strains.

65. J. S. C. Eagan, *The Nilgiri Guide and Directory* (Mysore, 1911), 146–47.
66. Nora Mitchell, "The Indian Hill-Station: Kodaikanal," University of Chicago Department of Geography Research Paper 141, 1972, 5. Also see Nutan Tyagi, *Hill Resorts of U.P. Himalaya: A Geographical Study* (New Delhi, 1991), 116, 130.
67. Kanwar, *Imperial Simla*, 56.
68. Major R. Bryson, "Nilgiri Sanitaria," in Eagan, *The Nilgiri Guide*, 81.
69. Constance F. Gordon Cumming, *From the Hebrides to the Himalayas*, vol. 2 (London, 1876), 122.

The first Indians to establish a palpable presence in those areas of the hill stations that the British held for themselves were the princes. Drawn by the political might and prestige that accrued to the larger stations when they became the summer headquarters of government, a number of wealthy princes began to take up seasonal residence there in the late nineteenth century. They expected the kinds of accommodations that could be obtained only in the station wards. By 1885, thirteen princes had purchased thirty-four of the finest houses in Simla, and others had acquired properties in Darjeeling, Ootacamund, Naini Tal, and elsewhere.[70] While many of these purchases were made as investments, with the houses leased to British tenants, more and more Indian princes took to the hills for their own pleasure.

British residents did not entirely object to the princes' entry onto the local scene. The lavish parties they hosted were welcomed, and they injected considerable capital into local civic and social projects. Their exotic splendor gave some color to hill-station society. One prominent official argued that it was a good thing that they were "brought more and more into social intercourse with the higher European community" since it would "promote a good understanding between European and Native." He compared the princes to "noblemen 'coming up to town' during 'the season' or for short periods when 'the Court' was there."[71]

Most officials, however, were disturbed by the influx of princes to the hill stations and particularly to Simla. After nervously tracking the princes' property purchases in the station for several years, the government moved to halt their encroachments. In 1890 the nizam of Hyderabad was prevented from purchasing the estate known as Snowden when its owner, Lord Roberts, the outgoing commander-in-chief of the army, put it up for sale. Lord Lansdowne, the viceroy responsible for prohibiting the transaction, issued an edict the following year that enjoined the princes from making further property purchases or visits to Simla without permission from the government.[72] Predictably, a sanitary rationale was offered for this regulation: the large entourages that accompanied the princes endangered the health of surrounding residents because of their deplorable hygiene. The secretary of the Simla municipality complained that "the hordes of ragamuffins who follow these Princes cause no end of trouble to our conser-

70. Memorandum regarding Simla houses, in file on acquisition by native chiefs of land in British territory, Sept. 1886, nos. 431–33, Foreign Dept. Proceedings, Secret-I, INA.

71. Minute by Sir Theodore Hope, in ibid.

72. See Kanwar, *Imperial Simla*, 95–98.

vancy officers.''[73] By pointing their fingers at the princes' retainers rather than at the princes themselves, the British sought to disguise their true concerns. But what really distressed Lansdowne and others was the simple fact that Indians were penetrating a British preserve—indeed, arguably their most important social and political preserve in India. It made little difference that the Indians who did this penetrating were princes. "My own idea is that the presence of these Chiefs at hill stations is distinctly undesirable," Lansdowne told the governor of Madras, "and that we ought to discourage it in every way."[74] And discourage it they did. Although the princes continued to come to the summer capital in substantial numbers, the government closely monitored their visits and often vetoed their attempts to purchase property, thereby ensuring that their presence was kept within carefully regulated limits.[75]

The princes, however, were not the only Indians to worry the British with their encroachments: a growing number of well-to-do commoners were entering the hill stations in the late nineteenth and early twentieth centuries as well. In 1902, Lord Curzon was outraged to learn that a Bengali zamindar had purchased a house in Simla. He demanded that action be taken "to exclude outsiders who have no lots or concern in the place, and who are best kept at a distance." His desire to place restrictions on the influx of nonprincely Indians was shared by other officials. One wrote that he had no objections to Indians who obtained property in the hill stations for investment purposes, but "what we want to prevent is the purchase of houses by wealthy natives who buy in order that they may live in them themselves." Another dusted off an old charge:

> [T]he social and sanitary conditions of the stations will be affected by the presence of a large number of natives living more or less in the European fashion, and gathering around them an increasing number of relatives and retainers. This is the state of things which we wish to guard against while there is still time.[76]

These calls to action were especially significant because they were not restricted to Simla, as earlier orders had been: top officials feared for hill

73. Newspaper clipping (unidentified) in Sir George Russell Clerk Collection, 68–69, MSS. Eur.D. 538/6, IOL.
74. Lansdowne to Wenlock, 24 June 1891, quoted in Kenny, "Constructing an Imperial Hill Station," 263.
75. See the annual reports on the visits of ruling princes to Simla in Simla Muncipal Corporation Records, 8/53/52/1912–26/I, HPSA.
76. See memoranda by Lord Curzon, H. S. Barnes, and H. H. Risley in no. 68, Dec. 1902, Home Dept. Proceedings, Public Branch (A), INA.

stations as a whole. The government of India polled all the provincial governments for their opinions on limiting the acquisition of property by wealthy Indians in the hill stations. Most favored imposing restrictions. Their replies detailed Indians' recent encroachments in Mahabaleshwar, Mussoorie, Naini Tal, Ootacamund, and elsewhere in tones of trepidation. The lieutenant-governor of the Punjab expressed a widely shared view when he declared that "there is a wide distinction between the European and the native. A Hill Station is a necessary health resort for the former or for his family. It is not so for the latter."[77] But if the "natives" did not observe this distinction, could they be made to do so? This was the crux of the government's dilemma. It had been possible to impose restrictions on the entry of the princes to the hill stations because their formal status as rulers of semi-autonomous states meant that they had no legal right to enter British-ruled territory or acquire property there without the permission of the government of India. But the raj had no such legal authority over its own Indian subjects. It was suggested by one official that the government sidestep the issue by arguing that its intent was to ensure adequate housing for civil servants not to prohibit the transfer of property to Indians.[78] But how then to explain the racially restrictive nature of its actions? Denzil Ibbetson cut to the heart of the matter when he declared that "we must make up our minds . . . whether we are prepared to avow that our main object is to exclude undesirable native occupants from hill stations." He and other advisers eventually persuaded Curzon that to do so would "arouse a storm of fury in the Native Press."[79] Thus, the effort to prohibit entry to the hill stations on explicitly racial grounds was reluctantly abandoned.

This debate within the upper echelons of the Indian government is significant for two reasons. First, it demonstrates that the British regarded the hill stations as their exclusive preserves, set apart from the rest of India and marked by boundaries that Indians had no right to penetrate. While Simla sometimes seemed to stand in a class all its own, its position with regard to the maintenance of a racial cordon sanitaire was simply the most acute example of a conundrum that affected all hill stations. Moreover, it was the hill stations alone that occupied the attention of officials in this

77. A. H. Diack, chief secretary to Punjab Government, to the Government of India, in no. 39, 1 June 1903, Home Dept. Proceedings, Public Branch (A), INA.

78. Minute by A. Williams in no. 41, 10 Dec. 1903, Home Dept. Proceedings, Public Branch (A), INA.

79. Minute by Ibbetson, in no. 41, 12 Dec. 1903, Home Dept. Proceedings, Public Branch (A), INA.

debate. No one suggested that Indians of wealth and title should be prohibited from inhabiting those districts of Calcutta or Madras or Bombay or other cities on the plains where the British congregated.

Second, this debate failed to accomplish what nearly all of its participants acknowledged as their goal: a policy that would protect the hill stations from further encroachments by Indians who sought to inhabit the areas that the British regarded as their own. Indians with titles, with wealth, and with Western values advanced upon the hill stations in increasing numbers after the turn of the century, and their presence transformed these mountain enclaves in profoundly important ways.

# 9 Arrivals and Departures

What I *do* see is the last feeble stirring of the instinct of self-preservation, the last remnant at the command of a condemned world-system. The catastrophe will and must come—it advances on every hand and in every way.

—Thomas Mann, *The Magic Mountain*

Half-an-hour by air . . . and then an hour's chug in the airport bus . . . had made the old hill station an attractive proposition for people who found an all night train and a six hour one back a high price to pay for a weekend in more invigorating air. . . . [It] attracted more people up than ever before: people in government, in commerce, the idle rich, the busy executives, and now even film stars and directors.

—Paul Scott, *Staying On*

The colonial hill stations reached the apex of their reputations as social and political centers for the British expatriate community at the turn of the century. By this time they had come to occupy positions of unprecedented importance in the public and private lives of the British in India. Simla could claim that it, rather than Calcutta, was the real capital of the raj. Its preeminence as a site of political power was evidenced by the presence there of the viceroy, the commander-in-chief, the members of the viceroy's council, and the battalions of bureaucrats who conducted the business of state. Similarly, Ootacamund, Darjeeling, Naini Tal, and Shillong had come into their own as regional seats of government, while a great many other stations operated as local political or military headquarters. The turn of the century also saw the hill stations consolidate their positions as centers of British social life. With the extension of the railway to the vicinity of most hill stations and the direct linkage of some of the most important ones by narrow-gauge track, it had become convenient for a great many of the British residents of India to take their holidays in the hills and to enroll their children in the educational institutions that clustered there. Schools, social and recreational clubs, and civic organizations prospered as never before, providing the inhabitants of the hill stations with social environments so welcoming and evocative of metropolitan models that they seemed utterly removed from the strange and uncomfortable realities of life on the plains.

Yet the hill stations' rise to prominence also set in motion some of the forces that led to their subsequent fall from British favor. Their reputations as enclaves where the colonizers could renew their sense of themselves as the agents of Western culture and imperial rule soon began to erode because of the presence of upper- and middle-class Indians whose own identities and destinies were increasingly bound up in the imperial system. These people sought access to the political power and social privilege that radiated from the highlands. Unlike the multitudes of common laborers whose places in the hill stations were sharply circumscribed, they could not easily be kept outside the physical and psychic walls that the British had built to protect themselves. Princes and professionals presented a far more complex predicament for the British because they sought to inhabit the same social space that the British themselves occupied.

Certain members of this Indian elite, moreover, were nationalist activists, and their attraction to the hills was shot through with antagonism toward the imperial power concentrated there. Consider two of India's most prominent nationalist families, the Boses and the Nehrus. The brothers Sarat and Subhas Chandra Bose were frequent visitors to Darjeeling in their youth, and they retained ties to the area throughout their careers. Yet the house that Sarat purchased in 1923 as a summer retreat for the family was located not in Darjeeling but in the smaller and less overweening satellite station of Kurseong.[1] Similarly, Motilal Nehru, Jawaharlal's father, had a seasonal residence in Mussoorie, another hill station without political resonance. Jawaharlal himself frequently took his family there for summer visits, and Mussoorie is where his daughter Indira spent a good part of her early life. Yet Jawaharlal also shared the antagonism that most Indian nationalists felt toward Simla and other hill headquarters. According to one of his biographers, Simla was "a town which he hated for its atmosphere of officialdom."[2] What Nehru and his nationalist colleagues found most objectionable about the concentration of imperial power in these remote resorts was that it allowed an autocratic regime to stand aloof and apart from its subjects. Even though their political attacks on these highland strongholds stood in ambivalent juxtaposition to their emulation of the rulers' seasonal sojourns in the hills, both actions had equally dire effects on the hill stations' reputations as ethnic enclaves whose inhabitants could

---

1. Leonard A. Gordon, *Brothers against the Raj* (New York, 1990), 46.
2. See Sarvepalli Gopal, *Jawaharlal Nehru: A Biography*, vol. 1 (Cambridge, Mass., 1976), 303, 41, 61.

feel confident of the unassailability of their position. The British saw their creations become riddled with the paradoxes of success: the hill stations' popularity as centers of British social activity made them increasingly popular sites for holidays by a Westernized Indian middle class, while their prominence as centers of British political power made them increasingly potent symbols of tyranny for an energetic Indian nationalist movement. As a result, they soon ceased to serve as British sanctums, as special sites set apart from the rest of India where the public and private spheres could recover their dialectical balance.

This was by no means the only reason that the hill stations lost their special standing in the imperial system. The greater ease and shrinking cost of travel to Europe, the Indianization of the government services, and various other factors contributed to their swift decline as centers of colonial influence in the twentieth century. The hill stations had become so intimately enmeshed in the structure and operation of the raj that their geographical isolation could no longer protect them from the storms that had begun to buffet the British and would eventually sweep them out of India.

———

The Indianization of the hill stations began long before India obtained independence in 1947. Its origins can be traced to the late nineteenth century, when the number of prosperous, professional, Westernized Indians began to reach the critical mass that would make them a conscious and influential class within colonial society. These people posed the greatest threat to the insular world the British had established for themselves in the hills.

The first hill stations to experience significant encroachment from middle-class Indians were those in the vicinity of Bombay, the boom city of modern India. Bombay's economy took off when the outbreak of the American Civil War created a demand for cotton from the city's hinterland and when the opening of the Suez Canal in 1867 established it as the gateway to India for British shipping. Indigenous commercial elites, most notably the Parsis, moved quickly to establish their predominance in the export trades and industries that sprang up around Bombay, and they soon played the same role that British firms played in Calcutta and Madras. The Parsis also acquired a great deal of property, much of it in the European areas, where they leased houses to British tenants. Their economic success eroded ethnic boundaries, allowing much more social intercourse with the British than occurred in other parts of India.[3] By the late nineteenth century, many of these newly prosperous Indians were following the British to Mahabaleshwar, Matheran, and the lesser hill stations of the region.

Matheran was near enough to Bombay—fifty-four miles by railway—for it to become a weekend retreat for that city's well-to-do residents. Founded at midcentury by Hugh Malet, the collector of Thana district, it was initially very much a British station: no more than sixteen of the first sixty-six applicants for building sites were non-Europeans.[4] By the 1880s, however, substantial numbers of Indian businessmen and professionals had begun to enjoy visits to Matheran. These included Bombay's most prominent industrialist, J. N. Tata, who acquired a weekend home in the station (as well as estates at Panchgani and Ootacamund).[5] One English visitor during this decade reported that a number of "handsome houses" had been built by Parsis and Jews, and that "crowds of [Parsis] are continually to be met with at the various [scenic] points."[6] According to Mrs. A. K. Oliver, a resident of Matheran, Indians from Bombay began to buy property and build houses at the station on a significant scale around 1893, and the outbreak of plague in Bombay in 1896 provided an additional impetus for its better-off residents to seek shelter in the hills. By 1905, more than ninety of the station's European-ward dwellings were Indian-owned, while Europeans owned just ten or eleven, which replicated the pattern of property ownership in Bombay. Two of the five hotels that had catered to Europeans in 1882 now served Parsis, and the remaining three were all Indian-owned; furthermore, all of the newer hotels served Indian clients, including one for Muslims, one for Hindus, and two more for Parsis.[7] A guidebook published a few years later claimed that just two cottages remained in European hands, though this figure seems improbably low.[8] By the late 1930s, Europeans owned perhaps 14 of the more than 190 private houses now spread across the station: nearly all the rest were held by Indians from Bombay. Parsis continued to hold sway, with more than a

3. Norma Evenson, *The Indian Metropolis: A View toward the West* (New Haven, 1989), 36–37.

4. A. F. Bellasis, *An Account of the Hill Station of Matharan, near Bombay* (Bombay, 1869), 7.

5. F. R. Harris, *Jamsetji Nusserwanji Tata* (London, 1925), 63, 74, 284.

6. Francesca H. Wilson, *My Trip to Matheran* (Madras, 1888), 40.

7. Mrs. A. K. Oliver, *The Hill Station of Matheran* (Bombay, 1905), 19, 108, and list of houses on 221–27.

8. J. T. Lewis, *The Rugby Guide to Matheran* (Poona, c. 1908), 9.

hundred properties in their possession, but the Hindu presence had grown, as evidenced by the 40-plus houses they owned and the five hotels (out of twelve) and three sanitaria (out of seven) that catered to Hindus.[9] The British had not abandoned Matheran altogether: enough of them leased houses and rented rooms for the season to sustain an exclusively European gymkhana. But Indians predominated, providing the station with much of its social and civic identity. Framjee Mehta founded a local biweekly newspaper in 1892; Sir Bomanji Dhunjibhoy established a race course in 1892–93; Damodhar Gordhandass sponsored a library in 1897; Byramjee Jeejeebhoy financed a hospital in 1902; Sir Adamji Peerbhoy constructed the light rail to the station in 1907. All of the members of the municipal board were Indians by the 1930s, if not earlier.[10] Matheran had become Indianized.

Mahabaleshwar followed much the same course. Even though it was far less convenient to the residents of Bombay than Matheran and retained a far more stable British clientele because of its status as the seasonal head-quarters of the Bombay government, it too saw the wholesale transfer of property and institutions into the hands of Indians. By 1903, Britons owned no more than 9 houses in the station, while Indians owned 128. Many of the Indian-owned houses were rented to Europeans for the season, but the majority were occupied by the proprietors themselves or their relatives and friends. Again, Bombay was the principal home of these Indians, though others came from Ahmedabad, Hyderabad, Jodhpur, and elsewhere.[11] And, again, they enriched the community with their philanthropic activities: Sir Morarji Gokuldas, a Bombay merchant, financed the construction of a hospital; Framji Nasserwanji Patel of Bombay provided a dharmsala for travelers; Seth Purushottam Mawji, a wealthy Bhattia from Bombay, built a Hindu sanitarium.[12] One measure of their influence upon the station's character was the evolution of membership in the Mahabaleshwar Club. When founded in 1881, the club had prohibited Indians from entry as members, but it began to admit some princes as honorary members around

9. Hansraj Parmanand, *Key to Matheran*, 2d ed. (Bombay, 1935), 55; Vishnu Bhikaji Dabake, *Hand Book to Matheran*, 3d ed. (Poona, 1938), 24–30, 97, and list of houses on 137–54.

10. Parmanand, *Key to Matheran*, 98; Oliver, *The Hill Station of Matheran*, 34, 40, 86.

11. J.W.P. Muir-MacKenzie, chief secretary to Government of Bombay, to Government of India, no. 38, 27 May 1903, Home Dept. Proceedings, Public Branch (A), INA.

12. N. M. Dastur, *Pocket Book of Mahabaleshwar and Panchgani*, 3d ed. (Poona, 1944), 107–9.

the turn of the century, and restrictions were loosened further because of financial exigencies during and after World War I. By 1924, an Indian was on the club's governing committee, and Gulam Hussain Hidayattallah, a soda-water manufacturer, became the first Indian president of the club in 1933.[13] Nothing spoke more eloquently of the ethnic transformation of Mahabaleshwar than the Indians' capture of its club, that most exclusive and hidebound of British colonial institutions.

Hill stations in other parts of India were somewhat slower to undergo a similar metamorphosis, but many of them had begun to show the first signs of Indianization by the turn of the century. "There can be no doubt," reported an unhappy H. H. Risley, secretary to the home department of the government of India, in 1902, "that there is an increasing tendency on the part of wealthy natives to spend the hot weather in the hills."[14] The wealthiest of these individuals were the rulers of the princely states, and they forged a prominent place for themselves in the hill stations—so much so, as we have seen, that the government began to curtail their presence in Simla after 1890. By buying up a great deal of property and hosting large parties in their ostentatious residences, the princes parlayed their wealth and status into social intimacy with the stations' European inhabitants. In the early 1880s the maharaja of Cooch Behar invested part of his huge fortune in the construction of some of Darjeeling's "best and neatest" villas, and by the middle of the decade he was said to hold the titles to nearly half of the homes in the station (Figure 14). (The Bengal government purchased one of his handsomest estates for use as the lieutenant-governor's summer residence.) He also had four homes in Simla and at least one in Ootacamund.[15] In Naini Tal, the nawab of Rampur owned "a large area of the best part of the station," and the nawab of Dacca occupied what was considered the best house in Shillong.[16] "Mussoorie seems from the first to have been deemed an eligible residence for native princes," remarked one guidebook to the station. Those who sojourned there for the season in-

13. Perin Bharucha, *Mahabaleswar: The Club 1881–1981* (Bombay, c. 1981), 77–90.

14. Memorandum by H. H. Risley, no. 68, 17 Oct. 1902, Home Dept. Proceedings, Public Branch (A), INA.

15. R. D. O'Brien, *Darjeeling, the Sanitarium of Bengal; and Its Surroundings* (Calcutta, 1883), 25; F. B. Peacock to H. M. Durand, 12 Sept. 1886, no. 432, Foreign Dept. Proceedings, Secret-I, INA.

16. J.S.C. Davis, commissioner of Kumaun Division, to Government of United Provinces, 16 Feb. 1903, and F. J. Monahan, secretary to chief commissioner of Assam, to Government of India, 3 March 1903, nos. 35, 34, Home Dept. Proceedings, Public Branch (A), INA.

Figure 14. A maharaja's mansion in Darjeeling. Photograph by the author.

cluded the maharaja of Kapurthala, who lived in the lavish Chateau Kapurthala, and the maharaja of Nepal, whose Fairlawn Palace was the largest house in the station. In addition, two exiles, Yakub Khan, the ex-amir of Afghanistan, and Maharaja Dhulip Singh, son of Ranjit Singh, resided in Mussoorie the year round.[17] Far to the south, the maharaja of Mysore, the nizam of Hyderabad, the maharaja of Vizianagram, and the gaekwar of Baroda bought or built some of the largest and most luxurious estates in Ootacamund.[18] And so many of Rajasthan's rulers acquired summer residences in Mount Abu—the rajas of Jodhpur, Jaipur, Dholpur, Alwar, Sikar, Bharatpur, Bikaner, Kishengarh, Bundi, Jaisalmer, Kotha, Udaipur, Tonk, Sirohi, and Khetri were identified as property owners in a 1919 directory of the station—that the British could hardly help but view themselves as tourists in a regal retreat. There was no point in trying to keep Indian princes out of the local Rajasthan Club since its very existence was due to their contributions.[19]

If the princes drove the initial wedge into these highland enclaves of Britons, the Indian bourgeoisie split them wide open through the sheer

17. T. Kinney, *The Echo Guide to Mussoorie* (Mussoorie, 1908), 11. Also see A. W. Cornelius, *Dehra Dun—Mussoorie—Landour Guide* (n.p., 1947), 48.

18. Sir Frederick Price, *Ootacamund: A History* (Madras, 1908), ch. 18.

19. Hiralal Dayabhai Nanavati, *Mount Abu* (Bombay, 1919), 23, Appendix. Also see Charles Allen and Sharanda Dwivedi, *Lives of the Indian Princes* (London, 1984), 158.

force of their numbers. A prosperous, self-conscious Indian middle class first began to come into its own in the latter half of the nineteenth century, and while the great nursery of its commercial elite was Bombay, congeries of lawyers, doctors, civil servants, merchants, and other Westernized Indians appeared in regional entrepots across the subcontinent. The hills attracted them in increasing numbers. "I find," remarked a British member of the Legislative Council at one of its sessions, "that Indians who are possessed of any means—members of the Bar and those who conduct businesses—are just as anxious to get away to cooler climates [as the British]."[20]

Calcutta was home to the oldest and largest congregation of Westernized Indian professionals, and toward the end of the century increasing numbers of them began to go to the hills for holidays. Like the European inhabitants of Calcutta, they turned to Darjeeling as the most accessible and attractive hill station in the region. Kipling's snide remark about "the Babus . . . stealing to Darjeeling" in his poem "A Tale of Two Cities" evidenced its growing popularity. A more substantive sign of its appeal was the opening in 1887 of the Lowis Jubilee Sanitarium, a health resort that catered exclusively to Indian clients. Built on land donated by the maharaja of Cooch Behar with funds contributed by Maharaja Gobindo Lal Roy, this imposing facility had rooms to accommodate well over one hundred patients, and admission figures for 1910 indicated that about half of them hailed from Calcutta.[21] Other institutional evidence of a growing middle-class Indian presence included a branch of the Brahmo Samaj (founded 1880) and a Hindu public hall (1891, rebuilt 1907). "The influx of native visitors to the station of Darjeeling in recent years had been considerable," reported the chief secretary for the Bengal government in 1903. "They generally go to boarding-houses, or the Lowis Sanitarium . . . , or they rent existing houses."[22] Doorga Pooja, the chief Hindu festival in Bengal, became an especially popular occasion for a visit to Darjeeling, which was "at its gayest" during those ten days in September and October.[23]

20. Extract from Proceedings of Indian Legislative Council, 12 March 1917, no. 136, April 1917, Home Dept. Proceedings, Public-B, INA.

21. E. C. Dozey, *A Concise History of the Darjeeling District since 1835* (Calcutta, 1922), 131–32; George P. Robertson, *Darjeeling Route Guide* (Darjeeling, 1913), 16.

22. W. C. Macpherson to Government of India, no. 41, 22 Aug. 1903, Home Dept. Proceedings, Public Branch (A), INA.

23. G. Hutton Taylor, *Thacker's Guide Book to Darjeeling and Its Neighbourhood* (Calcutta, 1899), 63.

Calcutta had also long supplied most of the Indian clerks who participated in the migration of the government to Simla, and although these
bureaucrats knew their place in the station's hierarchy, they forged a
relationship between the two capitals that eased the way for less subordinate migrants from Calcutta, including bankers, businessmen, lawyers,
and other professionals. One manifestation of their presence was the Kali
Bari, a religious and social center founded by Bengali clerks in the mid-
nineteenth century, which expanded in the 1890s to serve an enlarged
clientele and expanded yet again in the early 1930s, when it occupied a
massive concrete structure near the heart of Simla that contained a public
hall large enough to accommodate eight hundred people.[24]

By the turn of the century, however, the Punjab had probably become
the principal source of Indian visitors to Simla. The deputy commissioner
for Lahore observed that "well-to-do natives in Lahore are now more and
more acquiring the habit of going to the hill station that is the headquarters of Government, i.e., Simla," just as the commissioner of the Delhi
division noticed "an increasing number of native gentlemen [who] are
coming to regard the escape from the heat of the plains as a necessity."[25]
And a Parsi who visited Simla in 1925 reported that "many well-to-do
Punjabis . . . own bungalows on the hill where they come for a change."[26]

The confluence of these two streams of visitors gave an increasingly
Indian cast to the summer capital of the raj. Even though British authorities
had forced the princes to reduce their property holdings in Simla, which
had numbered 34 in 1885 (including 14 owned by the raja of Nahan), the
total tally of station ward houses in the hands of Indians both titled and
untitled actually rose to 102 by 1903.[27] Between 1898 and 1912, 66 houses
were bought by Indians. Most continued to harbor British tenants, but local
officials charted a growing tendency for Indians to occupy the places they
purchased: twenty-eight did so in 1906, fifty in 1912.[28] Other Indian

24. Sudhir Chandra Sen, *The Simla Kali Bari* (Simla, 1932); Pamela Kanwar,
*Imperial Simla* (Delhi, 1990), 166.
25. Letters from C. H. Atkins and T. Gordon Walker, no. 39, 9 Feb. and 28 April
1903, Home Dept. Proceedings, Public Branch (A), INA.
26. D. S. Bastavala, *Simla* (Bombay, 1925), 125.
27. Correspondence and memoranda, Sept. 1886, nos. 432, 433, Foreign Dept.
Proceedings, Secret-I, INA; H.S.P. Davies to Commissioner, Delhi Division, no. 39,
15 April 1903, Home Dept. Proceedings, Public Branch (A), INA. Kanwar (*Imperial
Simla*, 141) mistakenly cites the number of station ward houses owned by Indians
in 1907 as twenty-nine—this was in fact the number *occupied* by Indians in that
year.
28. Memorandum, 12 July 1912, Simla Municipal Corporation Records, 8/53/
52/1912–26/I, HPSA.

visitors leased houses for the season or stayed in boardinghouses and hotels, and by the 1920s several of these hotels catered exclusively to orthodox Hindus and Muslims.[29] The interwar years brought an increasing number of Indians who occupied mid-level ranks in the Indian Civil Service or served as representatives in the Legislative Assembly, and they expected to reside in the same style and comfort as their British counterparts. Certainly this seems to have been the case for Ved Mehta's father, a public health official who took his family to Simla every summer.[30] Even the princes could not be kept away from the station, despite official disapproval. In what appears to have been a fairly typical year, the maji sahiba of Bharatpur, the maharaja of Dholpur, the Maharaja Rewa, the raj rana of Jhalawar, the Maharaja Bikaner, the nahrawan of Dangardar, the raja of Dewas, the maharawal of Dungarpur, the Maharaja Alwar, and the maharaja of Benares all obtained permission to spend part or all of the 1913 season in Simla, where they invariably leased houses in the station ward.[31]

Information about property ownership provides a revealing glimpse of the Indian influence in other hill stations as well. While these figures do not indicate how many Indians actually resided in the stations, they do measure the extent to which the homes the British had built as refuges for themselves had been transferred into Indian hands. An Ootacamund directory for 1897 identified Indians as the owners of 120 of the 328 properties listed in its pages. In Naini Tal, 120 of the 280 houses in the station ward were owned by Indians in 1903. The more remote hill stations, and especially those that housed military garrisons, attracted less interest from Indian investors. Murree, located in the far northwestern corner of India, remained firmly in the grasp of British landlords, who owned 148 of the station's 180 houses in 1903. The equally remote Dalhousie was even more British, with just 12 of its 117 houses in Indian hands at the turn of the century (including 4 held by the raja of Chamba and two by the raja of Kashmir.) However, 12 of the 32 houses in Nathiagali, a tiny station near Abbottabad on the northwest frontier, were owned by Indians, 9 of them by two bankers from Abbottabad who presumably saw the property as an attractive investment.[32]

29. F. Beresford Harrop, *Thacker's New Guide to Simla* (Simla, 1925), 60.

30. Ved Mehta, *Daddyji* (New York, 1972), 152.

31. List of ruling princes or chiefs who visited Simla in 1913, Simla Municipal Corporation Records, 8/53/52/1912–26/I, HPSA.

32. The Ootacamund data are derived from a property listing in *The Visitors' Handbook of the Nilgiris* (Madras, 1897), 74–78. The figures for Naini Tal, Murree, and Nathiagali come from letters by J.S.C. Davis, J. G. Silcock, and Lt.-Col. H. A.

Further evidence of the hill stations' appeal to the Indian elite can be found in the many guidebooks written by and for Indians in the period prior to independence. I have examined nearly a dozen of these publications, and others surely existed.[33] Those that have survived include guidebooks to Darjeeling, Mahabaleshwar and Panchgani, Matheran, Mount Abu, Shillong, and Simla. Some of these publications went through multiple editions, and several appeared in Gujarati and Marathi as well as English-language versions.

One can glean from these guidebooks some useful insights into the hill stations' attractions to Indians. They resembled British-authored guide-books in most respects. Their main purpose was the same—to provide practical information about transportation, accommodations, recreational activities, and the like. Yet they also sought to describe their subjects in ways that would appeal to their readers, and these efforts resulted in strikingly familiar images. They portrayed hill stations above all as refuges from the trials and tribulations of everyday life on the plains. Their therapeutic benefits were touted to the tubercular, the diabetic, the anemic, and other invalids. One author gives a testimonial to his rapid recovery from bouts of diarrhea and cholera in the salubrious environment of Matheran. Another informs his readers that "whenever I wanted to recoup my health" he escaped to Mahabaleshwar.[34] These guidebooks also praised the hill stations for the psychic relief they provided. Matheran was de-scribed as a place where a person "can forget all the troubles and respon-sibilities of his every-day life and plunge himself headlong into the de-lightful heaven of the peace of Nature."[35] The aesthetic appeal of the hill

Deane, respectively, nos. 35, 37, 39, Jan. 1904, Home Dept. Proceedings, Public Branch (A), INA. The Dalhousie figures come from *Report of the Commission Appointed to Deal with the Transfer of the Punjab Government to the Hill Station of Dalhousie* (Simla, 1902), app. E. A detailed listing of Indian owners in Naini Tal can be found in C. W. Murphy, *A Guide to Naini Tal and Kumaun* (Allahabad, 1906), app. 14. They included one individual, Rai K. Sah Bahadur, who owned eighteen houses.

33. The publications I refer to are Bastavala, *Simla;* K. C. Bhanja, *Darjeeling at a Glance* (Darjeeling, 1942); K. C. Bhanja, *Wonders of Darjeeling and the Sikkim Himalaya* (n.p., 1943); Sarabhai Choksi, *Mahabaleshwar and Panchgani Guide* (Bombay, n.d.); Dabake, *Hand Book to Matheran;* Dastur, *Pocket Book of Maha-baleshwar and Panchgani;* Om Prakash Gupta, *Mount Abu: The Olympus of Rajasthan* (Ajmer, 1939); Nanavati, *Mount Abu;* Rao Bahadur D. B. Parasnis, *Mahabaleshwar* (Bombay, 1916); Parmanand, *Key to Matheran;* H. C. Sarkar, *Guide to Shillong* (Calcutta, n.d.).

34. Parmanand, *Key to Matheran*, Preface; Choksi, *Mahableshwar*, 3.

35. Dabake, *Hand Book to Matheran*, 1.

stations received a great deal of attention, as in this overwrought passage about the natural wonders of Darjeeling: "the voice of the silence from afar will whisper into your ears and your fancy will lift you up on its wings and carry you to a region of heavenly ecstacy conjuring up an unspeakable sense of the infinite glory of the Great Unseen Hand behind."[36] The same scenic "points" that the British admired for their picturesque beauty were also recommended in these works. Indeed, little distinguished Indian-authored guidebooks from their British-authored counterparts. This can be attributed in part to the fact that they were meant to appeal to British as well as Indian buyers, and also perhaps because they took British guide-books as models. But it would be a mistake to dismiss these works as merely imitative, evoking images that had no resonance with their Indian readers. If they touched on many of the same topics and themes as the British-authored guidebooks, the primary reason must be that their Indian audience had many of the same reasons for going to the hills as did the British. They too were concerned about their physical well-being as well as eager to escape the hurly-burly of the workaday world, to enjoy the cool temperatures and mountain scenery, and to revel in the stations' social and recreational activities.

Needless to say, none of these motives evoked any empathy from the British. They viewed their not-so-secret sharers with distrust, disdain, and aversion. They were distressed by what they considered the violation by these newcomers of their social space. Far more than the stations' masses of porters, servants, and other laborers, the Indian upper and middle classes penetrated into the physical and social heart of the hill stations. Their occupation of houses in the station wards, their involvement in municipal affairs, their entry into gymkhanas and other social organizations, and even their presence on the malls for evening strolls all shattered the British illusion that the hill stations offered a realm apart from the rest of India, a refuge from its vexations and its terrors. Once that illusion was gone, it was only a matter of time before the British began to pack their bags and leave.

————

The first signs that the hill stations had begun to lose their special aura appeared shortly after the turn of the century. In Simla the completion of the railway line from Kalka was expected to produce a substantial increase

36. Bhanja, *Darjeeling at a Glance,* 28.

in the station's population.[37] Lord Curzon used predictions of overcrowding as a justification for his abortive effort to move the summer headquarters of the Punjab government from Simla to Dalhousie.[38] But the arrival of the railway in 1903 did not bring the influx of visitors anticipated by authorities. On the contrary, the number of people—particularly European women—actually declined. The author of the report on the 1911 summer census attributed this fact to "the tendency among married Europeans . . . more and more to send their wives home [to Britain] for the summer, as that is considered cheaper and is of course more convenient."[39]

Ootacamund, like Simla, should have seen its fortunes improve with the arrival of the railroad shortly after the turn of the century. But in 1903 the appearance in the station of the plague, which killed 262 of its poorer residents in the first year alone, scared off many potential visitors.[40] Nor did matters improve once the epidemic had died down. The 1908–9 municipal report for Ootacamund noted "the vacancy of a comparatively large number of European houses during the last season," and subsequent reports described even higher vacancy rates. The shortening of the official "season" was offered as an explanation for this loss of visitors.[41] However, Ootacamund's sister station, Coonoor, which had no official status, reported a similar rise in vacancies, as did the equally unofficial Kodaikanal, further to the south.[42]

Still another indication that the hill stations had entered an era of slippage were the troubles that began to afflict the hill schools. After enjoying unprecedented growth in the last quarter of the nineteenth century, some of the hill schools suddenly found themselves facing an unexpected decline in enrollments and revenues. In 1900, Mussoorie's Boys' School closed its doors for financial reasons, and the same year the Bishop Cotton School in Simla and St. Paul's School in Darjeeling turned to the state for financial assistance; the Diocesan School in Naini Tal did the same two years later. These were among the best known educational establish-

37. *Report of the Simla Extension Committee, 1898* (Simla, 1898), 2.
38. See Curzon's dispatch to Lord Hamilton, 24 Sept. 1903, L/PJ/6/650/2252, Public and Judicial Dept., IOL.
39. *Report on the Summer Census of Simla 1911* (Lahore, 1912), 7, 5. Also see *Report of the Simla Improvement Committee* (Simla, 1907), 4.
40. Ootacamund Municipal Report for 1903–4, 11, Municipal G.O. #1847, TNSA.
41. Ootacamund Municipal Reports for 1908–9, 5; 1909–10, 4; 1911–12, 3, 8, Municipal G.O. #1076, #1438, #1676, TNSA.
42. Coonoor Municipal Report for 1909–10, Municipal G.O. #1015, TNSA; Kodaikanal Municipal Report for 1910–11, Municipal G.O. #1008, TNSA.

ments in the country, and their financial difficulties spurred the government into convening a committee of investigation in 1904. The committee observed that the schools at greatest risk were mainly Anglican institutions patterned after English public schools and intended for male students from the better strata of British society in India, and its report warned that the perpetuation of "distinctively English traditions" in India depended on the survival of these hill schools.[43] The crisis was traced to two sources. First, the reduction in the costs of passage to Britain and the expansion in the number of home educational institutions made it feasible for a larger portion of the British population in India to ship their sons off for schooling. Second, an increase in the competition for entry into the elite imperial service made enrollment in a domestic British public school all but obligatory, while at the same time the opportunities for employment in the less prestigious provincial service were shrinking as more and more positions in departments such as public works, surveying, police, opium, salt, and post and telegraph went to Indians, who had been granted the opportunity to compete for these posts in 1886. This development was especially damaging to the hill schools since they had built their reputations in large measure on their ability to guide their graduates into the provincial service. The future appeared bleak. One witness after another told the committee that greater numbers of boys were going to Britain for their education every year, and none could see any way to stem the exodus. (Because girls had far fewer career expectations or opportunities, they had less reason to be sent to British schools, and hence the Indian institutions that catered to them remained relatively stable.) The private secretary to the archbishop of Agra neatly summarized the various forces at work when he remarked that "more parents now than formerly send their children to England, because the difficulties of travel and expense are not now so great and because the golden days are now gone when a boy even imperfectly educated could get a good appointment in India."[44] These trends were ominous not only for the hill schools but for the hill stations where they were located.

Equally ominous was the announcement at the imperial durbar of 1911 that the capital of India would be transferred from Calcutta to Delhi. Seldom is mention made of the fact that the decision to move the seat of

43. Committee upon the Financial Condition of Hill Schools for Europeans in Northern India, vol. 1: *Report* (Simla, 1904), 5.
44. Committee upon the Financial Condition of Hill Schools for Europeans in Northern India, vol. 2: *Evidence and Appendices* (Calcutta, 1905), 38–39.

government to Delhi was as much a blow to Simla as it was to Calcutta.[45] Not only did the decision end any chance that Simla itself might become the official capital of India, but it also undermined the prospects that it would remain the unofficial nerve center of the raj. Once the grandiose capital complex at New Delhi reached completion, the government of India would be obliged to transfer its agencies and operations to those new quarters, thereby emptying Simla of its trappings of officialdom. And once Simla's political position began to wane, the regional governments would find it increasingly difficult to continue their annual migrations to the hills. None of these repercussions would be felt before the interwar era, but Simla and the other stations that headquartered various branches of government found themselves operating on borrowed time after 1911.

The outbreak of World War I gave a temporary boost to the hill stations' fortunes. A great many schoolchildren, women, and others who would otherwise have gone back to Britain for various reasons were forced to remain in India during the duration of the war, and a substantial portion of these involuntary exiles congregated in the hill stations. Simla's local authorities reported overcrowding in the European as well as Indian wards of the station.[46] The story was much the same in other hill stations. A local gazetteer reports that Mussoorie "during the war had bumper years. Europeans were unable to send their families to Europe and hotels and boarding-houses reaped a rich harvest. Many new shops were built and tradesmen earned huge profits."[47]

Once the war ended, however, the pent-up demand for passages back to Britain led to the rapid exodus of wartime residents from the hill stations, and the upheavals of the subsequent years did little to encourage others to fill the void. The postwar reductions in military forces resulted in fewer officers in the hills, while the increased pace of Indianization produced a further contraction in the number of British personnel—both military and civil—who spent the summer season in a hill station. The rise of the new capital in New Delhi and the complaints of Indian nationalists caused the imperial and provincial governments to scale back the size of their annual migrations to the hills and the length of their stays. The government of Madras, for example, reduced its season in Ootacamund from six to three

45. For example, Robert Grant Irving, *Indian Summer: Lutyens, Baker, and Imperial Delhi* (New Haven, 1981), scarcely mentions Simla.

46. Annual Report of the Simla Municipality, 1917–18, 2, HPSA.

47. *District Gazetteers of the United Provinces of Agra and Oudh: Supplementary Notes and Statistics*, vol. l: *Dehra Dun District* (Allahabad, 1924), 8.

months in the late 1920s.[48] Perhaps the most dramatic blow to the hill stations came with the Lee Commission's recommendation in 1925 to provide passage subsidies for officials who wished to travel to Britain for their annual leaves.[49] Previously, members of the Indian services had been able to return to Britain only on the extended furloughs they received once every four years or so. The Lee Commission liberalized this policy, recognizing that improvements in transportation now made it possible to get "home" and back in the course of a typical two-month annual leave. Most hill stations' inordinate reliance on their official status and official clients began to tell against them.

Evidence of deterioration proliferated. Simla's property values plummeted after 1919, according to its resident historian Edward Buck.[50] "So many people are away on leave," wrote Lady Reading, wife of the viceroy, in 1924; "they tell me over 150 houses [in Simla] are empty this season. Formerly all the wives came up here from the Plains in the hot weather, but now they mostly go home for the children's summer holidays."[51] The gazetteer for Darjeeling observed that "in common with other hill stations in India its tourist traffic has suffered from the cheapening and acceleration of travel to Europe and its European educational development from the tendency of parents who can afford it to send their children to Europe at an early age to receive education."[52] An especially vivid description of decline came from the 1934 supplement to the Dehra Dun district gazetteer:

> Mussoorie has considerably declined in prosperity since 1920 owing to the great decrease in the number of Europeans who visit it or make it a place for retirement. Many houses lie vacant every season and, except in May and September, the hotels are usually half empty. The Happy Valley Club, which is referred to in the *Gazetteer* of 1911 as being "all too small", is to be closed next year; the race course and polo ground have been derelict for some years; the Himalaya Club was closed even before 1920, as were the two breweries; and the Castle Hill Estate of the Survey of India was vacated in 1932. The Municipal Hall . . . leaks badly, is hardly

48. *Madras District Gazetteers, Statistical Appendix for the Nilagiri District* (Madras, 1928), 79.

49. Vipin Pubby, *Simla Then and Now: Summer Capital of the Raj* (New Delhi, 1988), 93.

50. Edward J. Buck, *Simla Past and Present*, 2d ed. (1925; reprint, Simla, 1989), 111.

51. Iris Butler, *The Viceroy's Wife: Letters of Alice, Countess of Reading, from India, 1921–25* (London, 1969), 139. For a fuller account of Simla's postwar decline, see Kanwar, *Imperial Simla*, ch. 17.

52. Arthur Jules Dash, *Bengal District Gazetteers: Darjeeling* (Alipore, 1947), 42.

habitable and is now never used for "balls, theatricals and other entertain-ments." The Evelyn Hall nursing home (the best of several) is to close this year, and nearly all the English shops have disappeared or passed to Indian purchasers.[53]

Population statistics confirm these bleak impressions. The total population of Simla fell from a winter census total of 26,149 in 1921 to 18,144 in 1931, and the Christian population (our only indicator of European inhabitants) from 3,181 to 1,239.[54] Another Punjab district hill station, Dalhousie, experienced a far more precipitous drop in its total population—from a winter count of 2,405 in the 1921 imperial census to a count of 1,030 in the 1931 census.[55] Darjeeling's population remained relatively stable, but it slipped nonetheless from 22,258 to 21,185 over the decade 1921–1931.[56] The total population of Ootacamund actually grew, but the Europeans, who had numbered 4,627 in 1911, declined to 3,525 in 1921 and 3,246 a decade later.[57] Among the hill stations of the United Provinces, Naini Tal's population fell 5 percent between 1921 and 1931, Chakrata's 6 percent, Lansdowne's 13 percent, and Mussoorie's a precipitous 40 percent.[58] We can assume that the populations of the hill stations continued to decline through the rest of the 1930s, although the statistical evidence is distorted by the fact that the next census occurred in 1941, when another world war again inflated the stations' populations.

By the late 1930s most provincial governments had entirely given up their annual migrations to the hills, and the imperial government slashed its stay in Simla from six to two months in 1939. With hill stations no longer able to depend on official patronage, municipal officials scrambled to attract other visitors to ensure their stations' survival. When the government of the United Provinces abandoned Naini Tal as its summer

53. *District Gazetteers of the United Provinces of Agra and Oudh: Supplementary Notes and Statistics up to 1931–2*, vol. 1D: *Dehra Dun District* (Allahabad, 1934), 4. Also see the remarks in Capt. O.E.S. Powers, *Dehra Dun Past and Present: Guide and Directory to Dehra and the Doon District* (Dehra Dun, 1929), p. 31.
54. *Punjab District Gazetteers, Simla District Statistical Tables, 1936*, vol. 6B (Lahore, 1936), Table 7.
55. *Punjab District Gazetteers, Gurdaspur District Statistical Tables, 1936*, vol. 14B (Lahore, 1936), Table 7.
56. Dash, *Bengal District Gazetteers: Darjeeling*, 53.
57. Paul Hockings, "British Society in the Company, Crown and Congress Eras," in *Blue Mountains: The Ethnography and Biogeography of a South Indian Region*, ed. Paul Hockings (Delhi, 1989), 351.
58. Nutan Tyagi, *Hill Resorts of U.P. Himalaya: A Geographical Study* (New Delhi, 1991), 136.

headquarters, for example, the municipal board responded by establishing a publicity and development department that issued an illustrated tourist guide and other notices to advertise the charms of the station. The department's Indian director claimed an increase in tourist traffic in 1939.[59] But who were these tourists? Few of them were likely to have been Britons. Simla officials, who contemplated instituting a promotional campaign similar to Naini Tal's, were told by the sales manager for the North Western Railway that the most promising potential clients were middle-class Indians:

> Experience with our rail-cum-road schemes from Bengal, Bombay, United Provinces, Central India and the Punjab to Kashmir indicate that there is a new class of visitors increasing in numbers annually who visit hill stations. This class consists almost entirely of respectable Indian gentlemen and their families recruited from the professional classes, i.e., doctors, school teachers, students, small landlords and successful businessmen.[60]

The problems facing the hill schools led to a similar shift in the composition of their student bodies. Headmasters responded to the continued exodus of European pupils by opening the doors of their schools to the sons of Indian parents who were prepared to pay the boarding fees. In the European schools of the Bengal presidency, for example, the ratio of European to Indian students shrank from 5:1 in 1926–27 to 3:1 in 1931–32. Many school administrators were prepared to reduce the ratio even further, but the government imposed a cap on the proportion of Indian pupils in European schools.[61]

Thus, the Indian upper and middle classes' incursions into the hill stations were in a certain sense as much a consequence as a cause of British flight. They filled the vacuum left by the British, purchasing British property, occupying British cottages, enrolling their children in British schools. And in so doing they made the hill stations their own.

The outbreak of the European war in 1939 once again forced the British who were in India to remain there for the duration of the hostilities, and once again the hill stations experienced a corresponding boost in business. Several of the hill stations acquired even more prominence when Japan began its military advance across southeast Asia: Simla became the head-

59. G. G. Gupta to Chairman, Simla Municipal Board, 29 April 1939, Simla Municipal Corporation Records, 105/1176/31/1939, HPSA.

60. C. D. Jordan to Secretary, Municipal Committee, 12 Sept. 1939, Simla Municipal Corporation Records, 105/1176/31/1939, HPSA.

61. Austin A. D'Souza, *Anglo-Indian Education: A Study of Its Origins and Growth in Bengal up to 1960* (Delhi, 1976), 180.

quarters for the exiled Burmese government and Darjeeling the headquarters for the exiled Malayan government, while British refugees from Burma filled Shillong, and Pachmarhi became a center for jungle-warfare training. But the transitory nature of this revival was apparent to all who cared to contemplate it. British rule over India was near its end, and with it came the end of the British presence in the hill stations. So fully had the British relationship to these highland enclaves become woven within the fabric of the imperial system that its unraveling became the unraveling of the hill stations as well.

———

For the British, then, the mountains lost their magic in the first half of the twentieth century. Their mantle of inviolability was pierced, and the pressures forcing the raj into retreat rushed in. Yet, far from sweeping the hill stations to their destruction, these forces became a source of renewal. The mountains cast their spell over an incoming coterie of arrivistes, a Westernized, indigenous elite who laid claim to the imperial realm's inheritance. Thus, the end of British rule did not entail the end of the hill stations.

Independence did, to be sure, bring substantial changes to the hill stations. The British left. Even those who decided to stay on—typified by Colonel Tusker Smalley and his wife Lucy, the characters so wonderfully realized by Paul Scott in *Staying On*[62]—are with rare exception now dead or gone. The Indians took over, and they have since made these highland resorts conform to their needs and desires. The populations of many hill stations have doubled and even tripled in the last decades of the twentieth century. Millions of summer visitors squeeze into the stations' malls and shops and hotels during the summer season, most of them arriving by bus and auto for excursions that last no more than a few days.[63] Modern, multistoried concrete structures increasingly crowd out quainter colonial buildings, which gradually fall into ruin. Simla, Darjeeling, Shillong, Ootacamund, and other hill stations have become busy entrepots for regional trade, their main roadways clogged with people and goods and vehicles. Congestion has created environmental and health

62. Paul Scott, *Staying On* (New York, 1977).
63. Nora Mitchell, "The Indian Hill-Station: Kodaikanal," University of Chicago Deparment of Geography Research Paper 141, 1972, ch. 5; Tyagi, *Hill Resorts,* passim.

problems of far greater seriousness than those the British faced.[64] Western tourists who seek the remnants of a colonial past in these places are likely to leave dissatisfied.[65]

Yet the hill stations remain in spirit much as they were before. Indians go to the highlands for many of the same reasons the British did. They seek relief from the heat of the plains. They seek relaxation, diversion, communion with nature, and escape from the pressures of their daily lives. And they seek these things in ways that bear a striking similarity to the ways of their colonial predecessors. They congregate on the malls. They boat on the lakes. They stroll to the "points" and "vistas" that offer sanctioned views of surrounding scenery. They behave at times in ways that would be regarded as scandalous in their own communities. In Bharati Mukherjee's *The Tiger's Daughter,* several young Indian women from Calcutta agree to participate in a beauty contest in a Darjeeling hotel, a form of exhibitionism they never would have contemplated in Calcutta.[66] While this incident is fictional, it suggests the degree to which the highland resorts retain something of their colonial reputation for provoking risqué or unconventional conduct. Their associations with romance in Indian films and their popularity as places for honeymooners are further signs that hill stations are seen as places where individuals can procure the emotional freedom that eludes them elsewhere. They remain avenues of escape from the conventions and constraints placed on social behavior in the plains. They remain sites of alterity.

An appreciation of the hill station by a modern Tamil author calls "the notion of creating townships on mountains for the sake of coolness, health and happiness . . . a gift from the Britisher. Though it is not a straight and direct gift, we may be thankful to the giver all the same."[67] If the hill station was in fact a "gift," the Indians who accepted it did so in much the same spirit that the British offered it. Above all, they accepted it as a place apart from the influences of the plains, a refuge from its troubles. This is the dominant theme, for example, of Anita Desai's *Fire on the Mountain,* which takes place in the hill station of Kasauli. The novel's central character is a woman who seeks escape in the hills from an unhappy past, who "had

64. "The Downhill Stations," *India Today,* June 15, 1989, 42–45.

65. Graeme D. Westlake, *An Introduction to the Hill Stations of India* (New Delhi, 1993), pt. 2.

66. Bharati Mukherjee, *The Tiger's Daughter* (New York, 1971), pt. 4.

67. M. S. Kalyanasundaram, *Indian Hill Stations* (Madras, 1961), 10.

been glad to leave it all behind, in the plains."[68] What she comes to realize by the end of the story is that she cannot leave it behind. The world she wants no part of eventually intrudes itself into her highland haven, shattering her hard-won sense of security. The British, by the end of their stay in India, would have understood.

68. Anita Desai, *Fire on the Mountain* (London, 1981), 30.

# 10  Conclusion

This book has sought to show that the view from the hill stations reveals far more about the British colonial experience on the subcontinent than either the British themselves or their historians have suggested or supposed. Despite their reputations as isolated retreats, the hill stations were profoundly implicated in the imperial endeavor. Their engagement in that endeavor is most readily apparent in the role they played as centers of political and military power. Largely because of their physical remoteness, hill stations became highly prized in the second half of the nineteenth century as headquarters for the imperial government, the provincial governments, and the command structure of the army, while a growing portion of the British troops stationed in India found themselves billeted in highland cantonments as well. Less noticeable but no less important to the purposes of the raj was the fact that the physical and ideological reproduction of those who ruled the subcontinent tended to take place in the hill stations. By concentrating their women and children in these mountain enclaves, the British were able to replicate the domestic, educational, and social institutions of their homeland with startling exactitude. Here they endeavored to restore a sense of common identity and imperial purpose to their lives and to pass these convictions on to their offspring. Paradoxically, then, the hill stations' contribution to the colonial project derived in the final analysis from their aura of aloofness from the rest of the subcontinent. No wonder so many observers have failed to acknowledge their complicity in the system that sustained British predominance. Their popularity derived from the notion that they had none.

What are the implications of the reintegration of the hill stations into the social history of the British in India? To answer this question, we need to trace the trajectory this history has taken. The first generation of historians to study the British colonial community tended to portray it as socially cohesive, composed mainly of upper-middle-class officials interspersed with scattered pockets of planters and merchants.[1] Perhaps the

---

1. See R. Pearson, *Eastern Interlude: A Social History of the European Community in Calcutta* (Calcutta, 1933); Dennis Kincaid, *British Social Life in India*

culminating example of this approach, with its stress on the homogeneity and high social standing of the colonizers, was Francis Hutchins's graceful synthesis, *The Illusion of Permanence,* which referred to the ruling race as a "middle class aristocracy."[2]

This interpretation has been demolished by more recent scholarship. Probing past the easy generalizations that derived from exclusive emphasis on the mandarins of the Indian Civil Service, a second generation of historians has shown that the British Indian population was far less homogeneous than previously supposed: it was in fact fractured into many occupational, ethnic, and other groups with disparate interests and concerns.[3] The widest fissure was the one between officials and nonofficials, but the lines of stratification were far more complex and extensive than that binarism can connote. Merchants, missionaries, planters, railway workers, soldiers, and various other groups clung to their own distinct subcultures, each existing conspicuously apart from the others.[4] Women too operated within a world of their own, segregated from the activities and opportunities available to men.[5] British society in India was not merely highly

---

1608–1937 (London, 1938); Philip Woodruff, *The Men Who Ruled India,* vol. 1: *The Founders;* vol. 2: *The Guardians* (1953; reprint, New York, 1964); Percival Spear, *The Nabobs* (1963; reprint, Calcutta, 1991). A more recent example of this approach is the work of Michael Edwardes, especially *Bound to Exile: The Victorians in India* (New York, 1970).

2. Francis G. Hutchins, *The Illusion of Permanence: British Imperialism in India* (Princeton, 1967).

3. The work of Bernard S. Cohn, most notably the 1962 essay, "The British in Benares: A Nineteenth Century Colonial Society," reprinted in his *An Anthropologist among the Historians and Other Essays* (Delhi, 1987), is important to this shift of perspective.

4. See David Arnold, "White Colonization and Labour in Nineteenth-Century India," *Journal of Imperial and Commonwealth History* 9, no. 2 (Jan. 1983): 133–58; Kenneth Ballhatchet, *Race, Sex and Class under the Raj: Imperial Attitudes and Policies and Their Critics, 1793–1905* (New York, 1980); P. J. Marshall, "The Whites of British India, 1780–1830: A Failed Colonial Society?" *International History Review* 12, no. 1 (Feb. 1990): 26–44; P. J. Marshall, "British Immigration into India in the Nineteenth Century," in *European Expansion and Migration: Essays on the International Migration from Africa, Asia, and Europe,* ed. P. C. Emmer and M. Morner (New York, 1992), 179–96; Raymond K. Renford, *The Non-official British in India to 1920* (Delhi, 1987); and Zoe Yalland, *Traders and Nabobs: The British in Cawnpore 1765–1857* (Salisbury, Wiltshire, 1987).

5. See, for example, Pat Barr, *The Dust in the Balance: British Women in India 1905–1945* (London, 1989); Pat Barr, *The Memsahibs: The Women of Victorian India* (London, 1976); Nupur Chaudhuri, "Memsahibs and Motherhood in Nineteenth-Century Colonial India," *Victorian Studies* 31, no. 4 (summer 1988): 517–35; Margaret MacMillan, *Women of the Raj* (London, 1988); and Barbara N. Ramusack, "Cultural Missionaries, Maternal Imperialists, Feminist Allies: British

segmented; it was intensely hierarchical, as visitors to the subcontinent repeatedly observed. The Indian Civil Service held pride of place in this hierarchy, but this did not prevent it from being riven with its own internal struggles over status. And high officialdom's disdain for the uncovenanted classes, the boxwallahs, and others evidenced a deeply rooted inegalitarian ethos.[6] Hutchins's claims for the middle-class character of the British Indian population have been challenged by growing evidence of a surprisingly large pool of poor whites. A series of studies has focused attention on various groups on the margins of British society—vagrants, orphans, prostitutes, the insane, and, pushed to the social periphery by their mixed racial origins, the Anglo-Indians or Eurasians. As David Arnold has noted, "There was a glaring incongruity between the imperialist ideal of an ethnically discrete ruling class and the presence of large numbers of poor whites."[7]

While this scholarship has deepened our understanding of British Indian society in important ways, it has also provoked new questions that cannot be answered through the pursuit of particularism and diversity. What prevented these varied and often mutually antagonistic groups from spinning off into entirely separate paths? Where were the centripetal forces that kept them within a common orbit? How, in other words, did the diverse clusters of Britons in India sustain the sense of social cohesion necessary for the preservation of their powers and privileges as colonizers? Rather than confront these questions, most scholars have simply taken it as a given that an overarching and immutable affinity existed among Britons *as* Britons or, more generally, among Europeans *as* Europeans. This view simply assumes what should in fact be demonstrated. Britishness and Europeanness are socially and historically constructed identities, and their specific meanings and boundaries are contingent on the circumstances within which they arise. Those circumstances were quite different in the colonial world than they were in Europe itself. This point has been made with great cogency by Ann Stoler, who insists that the notion of what it

---

Women Activists in India, 1865–1945," *Women's Studies International Forum* 13, no. 4 (1990): 309–21.

6. See Bradford Spangenberg, *British Bureaucracy in India: Status, Policy and the I.C.S. in the Late 19th Century* (New Delhi, 1976).

7. David Arnold, "European Orphans and Vagrants in India in the Nineteenth Century," *Journal of Imperial and Commonwealth History* 7, no. 2 (Jan. 1979): 104. Also see Ballhatchet, *Race, Sex and Class;* Waltraud Ernst, *Mad Tales from the Raj: The European Insane in British India, 1800–1858* (London, 1991); and Richard Symonds, "Eurasians under British Rule," in *Oxford University Papers on India*, vol. 1, pt. 2 (Delhi, 1987), 28–42.

meant to be European in the colonies was never predetermined but, instead, was subject to unstable, socially constructed configurations.[8] Class, race, and other cultural markers of difference in the colonial world shifted with economic and political circumstances. Thus, the cohesion of European colonizers cannot be taken for granted: it arose from distinctive challenges and through deliberate means.

The main argument of this book is that hill stations were at the heart of the British effort to define and defend the boundaries that set them apart from Indians and that sustained their identity as agents of a superior culture. To be sure, a great many other mechanisms furthered this end: newcomers were socialized to the normative codes of colonial society through clubland's powers to enforce conformity; vagrants, prostitutes, and other social deviants were removed from the scene through incarceration or deportation; whites in general were taught to appreciate the precariousness of their position and the importance of racial solidarity through reminders about the events of 1857. While all these practices contributed to the cohesion of the British Indian population, none had as much influence as the retreat to the hill stations. The role of these enclaves in rendering what it meant to be a Briton in India was a vital one.

In the hill stations the British could replicate the bourgeois civic culture that characterized the social world they had left behind in Britain. At the heart of this culture was the dialectical interplay between the public and private spheres. The public sphere was the male-dominated world of politics, policy, and production; the private sphere was the female-dominated world of family, faith, and reproduction. The articulation of the two spheres gave British society its distinctive identity. But the public/private dichotomy did not hold up well when transferred to the colonial context. The authoritarian demands of imperial rule gave predominance to the public exhibition of power, imposing an inordinately masculine, official cast on the British presence in India. The raj left little room for women, for families, for a private sphere in general, and their attenuation inhibited the civic culture that was so important to the formation of a common identity among the agents of imperialism. Only the hill stations made it possible for such an identity to be conceived, nurtured, and perpetuated within the confines

8. Ann Laura Stoler, "Rethinking Colonial Categories: European Communities and the Boundaries of Rule," *Comparative Studies in Society and History* 13, no. 1 (1989): 134–61; Ann Laura Stoler, "Making Empire Respectable: The Politics of Race and Sexual Morality in 20th-Century Colonial Cultures," *American Ethnologist* 16, no. 4 (Nov. 1989), 634–59.

of the colonial experience. Only the hill stations created the conditions where the balance between public and private could be restored and a sense of community could be sustained.

The construction of a community is first and foremost an act of imagination, requiring the formulation of those qualities that distinguish "us" from "them." Just such an act occurred when the British began to turn their attention to India's mountains. Their decision to establish health sanitaria in the highlands was a significant step in the delineation of difference, which they articulated in the medico-climatic terms that most European expatriates could appreciate at a visceral level. The hills were cool, the plains hot; the hills were healthy, the plains disease-ridden; the hills were therefore safe, the plains dangerous. The British accentuated this contrast by evoking the aesthetics of the picturesque and the sublime in their representations of the highlands. They privileged the sites where their hill stations arose as places of beauty and splendor, places that resembled favorite landscapes back home. They made the resemblance compelling by radically reshaping the habitat of the hill stations—establishing artificial bodies of water and introducing exotic plants and animals—thereby imposing their aesthetic preferences on the physical environment. They even managed to incorporate the indigenous peoples within the framework of their efforts to create a contrast with the plains. They cast the Todas of the Nilgiris and their counterparts around other hill stations in the role of noble savages, whose supposed innocence, quiescence, and intimacy with nature could be taken as tokens of the secluded and Edenic character of the places they inhabited. Through these and other devices, the British were able to invent the hill stations as settings where they could renew their sense of themselves as members of a common community.

From the moment the first houses appeared on the ridges of the Himalayas and other highland sites, the British were faced with the task of defining and delimiting the boundaries of their community. The debate over the colonization of the highlands with pensioners, artisans, and other undercapitalized settlers was part of that process, and its outcome pointed to some of the parameters of sodality. But so too did the decision to establish the Lawrence Asylums and similar institutions in the hills for the education of orphans and other poor white children. What made the inclusion of the colonists undesirable made the inclusion of the children imperative. Nor were the young the only ones on the lower margins of white society to gain entry to the highlands. We should not forget the large numbers of British soldiers who were stationed in hill cantonments. Although Rudyard Kipling and others created the impression that the hill stations were monopolized by civil servants and army officials and their wives, they did in fact draw a surprisingly varied clientele. Merchants, missionaries, and other nonofficials enjoyed occasional sojourns in the highlands, particularly after the advance of the railway across the subcontinent reduced the time and cost of travel. These visitors may not have gone to the hills as frequently as government officials and their families, nor stayed quite as long, but neither were they strangers to them. They may also have preferred the smaller, cheaper, humbler stations over the famous ones where the "heaven-born" congregated, but this preference was consistent with the segmentary, hierarchical nature of British colonial society. Indeed, the tendency for different groups to gravitate to different hill stations was one of the ways by which the social hierarchy was maintained. But the more telling point is that the only elements among the British population who were not welcome in one hill station or another were those marginalized whites who were not welcome in India at all.

As a result, the various hill stations contributed to the construction of the colonial community even as they catered to different sectors of it. In nearly all the stations the British created environments that reminded residents and visitors of the homeland and heritage that bound them together. "You might be up there in the hills almost as much separated from the natives as in England," remarked an official in one variation of an oft-repeated claim.[9] The geographical isolation of the hill stations induced a sense of psychological distance from the colonized populace, offering an escape from anxieties about disease, degeneration, and rebellion. Each station resembled an English village or spa town, complete with a neo-Gothic church at its center, a pedestrian mall for evening strolls, and a medley of charming cottages framed in flowers. The social climate imitated metropolitan patterns of behavior, with an emphasis on etiquette and an enthusiasm for parties, picnics, and other entertainments that lubricated the wheels of social interaction. The demographic disequilibrium of the colonizer community was circumvented by drawing large numbers of women to the hill stations, where they helped to construct a bourgeois private sphere with its emphasis on love and matrimony, its attention to children and family, and its general atmosphere of domesticity. The ideological commitment to the colonial endeavor was transferred from one generation to the next through the proliferation of educational institutions

9. John Abraham Francis Hawkins, in PP, *Second Report from the Select Committee on Colonization and Settlement (India)* (1858), Session 1857–58, VII, pt. 1, 129.

modeled after English public schools, which provided children who could not or would not leave India with the skills and values appropriate to their place in the colonial order. Birth, education, courtship, marriage, retirement, death: most of the major transitions in the life-cycle of the colonizers occurred with far greater frequency in the hill stations than elsewhere in India. These were the places where the British in India went to cultivate a shared identity as a ruling race and to perpetuate its properties over time.

For this ruling race, the exigencies of ruling were no less important than the affinities of race, and here too the hill stations attained an importance out of all proportion to their reputations. They presented the British with the tempting prospect of governing the colonial state without interference from the governed. The imperial government's gradual shift of operations to Simla in the latter part of the nineteenth century and the equivalent seasonal transfer of the provincial governments to Darjeeling, Ootacamund, and other hill stations was a concerted effort to attain this ethereal political condition. Combined with the movement of large segments of the Indian Army's headquarters and troops to the hills, this relocation of power was intended to prolong the colonial enterprise. The British sought in this way to secure a vantage point from which they could oversee their subjects while remaining unassailable by them.

In the final analysis, of course, they failed. And their failure too can be written in the history of the hill stations. Even these remote and exclusive enclaves were not immune to the forces that overturned the raj. On the contrary, they exemplified some of the contradictions at the very core of the British endeavor. They were meant to provide a refuge from contact with the Indian masses, but they depended on the Indian masses for their construction and maintenance. They were meant to provide a setting in which the government could exercise its authority dispassionately, but they isolated the government from the public's interests and aroused the people's passionate ire. They were meant to be places where the British could define themselves according to an exclusive set of cultural values and practices, but they attracted a Westernized Indian elite whose adoption of some of the same values and practices subverted British claims of exclusivity. Thus, the hill stations must be considered not only in terms of the social history of the British, but of the Indians as well. The testimony to this fact is that they have not just survived but thrived since independence.

# Select Bibliography

ARCHIVAL RECORDS

The archival records are so vast and so widely scattered that it would have required a Herculean effort to work through all of them. My aim was more modest—a selective examination of material from some of the more important archives in the hope of obtaining a reasonably balanced appreciation of the public issues that arose regarding hill stations. A list of the principal archives and classes of documents I consulted follows.

*Himachal Pradesh State Archives, Simla*

Annual Reports of the Simla Municipality
Simla Municipal Corporation Records
Simla Municipal Proceedings

*India Office Library and Records, London*

Board's Collection
India and Bengal Dispatches
Madras Dispatches
Proceedings of the Government of the United Provinces
Public and Judicial Department

*Indian National Archives, New Delhi*

Home Department Proceedings
Foreign Department Proceedings

*Tamil Nadu State Archives, Madras*

Annual Reports, Coonoor Municipality
Annual Reports, Kodaikanal Municipality
Annual Reports, Ootacamund Municipality

*West Bengal State Archives, Calcutta*

Proceedings of the Lieutenant Governor of Bengal

GAZETTEERS

Atkinson, Edwin T. *The Himalayan Gazetteer.* 1882. 3 vols. Reprint, Delhi: Cosmo Publications, 1973.
*The Imperial Gazetteer of India.* New ed. 26 vols. Oxford: Clarendon Press, 1908.
Thornton, Edward, *A Gazetteer of the Territories under the Government of the East-India Company, and of the Native States on the Continent of India.* 1858. Reprint, Delhi: Neeraj, 1984.

Assam

Allen, B. C. *Assam District Gazetteers.* Vol. 10: *The Khasi and Jaintia Hills.* Allahabad: Pioneer Press, 1906.

Bengal

*Darjeeling District Gazetteer, Statistics, 1901–02.* Calcutta: Bengal Secretariat, 1905.
Dash, Arthur Jules. *Bengal District Gazetteers: Darjeeling.* Alipore, Bengal: Bengal Government Press, 1947.
Hunter, W. W. *A Statistical Account of Bengal.* Vol. 10: *Districts of Darjiling and Jalpaiguri, and State of Kuch Behar.* London: Trubner, 1876.
O'Malley, L.S.S. *Darjeeling.* Calcutta: Bengal Secretariat Book Depot, 1907.

Bombay

*Gazetteer of the Bombay Presidency.* Vol. 19: *Satara,* Bombay: Central Government Press, 1885; Vol. 19B: *Satara,* Bombay: Phaltan and Aundh, 1926.
*Imperial Gazetteer of India, Provincial Series, Bombay Presidency.* 2 vols. Calcutta: Superintendent of Government Printing, 1909.

Central Provinces

*Central Provinces District Gazetteers. Hoshangabad District.* Vol. B: *Statistical Tables.* Allahabad: Pioneer Press, 1904; *Statistical Tables 1891–1926.* Nagpur: Government Press, 1927.
Corbett, G. L., and R. V. Russell. *Central Provinces District Gazetteers: Hoshangabad District.* Vol. A. Calcutta: Thacker, Spink, 1908.

Madras

Francis, W. *The Nilgiris.* Madras: Government Press, 1908.
*Gazetteer of Southern India.* Madras: Pharoah, 1855.
Grigg, H. B. *A Manual of the Nilagiri District.* Madras: Government Press, 1880.
*Imperial Gazetteer of India, Provincial Series: Madras.* Vol. 2. Calcutta: Government Printing, 1908.
*Madras District Gazetteers, Statistical Appendix for Madura District.* Madras: Government Press, 1905, 1915, 1930, 1933.

*Madras District Gazetteers, Statistical Appendix for the Nilgiri District.* Madras: Government Press, 1905, 1928, 1933.

Richards, F. J. *Salem.* Madras: Government Press, 1913.

## Punjab

*Gazetteer of the Gurdaspur District 1883–84.* Lahore: Arya Press, 1884.

*Punjab District Gazetteers, Gurdaspur District, 1914.* Vol. 21A. Lahore: Government Printing, 1915.

*Punjab District Gazetteers, Gurdaspur District Statistical Tables, 1904.* Vol. 21B. Lahore: "Civil and Military Gazette" Press, 1904; *Statistical Tables, 1912.* Vol. 21B. Lahore: Singh and Sons, 1913; *Statistical Tables, 1936.* Vol. 14B. Lahore: Government Printing, 1936.

*Punjab District Gazetteers, Kangra District, 1924–25.* Vol. 7A. Lahore: Government Printing, 1926.

*Punjab District Gazetteers, Rawalpindi District, 1907.* Vol. 28A. Lahore: "Civil and Military Gazette" Press, 1909.

*Punjab District Gazetteers, Simla District, 1904.* Vol. 8A. Lahore: "Civil and Military Gazette" Press, 1908.

*Punjab District Gazetteers, Simla District Statistical Tables, 1904.* Vol. 7B. Lahore: "Civil and Military Gazette" Press, 1909.

*Punjab District Gazetteers, Simla District Statistical Tables, 1936.* Vol. 6B. Lahore: "Civil and Military Gazette" Press, 1936.

Punjab Government. *Gazetteer of the Simla District, 1888–89.* Calcutta: Central Press, n.d.

## United Provinces

*District Gazetteers of the United Provinces of Agra and Oudh: Supplementary Notes and Statistics.* Vol. 1: *Dehra Dun District.* Allahabad: Government Press, 1924.

*District Gazetteers of the United Provinces of Agra and Oudh: Supplementary Notes and Statistics up to 1931–2.* Vol. 1D: *Dehra Dun District.* Allahabad: Government Press, 1934.

*District Gazetteers of the United Provinces of Agra and Oudh: Supplementary Notes and Statistics.* Vol. 34: *Naini Tal District.* Allahabad: Government Press, 1925.

*Imperial Gazetteer of India, Provincial Series: United Provinces of Agra and Oudh.* 2 vols. Reprint, New Delhi: Usha Publications, 1984.

Neville, H. R. *Naini Tal: A Gazetteer, Being Volume XXXIV of the District Gazetteers of the United Provinces of Agra and Oudh.* Allahabad: Government Press, 1904.

Walton, H. G. *Almora: A Gazetteer, District Gazetteers of the United Provinces.* Vol. 35. Allahabad: Government Press, 1911.

———. *British Garhwal. A Gazetteer, Being Vol. XXXVI of the District Gazetteers of the United Provinces of Agra and Oudh.* Allahabad: Government Press, 1910.

————. *Dehra Dun: A Gazetteer, District Gazetteers of the United Provinces of Agra and Oudh.* Vol. 1. Allahabad: Government Press, 1911.

*Garhwal. Supplementary Notes and Statistics.* Vol. 36. N.p., 1914.


GOVERNMENT REPORTS

*Great Britain, Parliamentary Papers (PP) and Debates*

*Papers Connected with the Re-organization of the Army in India.* Session 2, VIII, 1859.

*Papers Relative to the Formation of a Sanitarium on the Neilgherries for European Troops.* Session 729, XLI, 1850.

*Report of the Commissioners Appointed to Inquire into the Sanitary State of the Army in India.* XIX, 1863.

*Reports from the Select Committee on Colonization and Settlement (India), 1857–59.*

*Hansard Parliamentary Debates,* 3d series, vol. 293 (1884) and vol. 336 (1889); 4th series, vol. 47 (1897) and vol. 50 (1897).


*India*

Bamber, C. J. *Report on an Outbreak of Enteric Fever in Simla during the Summer of 1904.* Lahore: "Civil and Military Gazette" Press, 1904.

Committee upon the Financial Condition of Hill Schools for Europeans in Northern India. Vol. 1: *Report.* Simla: Government Printing Office, 1904; Vol. 2: *Evidence and Appendices.* Calcutta: Government Printing Office, 1905.

Ellis, R. S. *Report on the Stations of Ootacamund and Coonoor.* Madras: Adelphi Press, 1865.

————. *Reports upon the Military and Civil Station of Bellary, and upon the Mountain Sanitarium of Ramandroog.* Madras: Adelphi Press, 1867.

*General Report on the Administration of the Several Presidencies and Provinces of British India, 1856–57.* Pt. 1. Calcutta: Calcutta Gazette Office, 1858.

*Guide to the Records of the Nilgiris District from 1827 to 1835.* Madras: Government Press, 1934.

Hamilton, Lt.-Col. Douglas. *Report on the High Ranges of the Annamullay Mountains.* Madras: Fort Saint George Gazette Press, 1866.

————. *Report on the Pulni Mountains.* Madras: United Scottish Press, 1864.

————. *Report on the Shevaroy Hills.* Madras: Fort Saint George Gazette Press, 1862.

————. *Sketches of the Shevaroy Hills.* London: War Office, 1865.

Ibbetson, Denzil. *Report on the Census of the Panjab, Taken on February 1881.* Calcutta: Superintendent of Government Printing, 1883.

Lawrence, A. J. *Report on the Existing Schools for Europeans and Eurasians throughout India.* Calcutta: Government Printing, 1873.

Medical Board Office, Madras Presidency. *Report on the Medical Topography and Statistics of Neilgherry Hills.* Madras: Vepery Mission Press, 1844.

Mercer, Alfred. *Report on the Progress of Education of European Children during the Quinquennium 1912–13—1916–17.* Calcutta: Bengal Secretariat Book Depot, 1917.

Palmer, C., W. G. Murray, and V. Ball. *Report on the Hill of Mahendragiri.* Calcutta: Calcutta Central Press, 1870.

Public Works Department. *Completion Report of the New Viceregal Lodge at Simla.* Serial no. 22. Calcutta: Government Printing, 1890.

Public Works Department. *Completion Reports of Public Office Buildings and Clerks' Cottages at Simla.* Serial no. 21. Calcutta: Government Printing, 1889.

Ranking, J. L. *Report upon the Sanitary Condition of Ootacamund.* Madras: Adelphi Press, 1868.

*Report of the Commission Appointed to Deal with the Transfer of the Punjab Government to the Hill Station of Dalhousie.* Simla: Government Printing Office, 1902.

*Report of the Conference on the Education of the Domiciled Community in India, Simla, July 1912.* Calcutta: Government Printing, 1912.

*Report of the Simla Extension Committee, 1898.* Simla: Punjab Government Branch Press, 1898.

*Report of the Simla Improvement Committee.* Simla: Government Monotype Press, 1907.

*Report of the Simla Sanitary Investigation Committee.* Simla: Punjab Government Branch Press, 1905.

*Report on the Administration of the Madras Presidency, 1874–75.* Madras: Government Press, 1876.

*Report on the Government Botanical and Horticultural Gardens, Ootacamund, for the Year 1854–55.* Madras: Fort Saint George Gazette Press, 1856.

*Report on the Summer Census of Dalhousie, 1911.* Lahore: Punjab Government Press, 1912.

*Report on the Summer Census of Murree, 1911.* Lahore: Punjab Government Press, 1912.

*Report on the Summer Census of Simla, 1911.* Lahore: Punjab Government Press, 1912.

Robertson, W. R. *Report on the Agricultural Conditions, Capabilities, and Prospects of the Neilgherry District.* Madras: Government Gazette Press, 1875.

*Selections from the Records of the Bengal Government.* No. 17: *Report on Darjeeling,* by W. B. Jackson. Calcutta: Thos. Jones, 1854.

*Selections from the Records of the Government of Bengal.* No. 36, pt. 2: *The Maghassani Hills as a Sanatarium.* Calcutta: Bengal Military Orphan Press, 1861.

*Selections from the Records of the Government of Bengal.* No. 38: *Papers Relating to a Sanatarium upon Mount Parisnath.* Calcutta: Bengal Military Orphan Press, 1861.

*Selections from the Records of the Government of India (Military Department).* Nos. 1–3: *Report on the Extent and Nature of the Sanitary Establishments for European Troops in India.* Calcutta: Military Department Press, 1861, 1862.

Statistics of the British-Born Subjects Recorded at the Census of India, 17th February 1881. Calcutta: Superintendent of Government Printing, 1883.

GUIDEBOOKS, MEMOIRS, OTHER PRIMARY SOURCES

Annesley, James. Researches into the Causes, Nature, and Treatment of the More Prevalent Diseases of India, and of Warm Climates Generally. 2 vols. London: Longman, Rees, Orme, Brown, and Green, 1828.

Baikie, Robert. The Neilgherries. 2d ed. Calcutta: J. Thomas, 1857.

———. Observations on the Neilgherries. Ed. W. H. Smoult. Calcutta: Baptist Mission Press, 1834.

Balfour, Edward. Statistical Data for Forming Troops and Maintaining Them in Health in Different Climates and Localities. London: Statistical Society of London, 1845.

Barron, Capt. Richard. Views in India, Chiefly among the Neelgherry Hills. London: Robert Havell, 1837.

Bastavala, D. S. Simla. Bombay: Tata, 1925.

Bayley, H. V. Dorje-ling. Calcutta: G. H. Huttman, 1838.

Bellasis, A. F. An Account of the Hill Station of Matharan, near Bombay. Bombay: Education Society's Press, 1869.

Bhanja, K. C. Darjeeling at a Glance. Darjeeling, 1942.

———. Wonders of Darjeeling and the Sikkim Himalaya. N.p., 1943.

Bharucha, Perin. Mahabaleswar: The Club 1881–1981. Bombay: Asian Printers, c. 1981.

Blackham, Col. Robert J. Scalpel, Sword and Stretcher. London: Sampson Law, Marston, 1931.

Blavatsky, H. P. The People of the Blue Mountains. 1893. Reprint, Wheaton, Ill.: Theosophical Press, 1930.

Bomwetsch, G. S. Before the Glory of the Snows: A Hand Book to Darjeeling. Calcutta: Central Press, 1899.

Bowen, F. O. Hand-Book of Kodaikanal. Trichinopoly: N.p., 1932.

Breeks, James Wilkinson. An Account of the Primitive Tribes and Monuments of the Nilagiris. London: India Museum, 1873.

Brown, Percy. Tours in Sikhim and the Darjeeling District. Calcutta: W. Newman, 1917.

Browning, Oscar. Impressions of Indian Travel. London: Hodder & Stoughton, 1903.

Buchanan, W. J. "Notes on Old Darjeeling." Bengal: Past and Present 2, no. 6 (Oct. 1908): 439–58.

Buck, Edward J. Simla Past and Present. 1904. Reprint, Delhi: Sumit Publications, 1979.

———. Simla Past and Present. 2d ed. 1925. Reprint, Simla: Minerva Book House, 1989.

Buckland, C. T. Sketches of Social Life in India. London: W. H. Allen, 1884.

Burton, E. F. An Indian Olio. London: Spencer Blackett, 1888.

Burton, Isabel. AEI: Arabia Egypt India, A Narrative of Travel. London and Belfast: William Mullan & Sons, 1879.

—————. *The Life of Captain Sir Richard F. Burton.* 2 vols. London: Chapman and Hall, 1893.

Burton, Richard F. *Goa, and the Blue Mountains.* 1851. Reprint, Berkeley: University of California Press, 1991.

Butler, Iris. *The Viceroy's Wife: Letters of Alice, Countess of Reading, from India, 1921–25.* London: Hodder & Stoughton, 1969.

Caine, W. S. *Picturesque India: A Handbook for European Travellers.* London: George Routledge & Sons, 1890.

*The Call of the Nilgiris.* Madras: Higginbotham, 1911.

Campbell, A. "Note on the Lepchas of Sikkim." *Journal of the Asiatic Society of Bengal* 92 (1840): 379–93.

Campbell, Major Walter. *The Old Forest Ranger; or, Wild Sports in India.* London: Virtue Brothers, 1863.

Carey, W. H., comp. *A Guide to Simla with a Descriptive Account of the Neighbouring Sanitaria.* Calcutta: Calcutta Central Press, 1870.

Charles, Sir R. Havelock. "Neurasthenia and Its Bearing on the Decay of Northern Peoples in India." *Transactions of the Society of Tropical Medicine and Hygiene* 7, no. 1 (Nov. 1913): 2–31.

Chesson, John. "Hill Sanitaria of Western India: Panchgunny." *Bombay Miscellany* 4 (1862): 335–70. Reprinted as *Second Report on the Hill-Station of Panchgunny, near Mahableshwur.* Bombay: Alliance Press, 1862.

Choksi, Sarabhai. *Mahableshwar and Panchgani Guide.* Bombay, n.d.

"Civilian." *The Civilian's South India.* London: John Lane, Bodley Head, 1921.

Clarke, Hyde. *Colonization, Defence and Railways in Our Indian Empire.* London: J. Weale, 1857.

—————. "The English Stations in the Hill Regions of India." *Journal of the Statistical Society* 44 (Sept. 1881): 528–73.

—————. "On the Organization of the Army of India, with Especial Reference to the Hill Regions." *Journal of the Royal United Service Institution* 3 (1860): 18–27.

Cornelius, A. W. *Dehra Dun—Mussoorie—Landour Guide.* N.p., 1947.

Cornish, W. R. "The Shervaroy Hills." In *The Hill Ranges of Southern India,* ed. John Shortt. Madras: Higginbotham, 1870–83.

Crawford, D. G. *A History of the Indian Medical Service 1600–1913.* Vol. 1. London: W. Thacker, 1914.

Crawfurd, John. *Notes on the Settlement or Colonization of British Subjects in India.* London: James Ridgeway, 1833.

Cullimore, D. H. *The Book of Climates.* 2d ed. London: Bailliere, Tindall, & Cox, 1891.

Cumming, Constance F. Gordon *From the Hebrides to the Himalayas.* 2 vols. London: Sampson Low, Marston, Searle, & Rivington, 1876.

—————. *In the Himalayas and on the Indian Plains.* London: Chatto & Windus, 1884.

Curran, William. "Further Evidence in Favour of a Hill Residence for European Soldiers in India." *Irish Journal of Medical Science* 52, no. 104 (1871): 391–416.

—————. "The Himalayas as a Health Resort." *Practitioner* (Jan. 1871): 27–44.

Dabake, Vishnu Bhikaji. *Hand Book to Matheran.* 3d ed. Poona: Pratibha Press, 1938.

Dalhousie, Marquess of. *Private Letters of the Marquess of Dalhousie.* Ed. J.G.A. Baird. Edinburgh and London: William Blackwood & Sons, 1910.

*Darjeeling.* Pamphlet reprinted from the *Calcutta Review,* no. 55 (1857).

*Darjeeling and Its Mountain Railway.* Calcutta: Darjeeling Himalayan Railway Co., 1921.

Darjeeling Himalayan Railway Company. *The Darjeeling Himalayan Railway. Illustrated Guide for Tourists.* London: McCorquodale, 1896.

Dastur, N. M. *Pocket Book of Mahabaleshwar and Panchgani.* 3d ed. Poona: Chitrashala Press, 1944.

Denning, Margaret B. *Mosaics from India.* Chicago: Fleming H. Revell, 1902.

Dilke, Charles Wentworth. *Greater Britain: A Record of Travel in English-Speaking Countries.* Vol. 2. London: Macmillan, 1869.

Diver, Maud. *The Englishwoman in India.* Edinburgh and London: William Blackwood & Sons, 1909.

Donaldson, Florence. *Lepcha Land.* London: Sampson Low, Marston, 1900.

*The Dorjeeling Guide.* Calcutta: Samuel Smith, 1845.

Douglas, James. *Bombay and Western India.* 2 vols. London: Sampson Low, Marston, 1893.

"Doz." *Simla in Ragtime: An Illustrated Guide Book.* Simla: Station Press, 1913.

Drummond, Capt. H. *Notes on the Colonization of the Himalayas.* Edinburgh, 1845.

Dufferin and Ava, Marchioness of. *Our Viceregal Life in India: Selections from My Journal 1884–1888.* London: John Murray, 1890.

Duke, Joshua. *Kashmir and Jammu: A Guide for Visitors.* Calcutta: Thacker, Spink, 1903.

Dulles, Rev. John W. *Life in India; or Madras, the Neilgherries, and Calcutta.* Philadephia: American Sunday-School Union, 1855.

Duncan, Sara Jeannette. *The Pool in the Desert.* 1903. Reprint, Harmondsworth: Penguin, 1984.

Eagan, J.S.C. *The Nilgiri Guide and Directory.* Mysore: Wesleyan Mission Press, 1911.

Eastern Bengal State Railway. *From the Hooghly to the Himalayas.* Bombay: Times Press, 1913.

Eden, Emily. *Up the Country: Letters from India.* 1930. Reprint, London: Virago, 1984.

Edwardes, Sir Herbert Benjamin, and Herman Merivale. *Life of Sir Henry Lawrence.* 2d ed. 2 vols. London: Smith, Elder, 1872.

Ewart, Joseph. *Goodeve's Hints for the General Management of Children in India in the Absence of Professional Advice.* 6th ed. Calcutta: Thacker, Spink, 1872.

Fayrer, Sir Joseph. "The Hill Stations of India as Health Resorts." *British Medical Journal* 1 (June 9, 1900): 1393–97.

———. *Recollections of My Life.* Edinburgh and London: William Blackwood & Sons, 1900.

———. *Tropical Dysentery and Chronic Diarrhoea.* London: J. & A. Churchill, 1881.

Felkin, Robert W. "On Acclimatisation." *Scottish Geographical Magazine* 7 (1891): 647–56.

Ferguson, J. *Six Weeks' Trip through India.* Colombo: A. M. & J. Ferguson, 1902.

Fitzgerald-Lee, J. *Guide to Dharmsala and the Kangra Valley.* Lahore: "Civil and Military Gazette" Press, 1899.

Fletcher, F.W.F. *Sport on the Nilgiris and in Wynaad.* London: Macmillan, 1911.

Forsyth, Capt. J. *The Highlands of Central India.* London: Chapman & Hall, 1871.

Franks, H. George. *In and around Mahableshwar.* Poona: Poona Star Press, n.d.

Fraser, James Baillie, *Journal of a Tour through Part of the Snowy Range of the Himala Mountains and to the Sources of the Rivers Jumna and Ganges.* London: Rodwell & Martin, 1820.

Frazer, H. L. *Views of the Neilgherries.* Calcutta: H. M. Smith, 1856–57.

Fullerton, Lt.-Col. James. *Views in the Himalaya and Neilgherry Hills.* London: Dickinson, c. 1848.

Gandhi, Mahatma. "Five Hundredth Storey." In *Collected Works,* vol. 20. Delhi: Government of India, 1966.

Gay, F. Drew. *The Prince of Wales; or, From Pall Mall to the Punjaub.* Detroit: Craig and Taylor, 1878.

Geofry [pseud.]. *Ooty and Her Sisters, or Our Hill Stations in South India.* Madras: Higginbotham, 1881.

Giles, Lt.-Col. G. M. *Climate and Health in Hot Countries.* London: John Bale, Sons, 1904.

Gleig, G. R. *The Life of Major-General Sir Thomas Munro, Bart.* 3 vols. London: Henry Colburn & Richard Bentley, 1830.

Gore, F. St. J. *Lights and Shades of Hill Life.* 1895. Reprint, Delhi: Oriental Publishers, 1972.

Graham, Rev. J. A. *On the Threshold of Three Closed Lands.* Edinburgh: R. & R. Clark, 1897.

Grant Duff, Sir Mountstuart E. *Notes from a Diary Kept Chiefly in Southern India 1881–1886.* 2 vols. London: John Murray, 1899.

———. *Notes of an Indian Journey.* London: Macmillan, 1876.

*Guide to Mussoorie.* Mussoorie: Mafasilite Printing Works, c. 1907.

*A Guide to Ootacamund and Its Neighbourhood.* Madras: Lawrence Asylum Press, 1889.

*A Guide to the Neilgherries.* Madras: Thomas & Davis, 1886.

Gupta, Om Prakash. *Mount Abu: The Olympus of Rajasthan.* Ajmer, 1939.

Gurdon, Major P.R.T. *The Khasis.* London: David Nutt, 1907.

Hamilton, Gen. Douglas. *Records of Sport in Southern India.* London: R. H. Porter, 1892.

*A Handbook for Travellers in India, Burma and Ceylon.* 10th ed. London: John Murray, 1920.

Hare, Augustus J. C. *The Story of Two Noble Lives.* Vol. 2. London: George Allen, 1893.

Harkness, Capt. Henry. *A Description of a Singular Aboriginal Race Inhabiting the Summit of the Neilgherry Hills.* London: Smith, Elder, 1832.

Harrop, F. Beresford. *Thacker's New Guide to Simla.* Simla: Thacker, Spink, 1925.

Hathorn, Capt. J. G. *A Hand-Book of Darjeeling.* Calcutta: R. C. Lepage, 1863.

Heber, Bishop. *Bishop Heber in Northern India: Selections from Heber's Journal.* Ed. M. A. Laird. Cambridge: Cambridge University Press, 1971.

Hervey, H. *The European in India.* London: Stanley Paul, 1913.

Hill, Sir Claude H. *India—Stepmother.* Edinburgh: William Blackwood, 1929.

"Hill Stations of India as Sanitaria for the British Soldier." *Calcutta Journal of Medicine* 1, no. 8 (Aug. 1868): 308–13.

Hodgson, B. H. *Essays on the Languages, Literature and Religion of Nepal and Tibet.* Part 2. 1874. Reprint, Varanasi: Bharat-Bharati, 1971.

Hogg, Francis R. *Practical Remarks Chiefly concerning the Health and Ailments of European Families in India.* Benares: Medical Hall Press, 1877.

Hooker, Joseph Dalton. *Himalayan Journals.* 2 vols. London: John Murray, 1854.

Hornaday, William T. *Two Years in the Jungle: The Experience of a Hunter and Naturalist in India, Ceylon, the Malay Peninsula and Borneo.* New York: Scribner's, 1908.

Hosten, H. "The Centenary of Darjeeling." *Bengal: Past and Present* 39, pt. 2, no. 78 (April-June 1930): 106–23.

Hough, James. *Letters on the Climate, Inhabitants, Productions, etc. of the Neilgherries, or Blue Mountains of Coimbatoor.* London: John Hatchard, 1829.

Hull, Edmund C. P. *The European in India; or, Anglo-Indian's Vade-Mecum.* 2d ed. London: Henry S. King, 1872.

Hunt, Major S. Leigh, and Alexander S. Kenny. *On Duty under a Tropical Sun.* London: W. H. Allen, 1882.

———. *Tropical Trials: A Handbook for Women in the Tropics.* London: W. H. Allen, 1883.

Hutchinson, Capt. J. B. *Guide to Dalhousie and the Neighbouring Hills.* 2d ed. Rev. H. A. Rose. Lahore: "Civil and Military Gazette" Press, 1898.

*Illustrated Guide to the Nilgiris.* Madras: Higginbotham, 1912.

Indian Railways. *Mussoorie.* Calcutta: East India Railway Press, 1931.

Jacquemont, Victor. *Letters from India.* Vol. 1. London: Edward Churton, 1834.

Jervis, Lt. H. *Narrative of a Journey to the Falls of the Cavery with an Historical and Descriptive Account of the Neilgherry Hills.* London: Smith, Elder, 1834.

Johnson, James. *The Influence of Tropical Climates on European Constitutions.* 3d ed. New York: Evert Duyckinck, George Long, Collins, 1826.

Kail, Owen C. *The Hill Station of Matheran.* Bombay: Thacker, 1947.

Kaye, M. M. *The Sun in the Morning: My Early Years in India and England.* New York: St. Martin's Press, 1990.

King, Mrs. Robert Moss. *The Diary of a Civilian's Wife in India 1877–1882.* 2 vols. London: Richard Bentley & Son, 1884.

Kinney, T. *The Echo Guide to Mussoorie.* Mussoorie: Echo Press, 1908.

Kipling, Rudyard. "His Private Honour." In *Many Inventions*, 126–49. New York: Doubleday, 1925.

———. *Kim.* New York: Dell, 1959.

———. *Plain Tales from the Hills.* London: Penguin, 1987.

———. *Something of Myself and Other Autobiographical Writings.* Ed. Thomas Pinney. Cambridge: Cambridge University Press, 1990.

————. *Verse: Definitive Edition.* Garden City, N.Y.: Doubleday, 1952.

Kisch, H. M. *A Young Victorian in India: Letters.* Ed. Ethel A. Waley Cohen. London: Jonathan Cape, 1957.

"Kumaon and Its Hill-Stations." *Calcutta Review* 26 (Jan.-June 1856): 373–97.

"A Lady Resident." *The Englishwoman in India.* London: Smith, Elder, 1865.

Lang, John. *Wanderings in India: And Other Sketches of Life in Hindostan.* London: Routledge, Warne, and Routledge, 1859.

Lawrence, Sir Walter Roper. *The India We Served.* London: Cassell, 1928.

*The Lawrence Military Asylum.* Sanawur: Lawrence Military Asylum Press, 1858.

Lear, Edward. *Indian Journal.* Ed. Ray Murphy. London: Jarrolds, 1953.

*Letters from India and Kashmir.* London: George Bell & Sons, 1874.

Lewis, J. T. *The Rugby Guide to Matheran.* Poona: Deccan Herald, c. 1908.

Lowrie, John C. *Two Years in Upper India.* New York: Robert Carter, 1850.

Macaulay, Thomas Babington. *Letters.* Ed. Thomas Pinney. Vol. 3. Cambridge: Cambridge University Press, 1976.

McCurdy, Major E. A. *Three Panoramic Views of Ootacamund.* London: Smith, Elder, c. 1830.

McCurdy, Capt. E. A. *Views of the Neilgherries, or Blue Mountains of Coimbetoor.* London: Smith, Elder, c. 1830.

Maclean, William Campbell. *Diseases of Tropical Climates.* London: Macmillan, 1886.

MacPherson, Duncan. *Reports on Mountain and Marine Sanitaria.* Madras: Fort Saint George Gazette Press, 1862.

*Mahableshwur Guide.* Bombay: Education Society's Press, 1875.

Mainwaring, Col. G. B. *A Grammar of the Rong (Lepcha) Language.* 1876. Reprint, Delhi: Daya Publishing House, 1985.

Makay, George. *Remarks on the Climate, with Advice to Invalids and Others Visiting the Neilgherry Hills.* Madras: Gantz Brothers, 1870.

Marryat, Florence. *"Gup." Sketches of Anglo-Indian Life and Character.* London: Richard Bentley, 1868.

Marshall, William E. *A Phrenologist amongst the Todas.* London: Longmans, Green, 1873.

Martin, Sir James Ranald. *Influence of Tropical Climates in Producing the Acute Endemic Diseases of Europeans,* 2d ed. London: John Churchill, 1861.

Masters, John. *Bugles and a Tiger.* New York: Ballantine, 1968.

Mehta, Ved. *Daddyji.* New York: Norton, 1972.

Metz, F. *The Tribes Inhabiting the Neilgherry Hills.* 2d ed. Mangalore: Bazel Mission Press, 1864.

Mignan, Capt. Robert. *Notes Extracted from a Private Journal, Written during a Tour through a Part of Malabar, and among the Neilgherries.* Bombay: American Mission Press, 1834.

Mitchell, Mrs. Murray. *In Southern India.* London: Religious Tract Society, 1885.

Molony, J. Chartres. "An Indian Hill Station." *Blackwood's Magazine* 247, no. 1495 (May 1940): 625–39.

Moore, W. J. *Health Resorts for Tropical Invalids in India, at Home, and Abroad.* London: J. & A. Churchill, 1881.

———. *A Manual of Family Medicine and Hygiene for India.* 7th ed. London: J. & A. Churchill, 1903.

———. *A Manual of the Diseases of India.* 2d ed. London: J. & A. Churchill, 1886.

Morris, John. *Eating the Indian Air.* London: Hamish Hamilton, 1968.

"Mountaineer." *A Summer Ramble in the Himalayas.* London: Hurst & Blackett, 1860.

Murphy, C. W. *A Guide to Naini Tal and Kumaun.* Allahabad: Pioneer Press, 1906.

Murray, James. *Account of Malcolm Pait, on the Mahableshwur Hills.* Bombay: Chesson & Woodhall, 1863.

Murray, Major William. *An Account of the Neilgherries, or, Blue Mountains of Coimbatore, in Southern India.* London: Smith, Elder, 1834.

Murray-Aynsley, Mrs. J. C. *Our Tour in Southern India.* London: F. V. White, 1883.

Nanavati, Hiralal Dayabhai. *Mount Abu.* Bombay: N.p., 1919.

Newall, Major-Gen. D.J.F. *The Highlands of India Strategically Considered.* London: Harrison & Sons, 1882.

*Newman's Guide to Darjeeling and Neighbourhood.* Calcutta: W. Newman, 1900, 1919.

Nicholl, Major-Gen. T. *A Hand-Book to Coonoor and Neighbourhood.* Madras: Lawrence Asylum Press, 1888.

Northam, John. *Guide to Masuri, Landaur, Dehra Dun, and the Hills North of Dehra.* Calcutta: Thacker, Spink, 1884.

O'Brien, R. D. *Darjeeling, the Sanitarium of Bengal; and Its Surroundings.* Calcutta: W. Newman, 1883.

O'Donnell, C. J. "Simla, Calcutta and Darjeeling as Centres of Government." *Calcutta Review* 83 (Oct. 1886): 398–419.

O'Dwyer, Sir Michael. *India As I Knew It 1885–1925.* 2d ed. London: Constable, 1925.

"An Old Indian." *From Calcutta to the Snowy Range.* London: Tinsley Brothers, 1866.

Oliver, Mrs. A. K. *The Hill Station of Matheran.* Bombay: Times of India, 1905.

*Ootacamund as the Seat of the Madras Government.* Pamphlet reprinted from the *Madras Mail,* 1869.

Ormsley, Capt. V. *Almoriana: Leaves from a Hill Journal.* [Allahabad:] Pioneer Press, 1901.

Ouchterlony, Capt. J. *Geographical and Statistical Memoir of a Survey of the Neilgherry Mountains.* Madras: Higginbotham, 1868.

Parasnis, Rao Bahadur D. B. *Mahabaleshwar.* Bombay: Lakshmi Art Printing Works, 1916.

Parks, Fanny. *Wanderings of a Pilgrim, in Search of the Picturesque.* 2 vols. London: Pelham Richardson, 1850.

Parmanand, Hansraj. *Key to Matheran.* 2d ed. Bombay: Free Press Bulletin Press, 1935.

Peacock, E. B. *A Guide to Murree and Its Neighbourhood.* Lahore: W. Ball, 1883.

Pearson, J. T. "A Note on Darjeeling." Bound newspaper article, 1839. Reprinted in Fred Pinn, *The Road to Destiny: Darjeeling Letters 1839.* Calcutta: Oxford University Press, 1986).

Philips, C. H., ed. *The Correspondence of Lord William Cavendish Bentinck.* 2 vols. Oxford: Oxford University Press, 1977.

"Pilgrim" [P. Barron]. *Notes of Wanderings in the Himmala.* Agra: Agra Ukhbar Press, 1844.

Pinn, Fred. *The Road to Destiny: Darjeeling Letters 1839.* Calcutta: Oxford University Press, 1986.

Platt, Kate. *The Home and Health in India and the Tropical Colonies.* London: Bailliere, Tindall & Cox, 1923.

Powers, Capt. O.E.S. *Dehra Dun Past and Present: Guide and Directory to Dehra and the Doon District.* Dehra Dun: Goorkha Press, 1929.

Price, Sir Frederick. *Ootacamund: A History.* Madras: Government Press, 1908.

Prinsep, Val C. *Imperial India: An Artist's Journals.* 2d ed. London: Chapman & Hall, 1879.

Rees, J. D. *Lord Connemara's Tours in India.* London: Kegan Paul, Trench, Trubner, 1892.

Reynolds-Ball, Eustace. *The Tourist's India.* London: Swan Sonnenschein, 1907.

Ricketts, L. C. "English Society in India." *Contemporary Review* 101 (1912): 681–88.

Roberts, Lord. *Forty-One Years in India.* 2 vols. London: Macmillan, 1900.

Robertson, George P. *Darjeeling Route Guide.* Darjeeling: Bose Press, 1913.

Russell, William Howard. *My Diary in India.* 2 vols. London: Routledge, Warne, & Routledge, 1860.

Sandwith, F. M. "Hill Stations and Other Health Resorts in the British Tropics." *Journal of Tropical Medicine and Hygiene* 10, no. 22 (Nov. 15, 1907): 361–70.

Sarkar, H. C. *Guide to Shillong.* Calcutta: W. Newman, n.d.

Savory, Isabel. *A Sportswoman in India.* London: Hutchinson, 1900.

Schmid, Rev. B. "Remarks on the Origin and Languages of the Aborigines of the Nilgiris." *Journal of the Bombay Branch of the Royal Asiatic Society* 3, pt. 1, no. 12 (Jan. 1849): 50–53.

Scott, Alicia Eliza. *A Lady's Narrative, 1834.* London: Webster & Larkin, 1874.
———. *Simla Scenes Drawn from Nature.* London: Dickinson, c. 1846.

Scott, Paul. *Staying On.* New York: Avon, 1977.

Scott, W.L.L. *Views of the Himalayas.* London: N.p., 1852.

Scudder, Horace E. *Life and Letters of David Coit Scudder, Missionary in Southern India.* New York: Hurd & Houghton, 1864.

Sen, Sudhir Chandra. *The Simla Kali Bari.* Simla: N.p., 1932.

Shaw, Mary. "Some South India Hill Stations." *Scottish Geographical Magazine* 59, no. 3 (Jan. 1944): 81–87, and 60, no. 3 (Dec. 1944): 80–85.

*Shillong and Its Neighbourhood.* N.p., c. 1913.

Shortt, John. *An Account of the Tribes on the Neilgherries.* Madras: Higginbotham, 1868.
———, ed. *The Hill Ranges of Southern India.* Madras: Higginbotham, 1870–83.

Smith, J. Y. *Matheran Hills: Its People, Plants, and Animals.* Edinburgh: Maclachlan & Stewart, 1871.

Sprawson, Cuthbert Allan. *Moore's Manual of Family Medicine and Hygiene for India.* 8th ed. London: J. & A. Churchill, 1916.

Steel, Flora Annie. *The Garden of Fidelity.* London: Macmillan, 1929.

————, and G. Gardiner. *The Complete Indian Housekeeper and Cook.* Rev. ed. London: William Heinemann, 1917.

Stevenson, Rev. Dr. "A Collection of Words from the Languages of the Todas, the Chief Tribe on the Nilgiri Hills." *Journal of the Bombay Branch of the Royal Asiatic Society* 1, no. 4 (April 1842): 155–67.

Taylor, G. Hutton. *Thacker's Guide Book to Darjeeling and Its Neighbourhood.* Calcutta: Thacker, Spink, 1899.

Thomas, Capt. George Powell. *Views of Simla.* London: Dickinson, c. 1846.

Thurston, Edgar. *Anthropology of the Todas and Kotas of the Nilgiri Hills.* Madras: Government Press, 1896.

Tilt, Edward John. *Health in India for British Women.* 4th ed. London: J. & A. Churchill, 1875.

Towelle, W. Martin. *Towelle's Hand Book and Guide to Simla.* Simla: Station Press, 1877.

Trevelyan, G. O. *The Competition Wallah.* 2d ed. London: Macmillan, 1866.

Tull, Barbara Mitchell, ed. *Affectionately, Rachel: Letters from India 1860–1884.* Kent, Ohio: Kent State University Press, 1992.

*The Visitors' Handbook of the Nilgiris.* Madras: G. Ramasawmy Chetty, 1897.

Waddell, L. A. *Among the Himalayas.* 1899. Reprint, Delhi: Mittal Publications, 1979.

White, Lt. George Francis. *Views in India, Chiefly among the Himalaya Mountains.* Ed. Emma Roberts. London and Paris: Fisher, Son, 1838.

Williams, G.R.C. *Historical and Statistical Memoir of Dehra Doon.* Roorkee: Thomason Civil Engineering College Press, 1874.

Wilson, Andrew. *The Abode of Snow: Observations on a Journey from Chinese Tibet to the Indian Caucasus.* Edinburgh and London: William Blackwood & Sons, 1875.

Wilson, Francesca H. *My Trip to Matheran.* Madras: Higginbotham, 1888.

————. *The Shevaroys.* Madras: Higginbotham, 1888.

Wilson, Lady. *Letters from India.* 1911. Reprint, London: Century Publishing, 1984.

Younghusband, Sir Francis. *Kashmir.* London: Adam and Charles Black, 1911.


SECONDARY SOURCES

Adas, Michael. "From Avoidance to Confrontation: Peasant Protest in Precolonial and Colonial Southeast Asia." In *Colonialism and Culture,* ed. Nicholas B. Dirks, 89–126. Ann Arbor: University of Michigan Press, 1992.

Aiken, S. Robert. "Early Penang Hill Station." *Geographical Review* 77, no. 4 (Oct. 1987): 421–39.

Allen, Charles. *Plain Tales from the Raj.* London: Futura Publications, 1976.

————, and Sharanda Dwivedi. *Lives of the Indian Princes.* London: Century, 1984.

Anderson, David, and Richard Grove, eds. *Conservation in Africa: People, Policies, Practices.* Cambridge: Cambridge University Press, 1987.

Andrews, Malcolm. *The Search for the Picturesque: Landscape Aesthetics and Tourism in Britain, 1760–1800.* Stanford: Stanford University Press, 1989.

Archer, Mildred. *Early Views of India: The Picturesque Journeys of Thomas and William Daniell 1782–1794.* London: Thames and Hudson, 1980.

————, and Ronald Lightbown. *India Observed: India as Viewed by British Artists 1760–1860.* London: Victoria and Albert Museum, 1982.

Arnold, David. "Cholera and Colonialism in British India." *Past and Present* 113 (Nov. 1986): 118–51.

————. *Colonizing the Body: State Medicine and Epidemic Disease in Nineteenth-Century India.* Berkeley: University of California Press, 1993.

————. "European Orphans and Vagrants in India in the Nineteenth Century." *Journal of Imperial and Commonwealth History* 7, no. 2 (Jan. 1979): 104–27.

————, ed. *Imperial Medicine and Indigenous Societies.* Manchester: Manchester University Press, 1988.

————. "Touching the Body: Perspectives on the Indian Plague." In *Selected Subaltern Studies,* ed. Ranajit Guha and Gayatri ChakravortySpivak, 391–426. New York: Oxford University Press, 1988.

————. "White Colonization and Labour in Nineteenth-Century India." *Journal of Imperial and Commonwealth History* 9, no. 2 (Jan. 1983): 133–58.

Balfour, Lady Betty. *The History of Lord Lytton's Indian Administration, 1876 to 1880.* London: Longmans, Green, 1899.

Ballhatchet, Kenneth. *Race, Sex and Class under the Raj: Imperial Attitudes and Policies and Their Critics, 1793–1905.* New York: St. Martin's Press, 1980.

Barr, Pat. *The Dust in the Balance: British Women in India 1905–1945.* London: Hamish Hamilton, 1989.

————. *The Memsahibs: The Women of Victorian India.* London: Secker & Warburg, 1976.

————, and Ray Desmond. *Simla: A Hill Station in British India.* New York: Scribner's, 1978.

Bayly, C. A. *Imperial Meridian: The British Empire and the World, 1780–1830.* London: Longman, 1989.

————. *Indian Society and the Making of the British Empire.* New Cambridge History of India II.1. Cambridge: Cambridge University Press, 1988.

Bence-Jones, Mark. *Palaces of the Raj.* London: Allen & Unwin, 1973.

Berreman, Gerald D. *Hindus of the Himalayas.* Berkeley and Los Angeles: University of California Press, 1963.

————. "The U.P. Himalaya: Culture, Cultures and Regionalism." In *The Himalaya: Nature, Man and Culture,* ed. O. P. Singh, 227–65. New Delhi: Rajesh Publications, 1983.

Bhasin, Raja. *Simla: The Summer Capital of British India.* New Delhi: Viking, 1992.

Bhasin, Veena. *Ecology, Culture and Change: Tribals of Sikkim Himalayas.* New Delhi: Inter-India Publications, 1989.

Bishop, Peter. *The Myth of Shangri-La: Tibet, Travel Writing and the Western Creation of Sacred Landscape.* Berkeley and Los Angeles: University of California Press, 1989.

Bond, Ruskin, and Ganesh Saili. *Mussoorie and Landour: Days of Wine and Roses.* New Delhi: Lustre Press, 1992.

Booth, Martin. *Carpet Sahib: A Life of Jim Corbett.* Delhi: Oxford University Press, 1990.

Bose, M. L. *Social History of Assam*. New Delhi: Concept, 1989.

Brockway, Lucile H. *Science and Colonial Expansion: The Role of the British Royal Botanic Gardens*. New York: Academic Press, 1979.

Bruce-Chwatt, Leonard Jan. *Essential Malariology*. London: Heinemann, 1980.

Bührlein, Monika. *Nuwara Eliya: "Hill Station" und Zentraler Ort im Hochland der Insel Ceylon (Sri Lanka)*. Stuttgart: Steiner Verlag, 1991.

Calhoun, Craig, ed. *Habermas and the Public Sphere*. Cambridge, Mass.: MIT Press, 1992.

Callan, Hilary, and Shirley Ardener, eds. *The Incorporated Wife*. London: Croom Helm, 1984.

Carter, Paul. *The Road to Botany Bay: An Essay in Spatial History*. London: Faber & Faber, 1987.

Cell, John W. "Anglo-Indian Medical Theory and the Origins of Segregation in West Africa." *American Historical Review* 91, no. 2 (April 1986): 307–35.

Chamberlin, J. Edward, and Sander L. Gilman, eds. *Degeneration: The Dark Side of Progress*. New York: Columbia University Press, 1985.

Chaudhuri, Nupur. "Memsahibs and Motherhood in Nineteenth-Century Colonial India." *Victorian Studies* 31, no. 4 (summer 1988): 517–35.

———, and Margaret Strobel, eds. *Western Women and Imperialism: Complicity and Resistance*. Bloomington: Indiana University Press, 1992.

Clifford, James, and George E. Marcus, eds. *Writing Culture: The Poetics and Politics of Ethnography*. Berkeley and Los Angeles: University of California Press, 1986.

Cohn, Bernard S. *An Anthropologist among the Historians and Other Essays*. Delhi: Oxford University Press, 1987.

———. "The Census, Social Stratification and Objectification in South Asia." *Folk* 26 (1984): 25–49.

———. "Clothes and Colonialism in British India." Paper presented to symposium on Clothes and Organization of Human Experience, Aug. 1983.

———. "The Command of Language and the Language of Command." In *Subaltern Studies*, vol. 4, ed. Ranajit Guha, 276–329. Delhi: Oxford University Press, 1985.

———. "Law and the Colonial State in India." In *History and Power in the Study of Law*, ed. June Starr and Jane F. Collier, 131–52 Ithaca: Cornell University Press, 1989.

———. "Representing Authority in Victorian India." In *The Invention of Tradition*, ed. Eric Hobsbawm and Terence Ranger, 165–209. Cambridge: Cambridge University Press, 1982.

Colley, Linda. *Britons: Forging the Nation 1707–1837*. New Haven: Yale University Press, 1992.

Corfield, P. J. *The Impact of English Towns 1700–1800*. Oxford: Oxford University Press.

Curtin, Philip D. *Death by Migration: Europe's Encounter with the Tropical World in the Nineteenth Century*. Cambridge: Cambridge University Press, 1989.

———. "Medical Knowledge and Urban Planning in Tropical Africa." *American Historical Review* 90, no. 3 (June 1985): 594–613.

Davidoff, Leonore. *The Best Circles: Women and Society in Victorian England.* Totowa, N.J.: Rowman and Littlefield, 1973.

————, and Catherine Hall. *Family Fortunes: Men and Women of the English Middle Class 1780–1850.* London: Hutchinson, 1987.

Davies, Philip. *Splendours of the Raj: British Architecture in India 1660–1947.* Harmondsworth: Penguin, 1987.

Desai, Anita. *Fire on the Mountain.* London: Penguin, 1981.

Dewan, Dick B. *Education in the Darjeeling Hills: An Historical Survey, 1835–1985.* New Delhi: Indus, 1991.

Dozey, E. C. *A Concise History of the Darjeeling District since 1835.* Calcutta: N. Mukherjee, 1922.

D'Souza, Austin A. *Anglo-Indian Education: A Study of Its Origins and Growth in Bengal up to 1960.* Delhi: Oxford University Press, 1976.

Edwardes, Michael. *Bound to Exile: The Victorians in India.* New York: Praeger, 1970.

Ellsworth, Edward W. *Science and Social Science Research in British India, 1780–1880.* New York: Greenwood Press, 1991.

Ernst, Waltraud. *Mad Tales from the Raj: The European Insane in British India, 1800–1858.* London: Routledge, 1991.

Evenson, Norma. *The Indian Metropolis: A View toward the West.* New Haven: Yale University Press, 1989.

Farrell, J. G. *The Hill Station.* Ed. John Spurling. London: Fontana, 1987.

Farwell, Byron. *Armies of the Raj.* New York: Norton, 1989.

Ford, George H. "Felicitous Space: The Cottage Controversy." In *Nature and the Victorian Imagination,* ed. U. C. Knoepflmacher and G. B. Tennyson, 29–48. Berkeley: University of California Press, 1977.

Freitag, Sandria B. "Enactments of Ram's Story and the Changing Nature of 'The Public' in British India." *South Asia* 14, no. 1 (June 1991): 65–90.

Fyson, P. F. *The Flora of the South Indian Hill Stations.* Vol. 1. Madras: Superintendent Government Press, 1932.

Gadd, David. *Georgian Summer: Bath in the Eighteenth Century.* Ridge Park, N.J.: Noyes Press, 1972.

Geertz, Clifford. *Works and Lives: The Anthropologist as Author.* Stanford: Stanford University Press, 1988.

Gilbert, Edmund W. *Brighton: Old Ocean's Bauble.* London: Methuen, 1954.

————. "The Growth of Inland and Seaside Health Resorts in England." *Scottish Geographical Magazine* 55, no. 1 (Jan. 1939): 16–35.

Goodman, Dena. "Public Sphere and Private Life: Toward a Synthesis of Current Historiographical Approaches to the Old Regime." *History and Theory* 31, no. 1 (1992): 1–20.

Gopal, Sarvepalli. *Jawaharlal Nehru: A Biography.* Vol. 1. Cambridge, Mass.: Harvard University Press, 1976.

Gordon, Leonard A. *Brothers against the Raj.* New York: Columbia University Press, 1990.

Gorer, Geoffrey. *Himalayan Village: An Account of the Lepchas of Sikkim.* London: Michael Joseph, 1938.

Goswami, B. B., ed. *Cultural Profile of Shillong*. Calcutta: Anthropological Survey of India, 1979.

Grove, Richard H. "Colonial Conservation, Ecological Hegemony and Popular Resistance: Towards a Global Synthesis." In *Imperialism and the Natural World*, ed. John M. MacKenzie, 15–50. Manchester: Manchester University Press, 1990.

———. "Conserving Eden: The (European) East India Companies and Their Environmental Policies on St. Helena, Mauritius and in Western India, 1660 to 1854." *Comparative Studies in Society and History* 35, no. 2 (April 1993): 318–351.

Guha, Ramachandra. "Saboteurs in the Forest: Colonialism and Peasant Resistance in the Indian Himalaya." In *Everyday Forms of Peasant Resistance*, ed. Forrest D. Colburn, 64–92. New York and London: M. E. Sharpe, 1989.

———. *The Unquiet Woods: Ecological Change and Peasant Resistance in the Himalaya*. Berkeley: University of California Press, 1989.

———, and Madhav Gadgil. "State Forestry and Social Conflict in British India." *Past and Present* 123 (May 1989): 141–77.

Habermas, Jürgen. *The Structural Transformation of the Public Sphere: An Inquiry into a Category of Bourgeois Society*. Trans. Thomas Burger. Cambridge, Mass.: MIT Press, 1989.

Harris, F. R. *Jamsetji Nusserwanji Tata*. London: Oxford University Press, 1925.

Headrick, Daniel R. *The Tentacles of Imperialism: Technology Transfer in the Age of Imperialism, 1850–1940*. New York: Oxford University Press, 1988.

Heathcote, T. A. *The Indian Army: Garrison of British Imperial India, 1822–1922*. London: David & Charles, 1974.

Helly, Dorothy O., and Susan M. Reverby, eds. *Gendered Domains: Rethinking Public and Private in Women's History*. Ithaca: Cornell University Press, 1992.

Hembry, Phyllis. *The English Spa 1560–1815*. Rutherford, N.J.: Fairleigh Dickinson University Press, 1990.

Hockings, Paul. *A Bibliography for the Nilgiri Hills of Southern India*. Rev. ed. 2 vols. New Haven: Human Relations Area Files, 1978.

———. "British Society in the Company, Crown and Congress Eras." In *Blue Mountains: The Ethnography and Biogeography of a South Indian Region*, ed. Paul Hockings, 334–59. Delhi: Oxford University Press, 1989.

———. "John Sullivan of Ootacamund." In *Journal of Indian History Golden Jubilee Volume*, ed. T. K. Ravindran, 863–71. Trivandrum: University of Kerala, 1973.

———. "Tourism and English National Identity: Corkaquiney and the Nilgiris." In *Dimensions of Social Life*, ed. Paul Hockings, 633–51. Berlin: Mouton de Gruyter, 1987.

Hutchins, Francis G. *The Illusion of Permanence: British Imperialism in India*. Princeton: Princeton University Press, 1967.

Hyam, Ronald. *Empire and Sexuality: The British Experience*. Manchester: Manchester University Press, 1990.

Hyde, H. Montgomery. *Simla and the Simla Hill States under British Protection 1815–1835*. Lahore: University of the Panjab, 1961.

Inden, Ronald. "Orientalist Constructions of India." *Modern Asian Studies* 20, no. 3 (July 1986): 401–46.

Irving, Robert Grant. *Indian Summer: Lutyens, Baker, and Imperial Delhi.* New Haven: Yale University Press, 1981.

Kalyanasundaram, M. S. *Indian Hill Stations.* Madras: Tamil Pathakalayam, 1961.

Kanwar, Pamela. "The Changing Image of Simla." Urban History Association Occasional Papers Series 10, 1989.

———. "The Changing Profile of the Summer Capital of British India: Simla 1864–1947." *Modern Asian Studies* 18, no. 2 (1984): 215–36.

———. *Imperial Simla.* Delhi: Oxford University Press, 1990.

Keay, John. *When Men and Mountains Meet: The Explorers of the Western Himalayas 1820–75.* London: John Murray, 1977.

Keenan, Brigid. *Travels in Kashmir: A Popular History of Its People, Places and Crafts.* Delhi: Oxford University Press, 1989.

Kelley, Theresa M. *Wordsworth's Revisionary Aesthetics.* Cambridge: Cambridge University Press, 1988.

Kennedy, Dane. "The Perils of the Midday Sun: Climatic Anxieties in the Colonial Tropics." In *Imperialism and the Natural World,* ed. John M. MacKenzie, 118–40. Manchester: Manchester University Press, 1990.

Kenny, Judith Theresa. "Constructing an Imperial Hill Station: The Representation of British Authority in Ootacamund." Ph.D. diss., Syracuse University, 1990.

Kincaid, Dennis. *British Social Life in India 1608–1937.* London: George Routledge & Sons, 1938.

King, Anthony D. *The Bungalow: The Production of a Global Culture.* London: Routledge & Kegan Paul, 1984.

———. *Colonial Urban Development: Culture, Social Power and Environment.* London: Routledge & Kegan Paul, 1976.

———. "Culture, Social Power and Environment: The Hill Station in Colonial Urban Development." *Social Action* 26, no. 3 (July-Sept. 1976): 195–213.

Kupperman, Karen Ordahl. "Fear of Hot Climates in the Anglo-American Colonial Experience." *William and Mary Quarterly,* 3d ser., 41 (April 1984): 213–40.

Lee-Warner, Sir William. *The Life of the Marquis of Dalhousie.* 2 vols. London: Macmillan, 1904.

Lind, Mary Ann. *The Compassionate Memsahibs: Welfare Activities of British Women in India, 1900–1947.* New York: Greenwood Press, 1988.

Livingstone, David N. "Human Acclimatization: Perspectives on a Contested Field of Inquiry in Science, Medicine and Geography." *History of Science* 25 (1987): 359–94.

Lunt, James. "Simla: The British in India." *History Today* 18, no. 9 (Sept. 1968): 599–605.

MacKenzie, John M. *The Empire of Nature: Hunting, Conservation and British Imperialism.* Manchester: Manchester University Press, 1988.

Macleod, Roy, and Milton Lewis, eds. *Disease, Medicine, and Empire: Perspectives on Western Medicine and the Experience of European Expansion.* London: Routledge, 1988.

MacMillan, Margaret. *Women of the Raj.* London: Thames & Hudson, 1988.

Mahajan, Jagmohan. *Picturesque India: Sketches and Travels of Thomas and William Daniell.* New Delhi: Lustre Press, 1983.

Mandelbaum, David G. "Culture Change among the Nilgiri Tribes." In *Beyond the Frontier: Social Process and Culture Change,* ed. Paul Bohannan and Fred Plog, 199–208. Garden City, N.Y.: Natural History Press, 1967.

Mann, Thomas. *The Magic Mountain.* Trans. H.–T. Lowe-Porter. New York: Knopf, 1946.

Marshall, P. J. "British Immigration into India in the Nineteenth Century." In *European Expansion and Migration: Essays on the International Migration from Africa, Asia, and Europe,* ed. P. C. Emmer and M. Morner, 179–96. New York: Berg, 1992.

———. "The Whites of British India, 1780–1830: A Failed Colonial Society?" *International History Review* 12, no. 1 (Feb. 1990): 26–44.

Mason, Philip. *A Matter of Honor.* New York: Holt, Rinehart & Winston, 1974.

Metcalf, Thomas R. *The Aftermath of Revolt: India 1857–1870.* Princeton: Princeton University Press, 1964.

———. *An Imperial Vision: Indian Architecture and Britain's Raj.* Berkeley: University of California Press, 1989.

Mitchell, Nora. "The Indian Hill-Station: Kodaikanal." University of Chicago Department of Geography Research Paper 141, 1972.

Mitchell, W.J.T. "Imperial Landscape." In *Landscape and Power,* ed. W.J.T. Mitchell, 5–34. Chicago: University of Chicago Press, 1994.

Moore-Gilbert, B. J. *Kipling and "Orientalism."* London: Croom Helm, 1986.

Morris, Jan, with Simon Winchester. *Stones of Empire: The Buildings of the Raj.* Oxford: Oxford University Press, 1983.

Morris, John. *Living with Lepchas.* London: Heinemann, 1938.

Mukherjee, Bharati. *The Tiger's Daughter.* New York: Fawcett Crest, 1971.

Nicolson, Marjorie Hope. *Mountain Gloom and Mountain Glory: The Development of an Aesthetics of the Infinite.* Ithaca: Cornell University Press, 1959.

Nightingale, Florence. *Cassandra.* Reprint, New York: Feminist Press, 1979.

Oldenburg, Veena Talwar. *The Making of Colonial Lucknow 1856–1877.* Delhi: Oxford University Press, 1989.

Ollman, Arthur. *Samuel Bourne: Images of India.* Carmel, Calif.: Friends of Photography, 1983.

Ousby, Ian. *The Englishman's England: Taste, Travel and the Rise of Tourism.* Cambridge: Cambridge University Press, 1990.

Pakenham, Simona. *Cheltenham.* London: Macmillan, 1971.

Pal, Pratapaditya, and Vidya Dehejia. *From Merchants to Emperors: British Artists and India 1757–1930.* Ithaca and London: Cornell University Press, 1986.

Panikar, K. M. *The Himalayas in Indian Life.* Bombay: Bharatiya Bhavan, 1963.

Panter-Downes, Mollie. *Ooty Preserved: A Victorian Hill Station in India.* New York: Farrar, Straus & Giroux, 1967.

Pearson, R. *Eastern Interlude: A Social History of the European Community in Calcutta.* Calcutta: Thacker, Spink, 1933.

Pemble, John. *The Mediterranean Passion: Victorians and Edwardians in the South.* Oxford: Clarendon Press, 1987.

Pick, Daniel. *Faces of Degeneration: A European Disorder, c. 1848–1918*. Cambridge: Cambridge University Press, 1989.

Pieper, Jan. *Die Anglo-Indische Station oder die Kolonialisierung des Götterberges.* Bonn: Rudolf Habelt Verlag, 1977.

Pinney, Christopher. "Classification and Fantasy in the Photographic Construction of Caste and Tribe." *Visual Anthropology* 3 (1990): 259–88.

Prest, John. *The Garden of Eden: The Botanic Garden and the Re-creation of Paradise.* New Haven: Yale University Press, 1981.

Pubby, Vipin. *Simla Then and Now: Summer Capital of the Raj.* New Delhi: Indus, 1988.

Ramusack, Barbara N. "Cultural Missionaries, Maternal Imperialists, Feminist Allies: British Women Activists in India, 1865–1945." *Women's Studies International Forum* 13, no. 4 (1990): 309–21.

Rawat, A. S. "Henry Ramsay: The Uncrowned King of Kumaon." In *Himalaya Frontier in Historical Perspective*, ed. N. R. Ray, 184–89. Calcutta: Institute of Historical Studies, 1986.

Reed, Robert R. "City of Pines: The Origins of Baguio as a Colonial Hill Station and Regional Capital." Center for South and Southeast Asia Studies Research Monograph 13, Berkeley, Calif., 1976.

———. "The Colonial Genesis of Hill Stations: The Genting Exception." *Geographical Review* 69, no. 4 (Oct. 1979): 463–68.

———. "Remarks on the Colonial Genesis of the Hill Station in Southeast Asia with Particular Reference to the Cities of Buitenzorg (Bogor) and Baguio." *Asian Profile* 4, no. 6 (Dec. 1976): 545–91.

Renford, Raymond K. *The Non-official British in India to 1920.* Delhi: Oxford University Press, 1987.

Riddy, John. "Some Official British Attitudes towards European Settlement and Colonization in India up to 1865." In *Essays in Indian History*, ed. Donovan Williams and E. Daniel Potts, 17–41. London: Asia Publishing House, 1973.

Rivers, W. H. R. *The Todas.* London: Macmillan, 1906.

Rooksby, R. L. "W.H.R. Rivers and the Todas." *South Asia* 1 (Aug. 1971): 109–21.

Rosaldo, Renato. "Imperialist Nostalgia." *Representations* 26 (spring 1989): 107–22.

Saha, K. D. "The Study of Community-wide Distribution and the Growth of Population in Shillong." In *Cultural Profile of Shillong*, ed. B. B. Goswami, 4–31. Calcutta: Anthropological Survey of India, 1979.

Said, Edward W. *Orientalism.* New York: Vintage, 1979.

Savage, Victor R. *Western Impressions of Nature and Landscape in Southeast Asia.* Singapore: Singapore University Press, 1984.

Schmiechen, James A. "The Victorians, the Historians, and the Idea of Modernism." *American Historical Review* 93, no. 2 (April 1988): 287–316.

Sen, Jahar. *Darjeeling: A Favoured Retreat.* New Delhi: Indus, 1989.

Senftleben, W. "Some Aspects of the Indian Hill Stations: A Contribution towards a Geography of Tourist Traffic." *Philippine Geographical Journal* 17, no. 1 (Jan.-March 1973): 21–29.

Showalter, Elaine. *The Female Malady: Women, Madness, and English Culture, 1830–1980.* New York: Penguin, 1985.

Singh, Amar Kaur Jasbir. *Himalayan Triangle: A Historical Survey of British India's Relations with Tibet, Sikkim and Bhutan 1765–1910*. London: British Library, 1988.

Spangenberg, Bradford. *British Bureaucracy in India: Status, Policy and the I.C.S. in the Late 19th Century*. New Delhi: Manohar Books, 1976.

Spear, Percival. *The Nabobs*. 1963. Reprint, Calcutta: Rupa, 1991.

Spencer, J. E., and W. L. Thomas. "The Hill Stations and Summer Resorts of the Orient." *Geographical Review* 38, no. 4 (Oct. 1948): 637–51.

Stanford, J. K. *Ladies in the Sun: The Memsahib's India 1790–1860*. London: Gallery Press, 1962.

Stoler, Ann Laura. "Making Empire Respectable: The Politics of Race and Sexual Morality in 20th-Century Colonial Cultures." *American Ethnologist* 16, no. 4 (Nov. 1989): 634–59.

———. "Rethinking Colonial Categories: European Communities and the Boundaries of Rule." *Comparative Studies in Society and History* 13, no. 1 (1989): 134–61.

Strobel, Margaret. *European Women and the Second British Empire*. Bloomington: Indiana University Press, 1991.

Subba, Tanka B. *Dynamics of a Hill Society*. Delhi: Mittal, 1989.

Swanson, Maynard W. "The Sanitation Syndrome: Bubonic Plague and Urban Native Policy in the Cape Colony, 1900–1909." *Journal of African History* 18, no. 3 (1977): 387–410.

Symonds, Richard. "Eurasians under British Rule." In *Oxford University Papers on India*, vol. 1, pt. 2, 28–42. Delhi: Oxford University Press, 1987.

Tanna, Kaku J. *Plantations in the Nilgiris: A Synoptic History*. N.p., c. 1969.

Tarapor, Mahrukh. "John Lockwood Kipling and British Art Education in India." *Victorian Studies* 24, no. 1 (autumn 1980): 53–81.

Thakur, R. N. *Himalayan Lepchas*. New Delhi: Archives Publishers, 1988.

Tinker, Hugh. *The Foundations of Local Self-Government in India, Pakistan and Burma*. New York: Praeger, 1968.

Trevelyan, Raleigh. *The Golden Oriole*. New York: Viking, 1987.

Tucker, Richard P. "The British Colonial System and the Forests of the Western Himalayas, 1815–1914." In *Global Deforestation and the Nineteenth-Century World Economy*, ed. Richard P. Tucker and J. F. Richards, 146–66. Durham: Duke University Press, 1983.

———. "The British Empire and India's Forest Resources: The Timberlands of Assam and Kumaon, 1914–1950." In *World Deforestation in the Twentieth Century*, ed. John F. Richards and Richard P. Tucker, 91–111. Durham: Duke University Press, 1988.

———. "The Depletion of India's Forests under British Imperialism: Planters, Foresters, and Peasants in Assam and Kerala." In *The Ends of the Earth: Perspectives on Modern Environmental History*, ed. Donald Worster, 118–40. Cambridge: Cambridge University Press, 1988.

Tyagi, Nutan. *Hill Resorts of U.P. Himalaya: A Geographical Study*. New Delhi: Indus, 1991.

Walker, Anthony R. *The Toda of South India: A New Look*. Delhi: Hindustan, 1986.

———. "Toda Society between Tradition and Modernity." In *Blue Mountains: The Ethnography and Biogeography of a South Indian Region,* ed. Paul Hockings, 186–205 (Delhi: Oxford University Press, 1989).

Waller, P. J. *Town, City, and Nation: England 1850–1914.* Oxford: Oxford University Press, 1983.

Ware, Vron. *Beyond the Pale: White Women, Racism and History.* London: Verso, 1992.

Westlake, Graeme D. *An Introduction to the Hill Stations of India.* New Delhi: Indus, 1993.

Woodruff, Philip [pseud. for Philip Mason]. *The Men Who Ruled India.* Vol. 1: *The Founders.* Vol. 2: *The Guardians.* Reprint, New York: Schocken, 1964.

Wright, Gillian. *The Hill Stations of India.* Lincolnwood, Ill.: Passport Books, 1991.

Wyckoff, Charlotte Chandler. *Kodaikanal: 1845–1945.* Nagercoil, Travancore: London Mission Press, 1945.

Yalland, Zoe. *Traders and Nabobs: The British in Cawnpore 1765–1857.* Salisbury, Wiltshire: Michael Joseph, 1987.

Yule, Col. Henry, and A. C. Burnell. *Hobson-Jobson.* New ed. 1886. Reprint, Delhi: Rupa, 1989.

# Index